The Camel and the Wheel

The Camel and the Wheel

Richard W. Bulliet

Columbia University Press
New York

Columbia University Press Morningside Edition 1990

Columbia University Press
New York   Oxford

Morningside Edition with New Preface
Copyright © 1990 by Columbia University Press
The Camel and the Wheel was originally published in 1975.
All rights reserved

Library of Congress Cataloging-in-Publication Data

Bulliet, Richard W.
    The camel and the wheel / Richard W. Bulliet.—Morningside ed.
      p. cm.
    Reprint, with new pref. Originally published:
   Cambridge, Mass. : Harvard University Press, 1975.
    Includes bibliographical references.
    ISBN 0-231-07234-1 (alk. paper).—ISBN 0-231-07235-X (pbk.)
    1. Camels—History. 2. Camels—Middle East—History.
   3. Dromedary—Africa, North—History.
   4. Wheels—Middle East—History.
   5. Wheels—Africa, North—History.
   6. Transportation—Middle East—History.
   7. Transportation—Africa, North—History.
   8. Animals and history—Middle East.
   9. Animals and history—Africa, North. I. Title.
   SF401.C2B84 1989
   636.2'95'09—dc20
   89-25121
   CIP

Casebound editions of Columbia University Press books are Smyth-sewn
and printed on permanent and durable acid-free paper

Printed in the United States of America

c 10 9 8 7 6 5 4 3 2 1
p 10 9 8 7 6 5 4 3 2

Contents

Preface to the Morningside Edition

When I first determined to write this book, D. W. Lock-ard, then near retirement as the Associate Director of Harvard's Center for Middle East Studies, advised me in avuncular fashion that writing a book on camels would ruin my career. Fortunately, his prediction proved untrue. But it did reflect an outlook on Middle East Studies that was then dominant and is still quite prevalent. It is not that the field is anti-camel, but that it is extremely wary of unusual or innovative scholarship.

In the fifteen years since it appeared, *The Camel and the Wheel* has found a favorable reception among scholars from a number of different fields, but it has had little impact on the field of Middle Eastern history where subjects like technology and economics remain peripheral to the traditional concerns of religion, philosophy, and literature. Though a few encouraging forays are being made into uncharted waters, the field of Middle Eastern technological history in the Islamic period remains largely unexplored.

The various ideas and arguments put forward in the book

have proved stimulating to many scholars in other fields, however, ranging from the biologist Stephen Jay Gould,[1] to the world historian William H. McNeill,[2] to the computer columnist Erik Sandberg-Diment.[3] George A. Theodorson reprinted pp. 224–28, dealing with the relationship between urban design and transportation systems, in the revised edition of his *Urban Patterns: Studies in Human Ecology* (University Park, Penn.: Pennsylvania State University Press, 1982), pp. 394–97. The most gratifying sign of appreciation of all, however, was my receipt of the Dexter Prize from the Society for the History of Technology.

My own research has traveled down largely different roads during the intervening years, but I have pursued inquiries into a few of the topics I raise in the book. The only published fruit of this new research is an article entitled "Botr et Beranès: Hypothèses sur l'Histoire des Berbères" that appeared in *Annales: Économies, Sociétés, Civilisations* (January–February 1981), pp. 104–16. There I expand upon my discussion in chapter 5 of plow and draft harnesses in Roman North Africa. I argue that the evidence relating to camel use and harnessing techniques may be crucial to understanding the well-attested but poorly understood division of medieval Berber tribes into two groups, Butr and Baranis. According to my hypothesis, the Butr Berbers originated in association with Roman agriculture and were accustomed to using camels for plowing. By contrast, the Baranis tribes were from mountainous areas that were more isolated from Roman agriculture and patterns of camel use. These identifications, in turn, have implications for the broader history of early Islamic North Africa that are spelled out in the article.

My other area of further inquiry takes off from chapter 7 and concerns the relationship between wheeled transport and camel use in Central Asia, India, and the Greco-Roman world. The central question is when and why draft harness designs were rationalized and made competitive with pack camels in the different zones. The Greco-Roman world, despite its high level of material culture, retained primitive harness designs that ultimately contributed to the disappearance of wheeled vehicles in camel-using areas because they obstructed the development of efficient horse-drawn wagons.

India, by contrast, adopted more advanced harness designs from Central Asia in the medieval period and adapted them for camels, but a mixed transport economy of camel-carts, ox-carts, and pack camels remained viable. The reason for this was presumably a comparative scarcity of horses that ruled out broad conversion to efficient horse-powered vehicle use, but the history of Indian transport technology needs further study.

As for Central Asia, it was the original home both of the war chariot and of the mounted warrior that rendered the war chariot obsolete. Peoples there also made the switch to efficient single-animal harnessing and continue to use camel carts to the present day. Rulers in derivative areas of chariot use in the Middle East, Europe, and Africa eventually followed the Central Asian lead and converted their armies from chariotry and cavalry, but this conversion contributed to the demise of wheeled transport because efficient horse harnessing remained unknown. It is curious, indeed, that so important an invention as the stirrup, which made heavy cavalry possible, found its way to Europe from its earliest attested appearance in northern Afghanistan while the equally important idea of single-animal draft using a breast-strap, attested in the same region, did not.

I believe that the reason for this selective adoption of new technology was a religiously based mindset among the western Indo-European peoples, and other peoples affected by Indo-European attitudes toward warfare. I believe they saw paired draft for chariots and elite vehicles as a terrestrial mirror of the chariots of the gods. Whatever its real battlefield utility, which is questionable, the war chariot drawn by two or four horses was a status indicator of the Indo-European warrior class. So mounted, they were imitating the celestial gods, and the idea of shifting to single-animal draft for efficiency's sake was virtually sacrilegious. In Central Asia, I would suggest that the easier conversion to cavalry and to efficient single-animal harnessing was due to the decline of an original Indo-European worldview brought about by the gradual ascendance of the Turko-Mongolian peoples, history's pre-eminent horse riders.

I expect in the future to write at length on this subject, but I feel the central core of my thinking is worth this brief outline here because it may help to make more understandable the mechanical obtuseness of the Romans and other sophisticated peoples in not thinking of and generally adopting efficient horse harnessing. It may also help to explain why the modern harnesses invented in Roman Tunisia and Libya, as described in chapter 7, did not have greater economic and technological impact.

As for the book's other major theses, some have been elaborated upon, conditioned, or questioned in reviews and articles by other scholars. I have also come across further material to buttress one or another of the book's ideas. In sum, however, the weight of changes that might be made in response to this accumulated criticism and corroboration has not been great enough to require a revision of the text. Instead, a few comments can be made here with reference to specific parts of the text, leaving it to the industrious reader to integrate them.

The most significant challenge to a major hypothesis is in an article by my colleague Roger S. Bagnall, "The Camel, the Wagon, and the Donkey in Later Roman Egypt," *Bulletin of the American Society of Papyrologists*, 22 (1985), 1–6. Bagnall supports my contention that the camel was established in Egypt in pre-Roman times, but he proves from papyrological evidence that wagons were still in use as late as the seventh century A.D., contrary to my surmise from much more limited evidence that they disappeared between the fourth and sixth centuries as they did further to the east. Bagnall also documents substantial camel use in Egypt and argues, with justification, that donkeys must be considered in any survey of Egypt's total land transportation system.

Bagnall's data are incontrovertible, and his argument that head-to-head rivalry between camels and ox-carts may not have been important in Egypt, at least before the Arab conquest, is persuasive. However, he also makes the crucial point that in Egypt land transportation is never very important because almost all habitable parts of the country lie within a mile or so of the Nile River. The true transport system of Egypt is riverine and therefore intrinsically cheaper than any form of land transportation. Therefore, the prolonged coexistence of camels and wagons may be more a consequence of their peripheral economic importance than anything else.

Bagnall concurs that wagons did eventually disappear in Egypt. Perhaps the resolution of the anomaly, then, is to argue that Egypt became integrated into the wheelless society of Western Asia as a consequence of being incorporated into the wheelless Arab caliphate from the seventh century onward rather than for more more localized economic and technological reasons.

The most notable new contribution to the transporation history of the Islamic Middle East is Suraiya Faroqhi's article "Camels, Wagons, and the Ottoman State in the Sixteenth and Seventeenth Centuries," *International Journal of Middle East Studies*, 14 (1982), 523–39. The data she has found in Ottoman documents greatly improves, but does not fundamentally change, the understanding of the Anatolian transport system I outline on pp. 231–35.

The question of the origin of camel domestication has been resurveyed by Ilse Köhler in her dissertation "Zur Domestikation des Kamels"[4] with results that are largely consonant with my own but focusing more on the southeastern extremity of the Arabian peninsula as the hearth of one-humped camel domestication.

Paula Wapnish has reported on camel bones, possibly of domesticated animals, from a site near Gaza in the Sinai that date to the fourteenth and thirteenth centuries B.C.[5] This tends to support my suggestion (pp. 235–36, 58ff) that camels were at least occasionally used in the Fertile Crescent before the twelfth century B.C.

Christopher J. Brunner kindly brought to my attention the two-humped camel images surmounting the crowns of certain Central Asian Khwarazmian rulers in the third–fourth centuries A.D.[6] This information relates to my discussion of camels on the Silk Route (pp. 168ff).

Other points have found support in pictorial evidence that

has come to hand from various sources. These items include a rock engraving with accompanying Safaitic inscription from southern Jordan depicting a rider on a North Arabian saddle dating from the first to third century A.D.,[7] which reinforces my dating of the earliest North Arabian camel saddles (pp. 90ff); a rock engraving from northern Jordan of a two-humped camel,[8] which substantiates the occasional use of two-humped camels around the Syrian desert in Parthian times (pp. 164–67); and a Tang Dynasty figurine of a cross between a one-humped and a two-humped camel,[9] which shows that hybrid camels were known on both ends of the Silk Route (pp. 164ff).

Finally, important additions have been made to the bibliography of camel literature since 1975. Some that specifically add to the documentation of this book are Bruno Campagnoni and Maurizio Tosi, "The Camel," in Richard H. Meadow and Melinda A. Zeder, *Approaches to Faunal Analysis in the Middle East* (Cambridge: Peabody Museum Bulletin no. 2, Harvard University), pp. 91–103, which gives the published version of material cited in chapter 7, footnote 13; and Ye. Ye. Kuz'mina, "Stages in the Evolution of Wheeled Transportation in Central Asia" (in Russian), *Vestnik drevnei istorii*, 154 (1980), pp. 11–35,[10] which discusses early camel cart use in Central Asia.

Some useful earlier works that have come to light are V. N. Kolpakov, *Matériaux de biologie et culture des chameaux* and S. N. Bogolubsky, *Essai sur la provenance des chameaux*, both published (in Russian) in Alma Alta in 1929 by the Society for the Study of Kazakhstan.[11] The former is an authoritative and well-illustrated treatise on camel breeding and use in Kazakhstan that can be used to flesh out the picture of Central Asian camel use presented in chapters 6 and 7. The latter is largely concerned with camel dentition and is worth adding to the literature on the origins of camel domestication.

More generally, camel scholarship in the fields of biology and animal husbandry has been booming. Three important books have appeared: Hilde Gauthier-Pilters and Anne Innis Dagg, *The Camel: Its Evolution, Ecology, Behavior, and Relation-*

ship to Man (Chicago: University of Chicago Press, 1981); **xiii**
R. T. Wilson, *The Camel* (Harlaw, Essex: Longman Group,
1984); and Reuven Yagil, *The Desert Camel: Comparative Physiological Adaptation* (New York: S. Karger, 1985). Finally, the
Arab Center for the Studies of Arid Zones and Dry Lands
(ASCAD) in Damascus began publication in 1984 of the
Camel Newsletter (in Arabic, *Al-Ibil*), which contains book reviews of important new works on camels, short articles, an-
nouncements of camel symposia and congresses, and an excellent updating of camel bibliography. English is the
primary language of the *Newsletter*, with some articles translated into Arabic and French.

Notes

1. See Stephen Jay Gould, "Kingdom Without Wheels," *Natural
History*, 90/3 (March 1984), 42–48.
2. See William H. McNeill, "The Eccentricity of Wheels, or
Eurasian Transportation in Historical Perspective," *The American
Historical Review* (December 1987), 1111–1126.
3. See Erik Sandberg-Diment, "Of Camels and Caliphates,
Mindsets and Computer Technology," *Infoworld*, January 5, 1987,
p. 35.
4. Ilse Köhler, "Zur Domestikation des Kamels," Inaugural-Dis-
sertation zur Erlangen des Grades eines Doctor Medicinae Veteri-
nariae durch die Tierärtzliche Hochschule Hannover, 1981.
5. Paula Wapnish, "Camel Caravans and Camel Patoralists at
Tell Jemmeh," paper presented at the annual conference of the
American Anthropological Association, 1980.
6. See B. I. Vainberg, *Monety drevnogo Khorezma* (Moscow, 1977),
pp. 23–28.
7. See "Nuqush jadida min junub al-Urdunn," *Newsletter of the
Institute of Archaeology and Anthropology, Yarmouk University*, no. 5
(Irbid, Jordan, 1988), p. 7 (Arabic section). Analysis of the probable date of the inscription, by George Mendenhall, Zaidun Mu-
haisin, and Rifat Haziem, was kindly made available to me by
Professor Martha Mundy.
8. See F. Winnet and L. Harding, *Inscriptions from Fifty Safaitic
Cairns*, Near and Middle East Series (Toronto: University of Toronto Press, 1978), p. 670, #476–77.
9. The figurine is apparently in a museum in Urumqi, China,

but I have been unable to confirm this. The picture I have is on a postcard sent to me by my colleague Klaus Herdeg.

10. I wish to thank my former student Uli Schamiloglu for bringing this to my attention.

11. I am most grateful to David Bauer for making a partial translation of Kolpakov's essay.

Acknowledgments

It is a bit difficult to know where to begin or where to end
in acknowledging assistance received in writing this book. It
has been, on the one hand, a somewhat lonely task that has
occasionally approached, so I have been told, becoming an
obsession. Those who have borne with it in this guise, the
ones who with suppressed yawns and sinking eyelids have
listened to me expatiate on the subject for hours on end over
the last several years, deserve my profoundest thanks. Chief
among these I must number my wife Lucy, Mrs. Leila Fawaz,
my parents, and the ten Harvard freshmen who endured
my freshman seminar on the subject in 1970. On the other
hand, I have received valuable assistance on specific matters
from literally dozens of individuals, some of whom were
doubtless unaware of the help they were giving. I have thanked
many of these people in the pertinent notes, but I should like
to acknowledge here the particularly valuable consultation
of Sir Richard Turnbull of Henley, England; Mr. George
Kendle of Kewanee, Illinois; and a young man in Tozeur, Tu-

xvi nisia, who answered or found people who could answer all of my questions regarding carts and camels. On the scholarly side, I particularly benefited from the advice of Professor A. Leo Oppenheim, Professor Richard N. Frye, Professor John Emerson, Dr. Prem Singh, Dr. Thomas Stauffer, Mr. A. Bernard Knapp, and again my wife Lucy. Credits for illustrations are recorded elsewhere, but I was gratified by unusually helpful responses from Mr. Wilfred Thesiger, Professor Johannes Nicolaisen, Professor Michael Bonine, and Mr. Ben Ahmed Abdel Hadi, Director of the museum in Sousse, Tunisia. Finally, my boundless thanks to Mrs. Barbara Henson, who typed the manuscript.

Figures

Figures

Figures

Maps

Charts

Apologia

Whoever reads this book will find out a very great deal about camels; of that I am sure. He will also be introduced to some new and different ideas on many historical problems ranging from 3000 B.C. to the present day. Some of these will be purely speculative, others well supported with facts. Yet altogether they should provide a reasonable description of the role of the camel in human history and explain why camel utilization had a profound impact on the course of Middle Eastern and North African history in particular, an impact that indelibly marked the culture of those areas from the third or fourth century A.D. until modern times. On these matters, I trust, the reader will not be disappointed even if he is not fully satisfied. But the writing of this book does not stem merely from a desire to chronicle the relationship between man and camel. My attitude toward the subject is more involved, and I believe its involutions are worth detailing since they may

1

afford the reader added perspective from which to consider the information and theories presented herein.

For the first time in human history whole societies numbering millions of people are living outside of close, conscious daily contact with other animal species. Over 70 percent of the U.S. population lives in cities where animal contact is restricted, by and large, to household pets, prepackaged meat, and vermin. Only a half century ago dwellers in those same cities were constantly aware of work horses pulling vehicles and took for granted the important role of animal energy in human life. Equally important, a much greater proportion of the population lived in the country in daily contact with farm animals.

The magnitude of the change that has taken place in the relationship between human beings and other animals over the last half century or so, not just in the United States but in other industrialized countries as well, cannot be overstated; but because it is only a part of the vast complex of changes associated with the term modernization, it is seldom singled out for specific recognition. However, once this particular change is recognized, its effects on the attitudes of people toward animals can readily be observed. In particular, it can be observed in such phenomena as the intensification of relationships with pets, aversion toward hunting, and revival of interest in vegetarianism. In short, a humanistic view of animals is gradually coming to replace the animalistic view which predominated only a short time ago.

Yet as emotional attitudes toward animals have changed, so have intellectual attitudes. Animal behavior has emerged as a subject of intense interest at both the scientific and the popular levels. But even though the attenuation of close contacts with domestic animals has played a crucial role in the emergence of new attitudes, domestic species themselves have not yet been subjected to the type of noninvolved study which for the first time in history has become possible. Meat animals, naturally, we are still in touch with, albeit through an intervening film of plastic; but work animals are now a part of history. The fact that a horse butcher in Connecticut was interviewed on television in 1973 because of the phenomenal demand for his meat shows how greatly the old sentimental

attachment to the horse has dwindled. Similar publicity for a **3**
rush on horsemeat would have been almost unimaginable
twenty years ago when most of the meat buying population
still had personal recollections of work horses known or seen.
My approach to camels is thus, in part, a product of the
distance between man and animal characteristic of our society
at the present time. I do not love camels; I was not reared
among them. I've never even become intimately acquainted
with one. One forty-five minute ride in Tunisia was sufficient
to show me how long it takes a nonrider to get sore that way.
In short, I am interested in the camel as a historical phenomenon, an animal that was domesticated, exploited in many ways
by many different peoples, and is now on the way out as a
significant factor in the world's economy. The use of the camel
as a source of labor, which is the aspect of camel history that
will be stressed throughout, is already a relic of bygone times
in many camel countries, and it will eventually become so in
most of them. Thus the history of the animal from this aspect
is essentially a completed one that can be approached as a
closed episode. As such it may hopefully be more clearly seen
in its totality.

The two primary themes that will be followed throughout
the camel's history are, first, the relationship between the pack
camel and wheeled transport as rival, or occasionally compatible, means of carrying loads; and second, the relationship
between people specializing in the breeding of camels, normally
nomadic tribes, and the non-camel-breeding societies they
interact with through their animals' being used for labor in
those societies. These two themes might be labeled respectively economic history and historical anthropology, but no
special effort has been made to adopt the focus of interest of
either the economist or the anthropologist. The actual style of
discussion fits more closely the rubric technological history
since the primary indicator of varying patterns of camel usage
in different ages and different areas is the type of equipment
used to harness the animal's energy. Yet my intention has
not been to write technological history any more than economic
history or historical anthropology.

My true intention has been to show as completely and as
concisely as possible how this one particular domestic animal

has fitted into the total context of human society throughout history. This intention has at its root a thought and an experience. In 1967 the thought occurred to me (and it has occurred to others before me) that there seemed to be no mention of wheeled vehicles in medieval Islamic source materials. Since I knew from the Bible, if from nowhere else, that chariots, and presumably carts and wagons, had existed in the Middle East in ancient times, I wondered what had caused the wheel to disappear. My investigations into this question led me to believe that the camel was at the heart of the problem, and I wrote two articles setting forth my conclusions.[1] I had no intention at that time of going further into the history of the camel, however. For one thing, I knew next to nothing about animals, being a medieval Islamic historian by training, and I also realized that seeking answers to the questions opened up by my research would involve me in lands, languages, and disciplines with which I had no familiarity.

The experience which in retrospect I believe helped push me into making a serious commitment to studying the relationship between man and the camel took place in Iran in 1966. On that, my first visit to the Middle East, I had frequently been struck by the ubiquity of domestic animals in everyday life. Sheep grazed in the courtyard of the great mosque of Mehmet the Conqueror in the heart of Istanbul, and horse-drawn carriages were more common than taxis in small towns in Turkey and Iran. A sheep was skinned in the driveway in front of the restaurant I had just eaten in, and a chicken was decapitated for a buyer in the middle of a busy sidewalk. On the whole, being largely unfamiliar with animals in American life, I looked upon this animal presence as picturesque, a touch of local quaintness.

This viewpoint underwent a change one day outside Nishapur in northeastern Iran when the country path that I was riding my bicycle on was obstructed by a small flock of sheep being driven toward town by a shepherd. I waited for the man to clear a way, but he was preoccupied: he was beating a sheep to death with his staff. Since I had no choice but to watch what to me was a horrifying scene, I began to think about it. The sheep were obviously being taken to market, and the one being beaten was just as obviously extremely weak, probably ill. It would walk a step or two, fall, and then be beaten by the shepherd. It became clear to me that the man was beating it to make it walk since he couldn't sell it if it died there on the path. I noticed that the man was close to tears as his blows evoked less and less movement on the sheep's part. I think he knew that the sheep would never reach Nishapur, but he couldn't bring himself to stop trying to get it to walk. If it didn't reach the city, it might as well not exist.

As I thought the incident over later, I concluded that that one sheep was probably the difference between a profit and a loss, a day of gainful industry and a day of wasted effort. If he was a hired shepherd, its loss may possibly have affected his reputation and hence his entire economic and social position. In short, I became aware for the first time of the interrelationship between men and domestic animals. Had I been born fifty years earlier I would surely have taken this interrelationship for granted, if I had given thought to the incident at all. As it was, it made a deep impression upon me and led me in my subsequent studies of the camel to keep foremost in my mind the human context that is the defining characteristic of domestic animals. I wanted to find out not just how camel herders regarded their livestock but how the animal affected the nonherding society it came into contact with as well.

Perhaps it is superfluous to remark at this point that this is not the definitive work on camels. This is a book about camels only as they have related to and affected human society. This means, unfortunately, that the kind of question that comes most readily to mind when camels are mentioned—how long can they go without water? does riding one make you seasick? do they spit a lot?—will be dealt with, if at all, only in passing. This book will propose instead new questions, some of which it will answer satisfactorily and all of which it will attempt to answer.

Yet even within its own scope this is not a definitive book on camels and society. The subject is vast; the talents required to plumb it thoroughly are many and, for the most part, not at my command. My research has been limited almost entirely to published sources with only a limited amount of field observation. And even within the area of published literature I have come up against limitations of language, availability of material, and volume of reading required. The vast library of travel literature from camel countries, for example, has only been sampled.

My main reason for publishing a work that has not been developed to its fullest potential is that further work in this direction should properly be done by those with the appropriate training in the many fields it touches upon. My hope is that even if some of the specifics of the analysis put forward are disproven, the broad sweep of the theory overall will be persuasive enough to establish the history of the development of camel breeding and utilization as a serious subject for detailed investigation and to put on a less narrowly zoological or anthropological footing the study of relationships between man and domestic animals in general.

Throughout this book, incidentally, *camelus dromedarius* will be referred to as the one-humped camel and *camelus bactrianus* as the two-humped camel. This is to avoid the great confusion in most people's minds on the subject of proper camel nomenclature.

1 The Camel and the Wheel

Traditional wisdom holds the wheel to be one of mankind's cleverest inventions and the camel to be one of God's clumsiest. By and large the history of the wheel has been well studied.[1] From its first invention to the development of the motor car every advance has been examined and speculated upon. Whippletree, leaf spring, cambered spoke, each has come in for its share of attention. There has even been speculation as to why relatively advanced societies such as those of pre-Columbian America never made use of this marvellous transportation device. Yet never has there been a general investigation of why a vast area of the globe encompassing some of its most advanced societies at a certain time in history abandoned its use. In fact, this apparently anomalous historical event has barely even been recognized.

As for the camel, a very great deal has been written on one aspect or another of this unwieldy looking beast, but most

8

speculation on the history of the domestic camel has centered upon two questions: Where and when were camels first domesticated? And when and by whom were they first introduced into North Africa? While each of these questions has its own elusive fascination and will be discussed in due course in this book, the most important question in camel history, important because of its social and economic ramifications for the world outside the restricted orbit of the camel-breeding tribesman, has been routinely overlooked. That question is why did the camel (one-humped) replace the wheeled vehicle as a standard means of transportation throughout virtually its entire range from Morocco to Afghanistan?

Before getting fully involved with the complex question of why the camel replaced the wheel, the fact that this wheelless situation so freely alleged in the last two paragraphs ever in fact existed should first be established. Surely proof that the camel was used as a beast of burden in traditional Middle Eastern and North African society is not called for since the camel caravan is almost an inevitable part of every stereotypical view of the area. The absence of wheeled vehicles, on the other hand, must be demonstrated.

Proving that something did not exist at some time and place in the past is every historian's nightmare because there is always a nagging fear that evidence of its existence may at some future date be found. Luckily, the evidence for the non-existence of wheeled vehicles is so widespread and so mutually reinforcing that the fear is in this case an insubstantial one. Three types of evidence are particularly persuasive: direct statements by travelers and other observers, pictorial representations, and Arabic and Persian vocabulary.

The limitation of direct statements is that they do not extend back very far in time. But they are plentiful from recent centuries. In the eighteenth century C. F. Volney wrote "it is noteworthy that in the whole of Syria no wagon or cart is seen,"[2] and Alexander Russell in Aleppo echoed him in remarking that the camel "is of infinite use in a country . . . where, except a clumsy kind of cart, sometimes employed for transporting large stones, wheel carriages are in a manner unknown."[3] In the mid-nineteenth century Xavier Raymond wrote that in Afghanistan "the use of wagons (*voitures*) is

unknown,"[4] and from the northern Algerian Sahara around
the same time comes the report of Henry Tristam that "the
wonder of Zouïa, the curiosity most triumphantly pointed
out to us, is a two-wheeled cart, also a gift of the Bey of Tunis,
the first ever seen here and very probably the last, transported piecemeal on the backs of camels for 700 miles, and now
housed in all but a glass-case."[5]

In more recent times scholars have remarked upon the
absence of wheeled vehicles in Muslim lands. E. Lévi-Provençal,
a specialist on Muslim Spain, has written that "there seems to
have existed in the Muslim West, at least throughout the
Middle Ages, a kind of interdiction on the use of wheeled
vehicles for which it would be interesting to find a plausible
explanation";[6] and in a study of Moroccan agriculture Jean Le
Coz writes "it is known that traditional Morocco did not know
roads, in the sense of a laid out and constructed route of circulation, or even practically the use of the wheel."[7] For medieval Egypt S. D. Goitein has observed that "carriages, so
common in the Roman period, had completely disappeared and
are nowhere referred to in the Geniza papers."[8] Similarly,
it has been noted that records of the Crusader states in the
Middle East never mention carts and wagons.[9]

Further testimony of this sort could be sought out, but the
general picture of a dearth of vehicular traffic from Morocco to
Afghanistan is already clear. The question, of course, is how
far back in time this wheelless society extends. A type of evidence that dates back further than most travel accounts is
pictorial representation. In studying Islamic art one is confronted, on the one hand, by the extreme rarity of representations of wheeled vehicles of any kind except in Indian and
Ottoman miniature paintings which reflect milieux that never
lost the use of the wheel;[10] but, on the other hand, one finds
that those vehicles which are depicted appear more often than
not in legendary scenes inspired by pre-Islamic sources and
show utterly irrational modes of harnessing. One scene from
the Shahnameh, the Iranian national epic, for example, shows
two horses harnessed to a two-wheeled cart by chains extending from a loose, lassolike collar around the horse's neck to
the hub of the wheel. There are no shafts, no yoke, no tongue,
no reins, no bridle, nothing that would indicate how the horses

10   were to be guided or how they were actually to pull the cart without strangling themselves. As for the wagon itself, it seems to be a box or casket, complete with little legs, set upon two spokeless wheels of unguessable construction.[11] In short, the picture is pure invention, and the artist had never laid eyes upon a wheeled vehicle. The same deduction can be made from other pictures, as well.

One shows a mule rationally harnessed with a rather interesting horse collar, but the vehicle it is drawing rolls on tiny nonrevolving wheels and is attached to the mule in such a way that it could not turn very easily.[12] Another artist shows some comprehension of a horse collar but none at all of how it is used to hitch an animal to a cart.[13] Still another shows no definite attachment between horse and cart at all.[14] Once again the conclusion is clearly that most medieval Muslim artists did not know what a cart looked like from their normal, everyday experience.[15]

Finally, there is the linguistic evidence. Prior to the fourteenth century there is but one word in Arabic for all wheeled vehicles. That word is Ꜥajala and derives from a root connoting swiftness.[16] This word appears on rare occasion in medieval Arabic works to describe either the vehicles of foreign peoples or certain extraordinary vehicles that appear from time to time in Islamic history. It is also used occasionally for a kind of water wheel, irrigation being, along with pottery, a field in which the technology of the wheel never suffered a recession. What is significant about the use of the word Ꜥajala is not simply the rarity of its occurrence, although this alone goes very far toward confirming the absence of wheels in the medieval transport economy, but the fact that it was the only word in common use. Although carts and wagons were known from ancient times in Iraq, Egypt, and Syria, no word denoting such a thing passed into Arabic from the languages of these conquered areas. One word, in fact, markavthā, from a root meaning "to mount," means, among other things, a wheeled vehicle in Syriac, while the related word in Arabic, markab, means a riding animal, a saddle or other animal-borne vehicle, or a ship, but not a wheeled vehicle. Clearly the addi-

1 Irrational harness shown in legendary scene from Persian epic *Shahnameh. (facing page)*

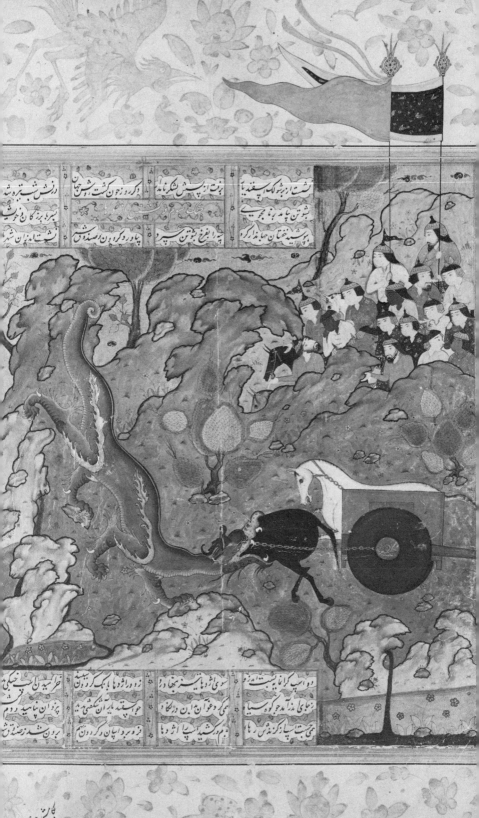

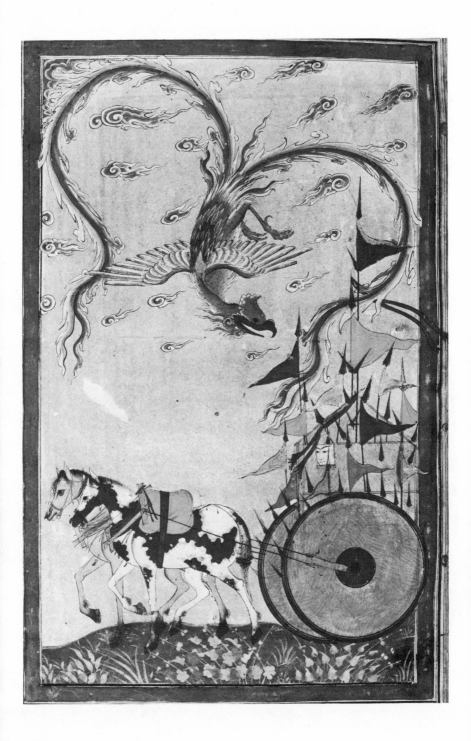

2 Realistic collar harness used with imaginary vehicle in Persian miniature. *(facing page)*

3 Imaginary draft harness in Persian miniature.

14 tional meaning found in Syriac had become obsolete by the time the Arabic language expanded into Aramaic or Syriac speaking territories.

The peculiarity of this absence of borrowed words is underscored by the ease with which Arabic accommodated foreign words for wheeled vehicles after the fourteenth century.[17] While ᶜaraba, the word which through Turkish influence replaces ᶜajala as the basic word for cart or wagon in the fourteenth century, apparently derives from a corruption of the Arabic word ᶜarrāda meaning a kind of siege weapon, other words are clearly of foreign origin, for example: karrūṣa from Italian carrozza, qarrīta from Italian carretta, hantūr through Turkish from Hungarian hinto, and faitūn from English phaeton. Furthermore, an identical situation exists in the Persian language. Throughout the medieval period the word gardūn easily suffices for those rare instances in which wheeled transport is mentioned. After the fourteenth century, however, words of foreign origin become common including ᶜaraba, doroshke from Russian, and gārī from Hindi.

Thus the linguistic evidence firmly supports that from pictorial sources and travel accounts, but it says more, as well. If the society in which the Arabic language slowly spread after the Islamic conquests of the seventh century had been a wheel-using society, some evidence of that should be discernible in loan words in Arabic. In Persian, of course, there is direct continuity between the spoken language of the time of the conquests and the Persian literary language which was reborn in the tenth century, and yet there, too, there exists a virtual blank when it comes to words dealing with wheeled transport. The only conclusion possible is that the wheel and its associated vocabulary had disappeared sometime prior to the Islamic conquests. This not only explains why Arabic and Persian are so deficient in vocabulary but also why carts and wagons are never mentioned in descriptions of conquered peoples.

If by the time of the Arab conquests the wheel had already disappeared from the Middle East, then the question to be asked is how long it had been gone by that date. Here, unfortunately, there is no great historical landmark to provide a limit such as that afforded by the conquests. It cannot even be

ascertained how commonplace carts and wagons were in the   **15**
area prior to their disappearance. Historians of transportation
have been able to find many representations of wheeled vehicles from ancient times; and even though the great prepon-
derance of them are military vehicles, understandably so given
the character of the kings and generals who commissioned
lasting works of art, there are enough pictures of carts being
used for common hauling purposes to prove that such popular
usage existed.[18] Yet it must be borne in mind that pack animals were also in common use from earliest times and may well
have been at all times a more significant part of the transpor-

4 Ancient chariot in Assyrian relief.

tation economy than wheeled vehicles.[19] Even so, whatever the exact proportion of wheels to pack animals in the transportation economy, the wheel did disappear, and it is the date of that disappearance that is being sought and not a precise index of the popularity of carts and wagons during the period when they were in normal use.

Since there is no reason to assume a priori that the disappearance of the wheel took place simultaneously in all parts of the Middle East and North Africa, the search for evidence indicating when the wheel disappeared is best carried out on an area by area basis. Unfortunately, areas such as the Persian Empire which the vagaries of history have stripped of most of their ancient literary products afford scant information. During the Achaemenid dynasty (sixth to fourth centuries B.C.) wheeled traffic is quite evident. Chariots in the army, mention of long paved roads, a stretch of road near Pasargadae still preserved complete with cart ruts, these things are conclusive. Even as late as the first century B.C. Diodorus the Sicilian, who regrettably tends to make use of earlier sources without notifying the reader, says that the main Persian road was up to taking wheeled traffic.[20] But the Parthians, who were the dominant power in the old Persian Empire from the third century B.C. to the third century A.D., are largely unknown to history, and by the time the Sasanian dynasty arises in the third century A.D. and information on Iran again becomes relatively plentiful, wheeled vehicles seem to have disappeared. Consequently, the date of the disappearance of the wheel in the Persian Empire is hard to pin down, and what few statements can be made are confined geographically to the western parts of the empire and do not refer to most of the Iranian plateau. The special problem of Iran will be taken up again in chapter six.

The remainder of the territory that experienced the wheel's disappearance was for the most part in the possession of the Romans. Roman Egypt (30 B.C. onwards) had both wagon transport and camel transport, the latter being a relatively recent and growing phenomenon. A specialist on the economy of this Roman province has written: "Transportation by land was usually by camel or donkey. Wagons were seldom used, although a tax found in Upper Egypt on wagons was paid by a private company engaged in transport, and some of the

5 Rock-painting of chariot from central Sahara.

large estates had wagons for farm work of various kinds."[21]
In addition, figures have been preserved from the first century A.D. detailing the specific cost of carrying sheaves of grain
by wagon, rents for wagons, and the price for which a wagon
was sold.[22] Therefore, the disappearance of the wheel in Egypt
must have been subsequent to the first century A.D. even
though the process would appear to have begun before that
time.

The history of wheeled vehicles in North Africa is particularly fascinating because of the abundant pictorial evidence
from the middle of the Sahara desert testifying to the use
there of horse-drawn chariots at some time in the distant past.[23]
Throughout Carthaginian times, as well, the chariot appears
to have held an important position even though it had long
disappeared from armies further east.[24] For nonmilitary vehicles, however, remains of the Roman period provide the most
significant evidence. Wagons appear not infrequently in mosaics from the first three centuries A.D., and road building
was carried out in Roman African territories in the first and
second centuries.[25] As will be discussed in detail in chapter
five, this is precisely the time that the camel was becoming
known in Tripolitania and Tunisia and being adapted to the
tasks of agricultural society. For quite specific reasons the
camel did not have quite the same impact on this particular
area that it did on others, and it would appear that carts never
passed out of use in southern Tunisia, if not in a broader
area. Thus the wheel's disappearance in North Africa is slightly
ambiguous. In non-Roman territory, wheeled vehicles other

6 Cart in Roman mosaic from Algeria.

than chariots may not have been used much at all. Evidence from beyond the Roman frontiers is very scarce. And within Roman territory, the wheel held its own in one limited area, apparently because of important technological improvements in harnessing. Where it did recede, however, it must have done so after the second century A.D.

Roman Syria, finally, by which is meant the entire Levant coast and the hinterland as far as the frontier of the Persian Empire, affords substantial evidence of the use of wheels. Roman armies campaigning in the area from the first century B.C. through the fourth century A.D. used many carts for baggage, siege engines, and even the transportation of pontoons for building bridges.[26] Yet they also made increasing use of pack camels, requisitioning them even from Egypt.[27] Of a more civilian character is a wall painting of the third century A.D. from Dura Europus, on the border between the Romans and the Persians, showing a team of oxen drawing a religious vehicle.[28] Since religious customs are extremely tenacious, however, this may not represent common, everyday usage. Carts are even mentioned as being used in Christian religious processions during the Islamic period.[29]

The system of Roman roads in Syria is also revealing. While the foremost purpose of the Roman road network was to serve the military, it also greatly increased the efficiency of civilian wheeled transport. Even when the road was unpaved, as most of them in Syria were until the time of Trajan (98–117 A.D.), it at least had been cleared of major obstructions such as boulders. During and after the reign of the emperor Trajan parts of Syria that had been newly incorporated into the empire were integrated into the imperial road network and important routes were paved.[30] This could only have improved conditions for wheeled vehicles, and evidence exists to show that carters took advantage of the situation. The fiscal law promulgated in 137 A.D. by the city of Palmyra, the great caravan center in the middle of the desert in northern Syria, decreed the duty upon a cartload of merchandise to be equivalent to the duty on four camel loads.[31] Clearly the road that had only shortly before that date been built to Palmyra had brought with it wheeled traffic to compete with the camel caravans.

The most interesting feature about this tax on carts at Palmyra, however, is not that it demonstrates the linkage between the road system and wheeled transport but that it gives a ratio of four to one between a camel load and a cartload. In this ratio lies an important clue to the entire transformation of the transport economy of the Middle East. To realize the significance of this ratio the Palmyrene fiscal law must be compared with the edict on prices issued in 301 A.D. by the emperor Diocletian in an abortive effort to stabilize prices and wages in at least the eastern provinces of the Roman Empire which were under his personal rule.

The edict specifies 20 denarii as the charge for carrying a wagonload of 1,200 Roman pounds one mile and 8 denarii as the charge for carrying a camel load of 600 Roman pounds the same distance.[32] Since the wagon was drawn by at least two oxen (eight and ten animals are mentioned, but these may include relief shifts),[33] the load per ox was almost equal to that of a camel while the cost per ox was 10 denarii. Thus, according to the edict on prices there was a savings of 20 percent to be made by shipping goods by camel instead of by wagon. Moreover, the ratio of a camel load to a wagonload is represented as being two to one as opposed to the Palmyrene four to one.

Although a century and a half separates the two documents in question, there is no reason to believe that the physical conditions of transport changed significantly during the intervening period. If a camel load was 600 Roman pounds in 301 A.D., as it very likely was since this is equivalent to 430 pounds avoirdupois and very much in line with medieval and modern camel loads,[34] it was surely about the same in 137 A.D. Furthermore, even though the figure of 500 pounds calculated by the historian of harnessing Lefebvre des Noëttes as the maximum load that could be drawn by horse or ox in Roman times has been disputed, the 1,200 Roman pounds (861 pounds avoirdupois) of the edict on prices is in line with this estimate and very far indeed from being double the estimate as would be required to explain the four to one ratio of the Palmyrene fiscal law.[35]

In short, a comparison of the two documents makes it quite evident that the lawmakers of Palmyra intended to levy a truly exorbitant tax upon anyone who drove a cartload of goods

into town. Carts were obviously not built in the treeless en- **21**
virons of Palmyra. Anyone setting up a carting business, therefore, must have been an outsider, a competitor trying to draw
off some of the lucrative caravan trade that had built Palmyra
into a luxurious city. There may have been no way to forbid
carts from following the new road into the desert, but the
businessmen who made Palmyra's laws could at least ensure
continued dominance of the caravan trade by their own strings
of camels by means of an inequitable taxation law.

The evidence from Palmyra, therefore, makes it quite clear
that carters and camel men in Roman Syria were in economic
competition with one another and more than willing to weight
the competition in their own favor when the opportunity arose.
Outside of Palmyra such clear evidence of direct competition
between the camel and the wheel is not readily available,
but certain figures from Roman Egypt indicate that similar
economy could be realized there by using camels.[36] Thus, overall, the 20 percent economy for the use of camels shown by
Diocletian's edict is a good indication that insofar as pack
camels did compete with wheeled vehicles, the advantage went
to the camel. In this connection, it is worth noting that when
pack camels and wagons have come into direct competition in
modern times, under circumstances of greatly improved harnessing and attendant improvement in the efficiency of the
vehicle, the camel has often proved to be the more economical
means of transport. This is true of Chinese Turkestan in the
1920s,[37] where the competing vehicles were camel drawn, and
of northeastern Iran a decade earlier.[38] Therefore, it may be
hypothesized that the primary reason for the abandonment of
wheeled transport in favor of camel transport was the greater
economy of the camel when it came into competition with
the wheel.

The questions that must be resolved to substantiate this
hypothesis are numerous and difficult. In point of fact, this entire book is largely the product of finally realizing just how
numerous and how difficult they are. In the first instance,
there is the problem of why camel transport could compete so
advantageously with wheeled transport. Secondly, why did th
competition result in the total abandonment of wheeled vehicles and not simply in their being superseded for purposes

of commercial transport? Most important, however, is the question that was mentioned earlier: Why did the camel replace the wheel at the particular point in history when it did, that is to say, apparently after the third and before the seventh century A.D.?

A diffuse but relatively satisfactory answer can be given to the first question, particularly since the vexing subissue of why the camel was not itself harnessed to a wagon and thus transformed into a yet more efficient hauler will be taken up separately in chapter seven. Given, for the time being, that the camel competed solely as a pack animal, numerous factors influenced the cost of transport. The most precise evaluations of the qualities of the camel as a pack animal have been made by military men in the nineteenth and twentieth centuries. Three independent specialists have written detailed summaries of their findings, and all have found the camel to be only slightly inferior to the mule in overall utility and decidedly more economical in care and maintenance. General Jean-Luc Carbuccia wrote a report in 1844 proposing the establishment of a permanent camel corps in French Algeria in which he enumerated no less than sixteen separate points wherein the camel was superior to the mule, most of them dealing with economies in feeding, watering, and care but also including greater strength, docility, and endurance.[39] The same conclusion was reached by the British military transport officer Major Arthur Glyn Leonard who wrote in 1894: "I have no hesitation in saying that, under existing conditions, mismanaged as the camel is, and taking him all round, for military purposes he is the best . . . Now as to the camel: (1) he has greater powers of abstinence from food and water [as compared to the mule]; (2) carries double; (3) requires fewer drivers; (4) is never shod; (5) procurable in greater numbers and more easily; (6) initial outlay less; (7) cost of maintenance less."[40] Captain A. S. Leese, finally, makes many of the same points on the basis of experience in India and east Africa.[41]

No similar comparison of a camel with a Roman ox is available, but Major Leonard did put in writing his estimation of the relative advantages of a pack camel and an oxcart in a proposal for the introduction of the former into South Africa. His conclusion is as follows:

And now in a few words let us sum up the special advan- **23**
tages of camel over ox transport.
  1. Can carry or draw twice as much.
  2. Faster, and able to cover more ground daily.
  3. Can do from 20 to 25 miles in one stretch.
  4. Will make many more journeys in a year and in their
respective lifetimes.
  5. Able to traverse ground that a wagon will stick in.
  6. No trouble fording rivers, where wagons would have
to be unloaded.
  7. [Not germane]
  8. Live and work four times as long.
  9. Greater powers of abstinence from food and water.
  10. Greater tenacity and endurance.
  11. Wagon liable to break down, upset, or stick. Conse-
quent loss of time and additional expense in former case,
besides inability or want of means to repair.
  12. Lastly, the additional dead weight of the wagon,
which is considerable—at least a ton, I should say.[42]

To be sure, Leonard and the others cited are enthusiastic
camel supporters and tend to state the animal's advantages in
glowing terms; but all were men of great practical experience
and their unanimous opinion must be taken seriously. Taking
them seriously, it becomes unimaginable that the cost of upkeep of a camel, calculated in terms of its work potential,
could have exceeded that of an ox or a mule in Roman Syria,
Egypt, and North Africa. Of course, a high purchase price
for camels could offset much of this savings, and livestock
prices from Egypt in the second century A.D. indicate that a
camel at that time cost on the order of twice as much as an ox
or four times as much as an ass.[43] Availability of camels, therefore, must be kept in mind as an additional factor in calculating
the comparative economy of using camels instead of oxen.
  Beyond the physical qualities that would tend to make the
camel a more efficient work animal than the ox, there are
technological factors involved with wagon use that must have
reinforced this potential economy. For one thing, the weight
an animal could draw in a wagon was severely restricted by
the prevailing state of wagon and harness design.[44] The great
potential of the horse could not be developed without a total

24 change of thinking in harness design, and judging from the ox-carts that have remained in use throughout the centuries in Anatolia, unsophisticated vehicles such as those that might have been used in farms and villages may still have been built with inefficient solid wheels. Roman oxcarts traveled only six to nine miles a day compared to fifteen to twenty for a pack camel.[45] Then again, the cost of a wagon and draught harness, even at its lowest, must have been far greater than the cost of a camel saddle, particularly in wood poor areas.[46] Moreover, additional economies could be realized from the camel's ability to travel as efficiently without a road as with one. Since the building of major roads was often subsidized by the imperial government for military purposes, its costs were not necessarily borne by the wagon owners who took advantage of it. Local roads from farm to village and village to town would not fall into this category, however. If wheeled vehicles were to be used efficiently in such local settings, some local

7 Chinese illustration of practical advantage of camel transport over road-bound transport.

investment in roads could not be avoided. Finally, a wagon re- **25**
quired one driver for every two animals, while a single person
could take care of a string of three to six camels.

As long as the loads for oxcarts remained as low as is indicated by contemporary sources, therefore, transport by pack
camel must surely have been cheaper. The true purpose of
Diocletian's edict on prices may be debatable, but the 20 percent competitive edge that it allows to the camel seems to
be well within reason. Nevertheless, this alone does not explain
the completeness of the wheel's disappearance.

How, then, did the competitive edge of the pack camel
translate into total or nearly total disappearance of wheeled
vehicles? There are several different ways of approaching this
question, and the true answer to it undoubtedly involves some
factors having little or nothing to do with camels. An important
instance is that of chariotry. For many centuries the chariot
dominated the battlefields of the Middle East; it was the
wheeled vehicle par excellence of ancient times although other
types of carts and wagons existed for more mundane transport purposes. From the technological point of view it seems
likely that then as now innovative design in devices used for
both military and civilian purposes came first from the military
side and that the art of the wheelwright and harness maker
benefited substantially from the military dominance of the
chariot.

Starting in the eighth century B.C., however, the military
chariot was slowly eclipsed by the adoption of mounted cavalry
as the main striking force first by the Assyrian empire and
eventually by virtually every state in the known world. The
use of the chariot by the Carthaginians in the fourth century
B.C. was almost anachronistic so far had the mounted horseman
displaced the charioteer in the military field. One eventual
result of this may have been technological stagnation in the
vehicle industry, but a result that is far better attested is a
shift in taste among ruling castes in the direction of riding.
Fancy chariots and private vehicles continued to be used, to be
sure. To pick a particularly egregious example, in 81 B.C.
Pompey announced his intention of celebrating his African
victories in Rome by entering the city in a chariot drawn by
four elephants only to be frustrated in his design by the narrow-

ness of the city's gates.[47] Nevertheless, chariots and carriages were definitely going out of style, and by the first century B.C. it was already considered improper for a man of station to ride in a vehicle if he was capable of riding a horse.[48] Obviously this contributing factor in the decline of the wheel has nothing to do with camels.

Another factor of questionable relationship to the camel is the decline of the Roman road system, which is difficult to date and in any case took place in different areas at different times.[49] Wheeled vehicles had made do without paved roads for many centuries prior to the expansion of Rome, but nevertheless vehicular traffic must surely have suffered as a result of Roman decline even though much local traffic probably never was served by official roads. As camels replaced wagons, of course, the need to maintain the roads steadily diminished, and the two processes seem to be reciprocally related. Whether increased camel traffic actually figured in the initial stages of road disrepair is to be doubted, however.

Perhaps the dominant factor in the whole process was the decline of harness and wagon manufacture. When the volume of business in any trade falls below some critical level, its continued existence falls into jeopardy. Horseshoeing in the twentieth century United States is a plausible model. In a single generation the once ubiquitous farrier has disappeared entirely from thousands of localities because of the obvious catastrophic decline in volume of business. The decline in the wagon building trades in imperial Roman times was probably much slower, but it was even more complete. In the area of commercial hauling the competition of the camel spurred the decline while changing tastes did the same thing at the luxury level. Once gone, the only way to regenerate such complex trades would have been to reintroduce craftsmen from areas where they continued to flourish. Whatever crude homemade vehicles may have remained would have been less competitive than the properly built ones.

On balance, the economy of the pack camel appears unquestionably to have been the crucial factor, albeit not the sole factor, in the wheel's disappearance. Without a suitable replacement, the carts would have kept on rolling however delapidated the roads became and however disdainful the aris-

tocracy. The fact that the wheel survived the collapse of
Roman power in Gaul is sufficient proof of this. But a replacement was at hand, a superior mode of transport, 900 pounds
of muscle, hauteur, and, for those who can come to appreciate
it, grace.

This brings us for the third and final time to the central
problem of chronology. The suitable replacement was no new-
comer; it had been patiently waiting for the creaky oxcarts
to get out of the way for centuries. Why, then, did the change-
over take place in the fourth, fifth, and sixth centuries A.D.
instead of five hundred years earlier or five hundred years later?
The answer that this book will offer to this question is an
elaborate one, one rooted in the entire long history of camel
domestication. It is, moreover, an answer that is inextricably
ensnarled with historical questions that bear only tangentially
upon the history of transportation. If, therefore, in the following chapters the train of argument follows unexpected path-
ways, I beg the reader not to despair that I have lost track
of my central theme.

2 The Origin of Camel Domestication

Looking at the small, delicate bones of the first rabbit-sized ancestor of the camel that lived in North America during the Eocene period when mammals first began to be an important class of animals, it is hard to imagine its evolution into the large, peculiar looking animal of today.[1] In fact, the living western hemisphere relatives of the camel, the llama, alpaca, guanaco, and vicuna, having neither the long curved neck nor the humps of stored fat that characterize the camel, look like much more reasonable extrapolations from the original Protylopus. How these and other less visible but peculiarly camelline characteristics have developed is not known in detail, but camelus as a distinct genus becomes recognizable in the Pleistocene period, a span of about half a million years ending about 8000 B.C., with its attendant waves of glaciation. During one of the glacial periods when low sea level exposed the floor of the Bering Strait and made possible dry land movement from North

America to Asia, the camel entered the eastern hemisphere where it flourished while its cousins left in North America migrated south or became extinct.

Remains of several different species of prehistoric camel have been discovered in excavations of various periods stretching from the Altantic Ocean to Russia and across Central Asia. While these remains testify to a very extensive expansion of camel terrritory from the original point of entry in eastern Siberia, they say very little about what the camel was actually like across this vast range. There is no way of telling from bone structure, for instance, whether a camel has one or two humps or none; and the designation of these prehistoric remains as belonging to either the one-humped or two-humped species is based almost exclusively on the distribution of the two species in historic times despite ample evidence of significant changes in their geographical distribution.

The most intriguing aspect of the distribution of prehistoric camels in the eastern hemisphere is unquestionably the extinction of the animal in the area of the Sahara desert where in historical times, after its reintroduction from Asia, it has proved its ability to survive. The fact that it was the one-humped camel that reentered the Sahara as a domestic animal and thrived there has caused prehistoric remains to be identified as one-humped, but more logically it suggests that the animal that did not survive in prehistoric times was of a different species, and this suggestion is supported by the evidence that will be presented in chapter six pointing to an enormous shrinkage of the territory of the two-humped camel in historic times. In other words, it seems possible that the original camel species distributed throughout the entire known range of prehistoric camels in Africa, Europe, and Asia resembled more closely in environmental adaptation the presently known two-humped animal than the one-humped.

The evolution of the one-humped camel from the two-humped camel has been put forward by numerous writers on the basis of the observation that the fetus of the one-humped camel goes through a two-humped phase; but it has also been suggested on the basis of data on hybridization of the two species that all camels have a genetic capacity for two humps.[2] However, number of humps may not be as important as other characteristics in determining the apparently superior adaptation of the two-humped camel to colder, moister climates and the one-humped to torrid ones.

Experimentation with camels has been confined for the most part to the one-humped species, and this is unfortunate since there is no sure evidence of the degree to which the two-humped animal shares with its cousin specific adaptations for combatting dehydration and high temperature.[3] Yet circumstantial evidence in the form of the traditional beliefs of camel breeders and users that the one-humped camel cannot flourish in cold or moist climates nor the two-humped camel in extremely hot climates strongly suggests that there is a degree of physiological difference between the two species large enough to have affected their geographical distribution.[4]

Many of the most visible environmental adaptations, of course, are common to both species and imply a shared evolution. Both store fat in humps; both have long necks suitable for feeding on bushes and trees; both have padded feet suited to travel on sand and ill suited to travel on mud although different breeds within each species may have feet better adapted to stony or mountainous travel;[5] both have the capacity to go long intervals without water although again certain breeds within each species require more frequent watering than others.[6] From these shared characteristics the impression emerges of the prehistoric camel as an animal living in bushy semiarid lands, almost completely defenseless against predators with its soft feet and ungainly run, trusting for survival primarily upon its ability to live in desolate areas and frequent only rarely the water holes where lions or other enemies could attack it.[7] As the pressure of predation became greater, the value of adaptation to desert life steadily increased, but in the emerging desert of the Sahara, at least, the camel seems to have been unable to hide sufficiently. The earliest periods of Saharan rock art depict animals now found only south of the desert, such as elephants and giraffes, but do not depict the camel which presumably had become extinct by that time, extinct because of predation coupled with an as yet incomplete adaptation to full desert life.

The ways in which the two species diverge can all be plausibly related to temperature. The domestic two-humped camel (since no wild one-humped camels exist no other comparision can be made) is darker in color, woolier, and shorter of leg than its one-humped cousin; and these traits correlate with the tendency of animals living in hot deserts to be light colored, short haired, and long limbed. Two additional traits of interest are the greater skin elasticity of the one-humped animal and, of course, the fact of having one hump instead of two. The possible connection of these two traits to environmental temperature is the following:

Camels do not store water as both folk belief and earlier scientific theory allege; they conserve it. Moreover, they conserve it in many ways.[8] Efficient kidneys allow for a high concentration of impurities in liquid waste; dehydration affects bodily fluids other than the blood; immense quantities of water can be consumed in one watering and the water consumed, which is normally equal to the level of loss from dehydration, is distributed throughout the body tissues within forty-eight hours. Most important, however, for camels living in very hot climates is their capacity to absorb heat by allowing their blood temperature to rise, without ill effect, over six degrees Fahrenheit in the course of a hot day before beginning to perspire. In this way water loss through perspiration is greatly minimized. During the chilly desert night the animal's body temperature falls to its base level ready to begin a new rise the next day. This particular adaptation has not been experimentally demonstrated for two-humped camels.

Ordinarily an animal living in a hot environment is adapted for efficient cooling of the blood. If the animal cools itself by perspiring, it tends to develop a high ratio of surface area to body volume so that less heat has to be dissipated by each square inch of skin. The large ears of African elephants are a notable adaptation of this sort. This principle cannot easily be applied to the camel, however, since it conflicts with the water hoarding principle according to which it begins to perspire only after absorbing as much heat as it can bear. An opposite principle, in fact, might be proposed, one that would favor a slow heating body configuration, that is, a low ratio of surface area to body volume.[9] The more slowly heat was absorbed, the later the onset of perspiration and consequently of water loss could be postponed. If such a principle were actually in effect, the consolidation of two humps into one (or super-

8 Two-humped stud camel from northwestern Iran. Note long hair, short legs.

9 Tuareg riding camels in the Sahara. Note short hair, long legs, light color.

development of the back hump and suppression of the front) would provide an apt illustration of it since the surface area of a single hump would be substantially smaller than the area of two humps whose combined volume equalled that of the single hump. Anatomically the change would not be terribly great since the humps have no bony structure. Furthermore, the fact that the humps of two-humped camels flop over in a flaccid manner when depleted by starvation while the more elastic skin of the one-humped camel causes a steady diminution in the size of the hump without flaccidity under similar conditions could be seen as a corroboration of the principle.[10]

Without confirmation through scientific experimentation, especially regarding the heat and dehydration adaptations of the two-humped camel, it is impossible to be certain of the actual process of evolution of the two known camel species. The differentiation suggested above along the lines of adaptation to high temperature is plausible at best. Nevertheless, it does suggest an explanation of the apparent geographical distribution of camels at the dawn of domestication. By 3000 B.C. or so the camel was extinct or nearly so in Africa and was probably uncommon as a wild animal in the Middle East and Central Asia. Its bones are infrequently encountered in stone age sites, and it is almost never depicted as a wild beast.[11] It is likely that it was in the process of becoming extinct through predation over much of its range and that where it did still survive it was encountered in only the most barren areas.

Desiccation was also progressing, however, both in North Africa and the Middle East. As the Arabian desert became increasingly desolate, camels that were poorly adapted to heat may have died out or migrated, leaving, perhaps, pockets of animals cut off in the better watered areas of eastern and southern Arabia in particular. If, in fact, the one-humped camel did evolve from the two-humped camel, it seems more than likely that it happened in Arabia since that is where all of our earliest positive indications of one-humped camels come from. While a non-heat-adapted camel, presumably two-humped, fought a losing battle for survival in the north, remnant populations in Arabia developed special adaptations for high temperature, including the single hump, and thus fitted themselves to move into a newly developing, predator free environmental niche, the

torrid wastes of Arabia. Thus the camel would have become
known to neolithic man in two different incarnations: in Mesopotamia, Anatolia, Iran and further east as a shy, uncommon
beast, most numerous in desert areas, to be hunted possibly for
food, and in Arabia as a common animal peculiarly adapted to
life in the hot desert and relatively fearless being without predators other than man. Both of these forms of prehistoric man-
camel contacts gave rise to domestication, probably, but not
necessarily, independently; but the one-humped camel is of
more immediate concern here, and further discussion of the
two-humped camel will be deferred to chapter six.

The question of the origin of camel domestication traditionally begins, as indeed does everything else, with the book of
Genesis. Among the bribes received by Abraham from the Phar-
aoh of Egypt in prospect of taking Sarah into his harem were
sheep, oxen, asses, and camels. Again in a later episode ten
camels were sent along by Abraham with his eldest servant who
was to seek out a wife for Isaac. His choice fell upon Rebekah
as the first maiden to come to the well where the servant had
stopped and offer drink not only to the servant but to the
camels as well. Since a camel can drink as much as twenty-eight
gallons of water in a single watering, the hospitality involved
in watering a stranger's string of ten animals may have been
a truly extraordinary token of potential wifely submission.[12]
One generation further on camels appear again when Rachel,
Jacob's wife, hides among the camel furnishings the images
stolen from her father and then sits upon them; and in the next
generation Joseph is sold by his jealous brothers to Ishmaelite
merchants from Gilead passing by with camels laden with
spice and incense.[13]

From these references a pattern of camel use can be extrapolated that seems very much in consonance with later Middle
Eastern society: the camel forming part of a bride price, a small
caravan of camels crossing the desert from Palestine to Iraq, a
woman perched atop a camel loaded with camp goods, merchants carrying incense to Egypt. This entire vision, however,
both original text and extrapolated image, has been categori-
caly rejected by W. F. Albright, one of the foremost scholars of
Biblical history and Palestinian archaeology and the person
whose opinion on camel domestication is most frequently en-

countered.[14] According to Albright, any mention of camels in the period of Abraham is a blatant anachronism, the product of later priestly tampering with the earlier texts in order to bring them more in line with altered social conditions. The Semites of the time of Abraham, he maintains, herded sheep, goats, and donkeys but not camels, for the latter had not yet been domesticated and did not really enter the orbit of Biblical history until about 1100-1000 B.C. with the coming of the Midianites, the camel riding foes of Gideon.[15]

Albright's firm and repeated advocacy of this date, which might be extended backwards several centuries to allow for early stages of domestication, has been taken up by many other scholars; but it has not gone without contention.[16] Although some students of camel domestication have ignored or been unaware of Albright's viewpoint, it has strongly colored most analyses of the problem; and what appears to be a debate about the date of first domestication concentrates more often than not upon whether Abraham's camels were real or interpolated. Consequently, any real or imagined depiction of a domestic camel antedating 1100 B.C. has been seized upon as conclusive proof by Albright's challengers or written off as spurious or misdated by his supporters, all without taking into consideration the actual process of domestication or its social ramifications.

There are no sound grounds for doubting Albright's contention that camel domestication first became a factor of importance in the Syrian and north Arabian deserts around the eleventh century B.C., and, as will be seen, there is much to support the contention besides the absence of camelline remains in Holy Land archaeological sites of earlier date, which was Albright's primary datum. On the other hand, this date need not be taken as the beginning date of camel domestication in an absolute sense. Closer attention to the process of domestication indicates that the camel was actually domesticated long before the year 1100 B.C., but in southern rather than northern Arabia where the practice did not indeed penetrate, although evidence of it may have, until the period put forward by Albright.

Modern anthropological studies prove the obvious, that there is more than one way to live with a camel. A camel can be milked, ridden, loaded with baggage, eaten, harnessed to a

plow or wagon, traded for goods or wives, exhibited in a zoo, **37**
or turned into sandals and camel's hair coats. No camel-using
group does all of these things nor is the balance in importance
between one use and another likely to be identical between two
unrelated groups. Some usages, such as eating, do not imply
domestication since they can be applied as well to the wild animal as to the domesticated one while others, such as riding and
use as a draught animal, imply thorough domestication. It is
through tracing the different usage patterns of camel people
that the process of camel domestication, dissemination, and
historical influence can best be understood.

Ideally, this approach should be followed up by the techniques of modern anthropological inquiry, but extrapolation
from studies of modern camel-breeding or using societies to
earlier societies is a delicate proposition, and the historical data
from early periods rarely display much anthropological sophis-
tication. The core of the hypothetical reconstruction of early
camel history to be presented in this and succeeding chapters
will thus center upon a different line of investigation, that of
technological history.

Technological historians share certain biases. They prefer
working with artifacts or pictures to working with descriptions.
They believe that technological change is, by and large, gradual
and that there is usually at least one middle stage to be discovered between one type of device or process and any significantly improved versions of the same device or process. And
they tend to favor diffusionist theories linking technological
developments into chains stretching back chronologically and
geographically to a single point of origin to theories of simul-
taneous discovery or parallel evolution. They are always ready,
naturally, to throw over these biases in the face of persuasive
evidence, but they influence nevertheless the direction they take
in investigating a problem, and they have influenced this study
of the camel.

The process of domestication of a single animal has never
been observed from start to finish, but various stages leading to
complete domestication have been observed separately. The
relationship between the Australian aborigine and the dingo,
for example, represents a stage of semidomestication, and even
a major herd animal like the reindeer can be said to be less fully

domesticated than the cow.[17] From observations such as these theoretical reconstructions of the complete process of domestication have been attempted, but their application to the case of a specific animal such as the camel is often quite difficult. Still, certain conclusions stemming from the theoretical study of domestication should be borne in mind. First, it takes a very long time to transform a wild animal into a domestic animal, almost certainly a matter of centuries, although this will obviously vary from one species to another. Second, only in the later stages of domestication is an animal likely to be used for riding, bearing burden, or draught. Before it is too wild, although here again there are exceptions such as the zebra which can be broken to the harness from the wild state. On the other hand, animal products—meat, milk, fiber, leather, dung—can be utilized at much earlier stages and often when the animal is still completely wild.[18] At every stage implements are used in some way or other, but only at fairly advanced stages do these implements become specialized and clearly differentiated from those used for other types of animal. The same stone ax can kill a wild horse or a wild camel, but whoever tries to nail a horseshoe to a camel's soft foot is in for a rude surprise. In terms of artifacts, then, evidence for the earliest stages of camel use is essentially untraceable. Nevertheless, the evolutionary development of relatively late implements can reveal something about the earlier stages.

The most primitive pattern of camel utilization appears, surprisingly, to be that of the Somali and related peoples of the eastern horn of Africa.[19] Presently divided among Ethiopia, Somalia, and the Territoire Français des Afars et des Issas directly opposite the southwestern tip of Arabia, the eastern horn of Africa forms a triangle bordered by the Indian Ocean on the east, the Gulf of Aden on the north, and the 10,000 foot high mountain wall of the Ethiopian highlands on the west. While its northward facing coastline consists of narrow plains backed by mountains that often exceed 5,000 feet and its eastward coastline is a virtually harborless desert, much of the interior of the country is well suited to camel herding, being suitably furnished with scrub vegetation but too dry for other uses.

Today Somalia alone has a camel population exceeding four million, and that excludes the camels of neighboring northern

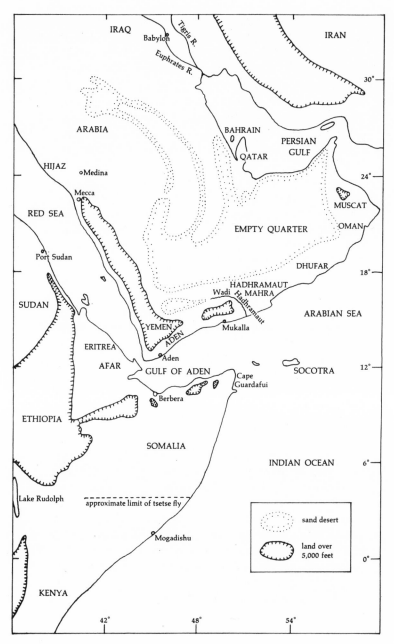

South Arabia and the Horn of Africa

Kenya, eastern Ethiopia, and Ethiopian Eritrea to the north.[20] Thus, the horn constitutes one of the largest and most abundant camel territories in the world, not to mention one of the least known. Unquestionably the most striking feature of Somali and related camel culture is the fact that unlike all other camel peoples they never ride their animals. Although the British and Italians gave ample proof of the suitability of Somali camels for riding and actually found that Somalis were willing to ride them as members of colonial military formations, Somali interest in the practice was and continued to be nonexistent. They complain that it makes them easy targets.[21]

Beyond this disinterest in riding, there are other singular characteristics of Somali camel culture as well. For one, the reliance upon camel's milk as a dietary staple is unusually heavy, especially during the wet seasons when men live apart from their families in herding camps where there is virtually no other form of sustenance. Futhermore, aside from a limited caravan trade in the north, camels are little used for carrying burdens.[22] A few animals are used for carrying camp goods, such as the curved poles that form the framework of Somali houses, from one campsite to another; but most exist simply as a form of wealth and source of nourishment. The Somali pack saddle, in fact, is almost unique, being related only to that in use on the island of Socotra which will be discussed later.

It is very difficult to brush aside these facts as mere local idiosyncracies since the camel is certainly not native to the area. The question is where the camel of the horn of Africa came from and when. The unique Somali pattern of camel usage points to the answer.

From the camel's point of view, the horn of Africa is not so much a triangle as an island. To the south the tsetse fly begins to be found in Somalia about four degrees north of the equator, and although tsetse fly country is not continuous, it affords an effective barrier to the spread of the camel southward where, in any case, high humidity would make camel breeding difficult. To the west is the high Ethiopian plateau to which the camel might possibly become adapted since mountain breeds are known elsewhere but where there is no evidence of camel breeding ever having been practiced.[23] To the east, of course, is the Indian Ocean, the Gulf of Aden, the Bab al-Mandab

strait at the mouth of the Red Sea, and the Red Sea. Only along
the Red Sea coast at the northern end of the region, where the
Ethiopian highlands meet the sea, is there a possible land route
for camels to go elsewhere in Africa, and the land just south of
that isthmus is the forbiddingly desolate and arid Danakil area
or Afar triangle which is far from being prime land even
for camels.[24]
Given this high degree of geographical isolation, there are
only two plausible ways in which the camel could have reached
the horn of Africa: either it came south by land along the coast,
which would make it a southern offshoot of Sudanese or
Saharan camel culture, or it came across the sea from the
Arabian peninsula. The peculiar usage pattern of the Somali
effectively rules out the former possibility. All Sudanese and
Saharan camel peoples ride their animals and have, in fact,
developed several types of saddles designed exclusively for
riding.[25] The pack saddles of the north also differ completely
from the Somali design, and the camel is used there extensively
as a beast of burden. Ethnically, the relation of the Somali to the
Beja camel breeders on the northern side of the coastal isthmus
is beyond question, but equally beyond question is the fact that
the Somali are latecomers to the African horn who found the
camel already there when they came and adopted indigenous
patterns of camel utilization. Today both the southernmost Beja
tribes in the hills on the northern side of the coastal isthmus and
the northernmost tribes on the southern side herd cattle rather
than camels, and there is no reason to suppose that this dis-
continuity between Sudanese camels and Somali camels does
not have a long history.[26]
Finally on the physiological side, the reproductive cycle of
the camel is governed by a male rutting period of two or three
months duration once a year during the best grazing season and
a twelve to thirteen month gestation period which causes mating
and calving to coincide. What triggers the period of rut is not
known, but since it always takes place during the rainy season,
whatever part of the year that is in a given locale, and since
camels do not seem to reproduce well in wet climates, some connection with the level of humidity is indicated.[27] Whatever the
exact cause of the onset of rut may be, however, animals that
are moved from one area of seasonal rainfall to another area

42   where the rainfall occurs in a different season cease almost entirely to reproduce.[28] In the case of Somalia and the Sudan just such a difference in climatic regime exists. The Sudan is summer rainfall country, with July and August being the wettest months at Khartoum, while Somalia's climate is governed by the monsoons which bring the heaviest rains, which are not very heavy, in May and June and lighter rains in October, November, and December. Consequently, it is unlikely that any efforts by camel breeders north of the coastal isthmus to penetrate south with their herds would have been pursued once it was discovered that reproduction was adversely affected.

Looking to the Arabian alternative, it must be observed that while the discrepancies cited between Somali and Saharan camel use hold true as well for Arabia, southern Arabia does fall under the monsoon climatic regime and for this reason alone is a more likely source for Somali camel culture.[29] Moreover, the introduction of the camel into North Africa occurred at a roughly determinable date and its utilization at the time of introduction is known through contemporary rock paintings and engravings to be approximately like that of present day Saharan tribes.[30] Therefore, it is out of the question that the Somali usage pattern could have been copied from an earlier stage of Saharan or Sudanese camel domestication. With Arabia the opposite case holds. The camel appears to be indigenous to Arabia, and present or historically determinable patterns to camel use may well, and in all probability do, derive from earlier stages of camel domestication within the Arabian peninsula. Therefore the Somali camels most probably stem from original stock imported from southern Arabia at a time when camel domestication in that area was in a relatively early stage, a stage which was preserved in the isolation of Somalia after being superseded in its original area.

Ideally, several crucial bits of information might be deduced from this. Knowledge of the date of the introduction of the camel into the horn of Africa might pin down an early stage of camel domestication chronologically, just as knowledge of the exact area from which the camels were imported might pin it down geographically. Unfortunately, these lines of inquiry are difficult to pursue. As already mentioned, the Somali themselves and related peoples like the Afar to the north appear on

the historical scene much too late to be considered the original
importers of the camel. Around the sixteenth century A.D. the
Somali pushed southward to occupy most of Somaliland driving
before them the related Galla peoples who had established
themselves in an earlier wave of expansion from the north. The
Galla of today keep only a very few camels and are primarily
cattle breeders. As for the inhabitants preceding the Galla,
remnants may survive in the Negro populations along and between the Juba and Shebelle rivers in southern Somalia, but this
is far from certain.

This extremely sketchy ethnological history does not correspond very conveniently with the almost equally sketchy
evidence of rock paintings and engravings. Classifying what
little rock art there is according to the various techniques developed for the relative dating of similar art in the Sahara,
three periods have been distinguished by J. D. Clark.[31] The
first period depicts a society of pastoral people herding long-
horned cattle and bears close resemblance to certain groups of
Saharan art. No camels are depicted. The second group con-
tinues to show long-horned cattle but also shows both the camel
and the zebu, the type of humped cattle presently found
among the Somali and Galla. It is questionable whether the
horse is depicted in this group. The third group, finally, is
clearly from the recent historical period and includes the tribal
marks of tribes still living in the same locations.

The dating of the first two groups is quite uncertain, but
there are indicators in the types of domestic animal depicted
along with the camel. The horse, significantly, appears only in
the third or, strictly speaking, Somali group. Its absence earlier
reinforces the notion that the camel did not enter the horn from
the north since the horse long precedes the camel in Saharan
rock art. If the camel preceded the horse, however, it succeeded
long-horned cattle and is not clearly prior to the zebu. Unfortunately, this data does not correspond readily to the sole datable
pictorial evidence, the reliefs at Deir al-Bahri, the funerary
temple of Queen Hatshepsut opposite Luxor, showing the expedition sent by the queen to the land of Punt between 1501 and
1479 B.C. There is no way of knowing for sure whether Punt
was situated in Somalia, in southern Arabia, or in both; but
since what is in question here is a possible linkage between

those two areas, exact certainty is not crucial. What is important is the fact that the land of Punt furnished at that time both long-horned and short-horned cattle but not the zebu. Representations of short-horned cattle, now no longer found in Somalia, do show up in both southern Arabia and Somalia,[32] but Clark makes no mention of them in his three period classification scheme for Somalia so there is no way of telling by this means whether or not they antedated the camel.

The appearance of short-horned cattle in southern Arabia, Somalia, and Punt, wherever it may have been, has been taken to indicate that the route of introduction of short-horned cattle from India or Iran, presumably, into Africa was by sea via southern Arabia, essentially the same route, although with southern Arabia as the starting point, being proposed here for the introduction of the camel into Somalia. Adding force to this argument is the continued existence to the present day of a dwarf breed of short-horned cattle on Socotra, a mountainous eighty mile long island located in the Indian Ocean 130 miles east of Cape Guardafui, the point of the African horn, and 190 miles southeast of the nearest point on the south coast of Arabia. Postulating an active sailing trade following the monsoons up the east African coast to southern Arabia and to the Persian Gulf and India beyond, a probable sequence of human and animal movements in ancient times can thus be suggested.[33] Short-horned cattle must have been brought from Arabia to Africa in the later half of the third millennium B.C. since they appear in Egyptian art of the Middle Kingdom (2200–1788 B.C.). During roughly the same period the ancestors of the dwarf cattle probably became established on Socotra, which along with Somalia and Dhufar on the Arabian coast is one of the three places in the world that produce high quality frankincense. Since from the third millennium B.C. onward the Egyptians sent expeditions by sea to bring back incense from Punt, it is likely that Socotra, which could hardly have been avoided by seamen traveling to or between Arabia and Somalia, was settled at this time by incense gatherers who sustained themselves in part with these cattle.[34]

The camel could have reached Socotra and Somalia as part of this same expansion based on the sea-borne incense trade, but it may have come later since it is found depicted in Somalia along with the substantially later zebu cattle.[35] The only rock **45** carvings found to date in Socotra depict the camel but cannot be dated much before the tenth century B.C.[36] The coexistence of long- and short-horned cattle in Punt about 1500 B.C. and of long-horned cattle and zebus in the second period of Somali rock art should not be overlooked, however. The zebu eventually replaced both types of cattle in Somalia so the period of coexistence shown in period two depictions presumably represents the early phase of the introduction of the zebu. It would also appear, however, that the zebu never reached Socotra just as the horse never did, and this suggests that Socotra experienced little introduction of new species after its initial settlement and exploitation as an incense island.[37] Yet the camel did reach Socotra, and, as will be seen later, at a stage of domestication much more similar to that of Somalia than to that of southern Arabia. Therefore a tentative deduction can be made that the camel came to both Somalia and Socotra at approximately the same time either with or somewhat after the short-horned cattle and in any case before the zebu. A date between 2500 and 1500 B.C. would thus seem reasonable, but this must be tested against further data to be brought up in the next chapter.

If the Somali pattern of camel use is the most primitive presently known, then it is evidently a pattern derived ultimately, though doubtless going through certain changes within Somalia, from someplace in southern Arabia.[38] Within southern Arabia the most probable point of origin is the central area of Hadhramaut, Mahrah, and Dhufar. Although Yemen in the southwest corner of the peninsula is closest to Africa, it is too wet and mountainous to be good camel country;[39] Muscat and Oman further to the east beyond Hadhramaut, Mahrah, and Dhufar are too distant to be given first consideration. The island of Socotra, it is worth mentioning, was ruled from coastal Arabia in Hellenistic times as it is today,[40] and the frankincense trees which grow there and in northern Somalia are not found in southern Arabia much west of Dhufar.

The fact that the Hadhramaut area (including Mahrah and Dhufar) probably gave rise to the camel cultures of Somalia and Socotra does not by itself prove that camels were first domesticated in southern Arabia.[41] Camel domestication would, however, appear to have been known there before it was

46   known in northern Arabia and Syria. Conceivably the camel
was domesticated elsewhere in the peninsula and reached the
Hadhramaut from there. One must rule out, however, the
Syrian desert, the northern part of the Arabian desert, and the
coastal oases of eastern Arabia from Bahrain northward since
these areas were well known to the literate societies of Mesopotamia and the Mediterranean Levant coast and it is unlikely,
as Albright has argued, that camel breeding would both have
escaped literary notice and failed to leave material traces up
until the eleventh century B.C. if it was known in the immediate
hinterland of these settled societies. To be sure, one or two
representations of camels from early Mesopotamia have been
alleged, but they are all either doubtfully camelline, as the
horsy looking clay plaque from the third dynasty of Ur (2345–
2308 B.C.),[42] or else not obviously domestic and hence possibly
depictions of wild animals, as is the case with the occasional
Ubaid and Uruk period (4000–3000 B.C.) examples.[43]

Excluding the Yemen, already mentioned as poor camel
country on climatic grounds, this leaves only central Arabia

10 Fragmentary clay plaque from Ur alleged to depict camel rider.
Animal is more probably an ox or ass.

and the Hijaz or Red Sea coastal highlands as possible alternative loci of original camel domestication, and in these desolate
areas incentive and feasibility loom as major questions. Herders
living on the fringes of the desert to the north were already
familiar with the domestic sheep, goat, cow, and donkey well
before the camel was domesticated. For almost any purpose
then imaginable, except for living out in the middle of the
desert, one of these existing domestic animals was perfectly
satisfactory. It could be argued, of course, that certain marginal
peoples were forced to move into the desert and that they
domesticated the camel in response to need, but such an argument would have to explain how those marginal peoples man-
aged to stay alive during the long early stages of domestication
when the camel was still more wild than tame. It is often stated
that life in the deep desert is impossible without the camel, but
to be precise it should be said that life is impossible without the
domestic camel. The Arabian desert offers little chance of
survival to anyone who does not already know how to live in it
before he gets there and who has no one to teach him how.
Thus it is difficult to see why anyone would be in a position to
domesticate the camel in either central Arabia or the Hijaz.[44]
Where would they have come from? And why? And how could
they have stayed alive long enough to pursue the work of
domestication?

In the face of these puzzling questions, the case for southern
Arabia becomes stronger. Much later Arab tradition from the
seventh century A.D. even contains some things that hint at a
south Arabian origin for the domestic camel. First is the well
known metaphor attested both in the Qur'an and in bedouin
poetry of the camel as the ship of the desert.[45] On the one hand,
the aptness of the image is obvious to anyone familiar with the
sea, but on the other, it is quite extraordinary to find it in use
among people who had little contact with or knowledge of the
sea and who otherwise used very few nautical images. Not
inconceivably the whole conception goes back to the seafaring
people of southern Arabia, the Red Sea coast never having
developed a significant seafaring tradition.

A more weighty hint is the close association in Arab folk
belief of camels with jinn, the sometimes benevolent sometimes
malevolent spirit beings that inhabit the desert. According to

different traditions, camels are related to jinn;[46] one of the four components of jinn along with man, the sea, and the four winds;[47] created from the eyes of jinn;[48] and created from devils.[49] Similarly, the resting places of camels are said to be the haunts of devils and hence improper places to pray as opposed to sheep and goat folds which are auspicious.[50] Overlaying these traditions are many others bespeaking the excellences of camels, and it is possible that the jinn traditions date from a period when the Arabs did not have camels but only knew them as the possessions of other peoples who lived in deserts that the Arabs themselves with their sheep and goats could not penetrate. The connection with southern Arabia comes from some additional traditions dealing with legendary wild camels (*ḥūsh*) said to live in the equally legendary land of Wabār which was once inhabited by the people of ʿĀd who were destroyed by God who then gave the land to the jinn. These wild camels are said to mate with the camels of the jinn to produce the breeds known as Mahrī, ʿUmānī, ʿĪdī, and ʿAsjadī or Dhahabī.[51] The land of Wabār itself is located by different authors in different places but always in southern Arabia,[52] and the camel breeds descended from the camels of the jinn are respectively those of Mahrah, Oman, and the tribe of ʿĪd which is a subtribe of Mahrah.[53] The name of the fourth breed means goldbearing but what significance this may have is uncertain. The Mahri and Omani camels even today, it should be noted, are classed as the finest riding camels in Arabia, and the word *mahri* has the specific meaning thoroughbred riding camel in North Africa.

Arguments from Arab folklore, therefore, buttress the idea that the camel was originally domesticated in the south whence it became known to the Arabs as the animal of an alien and perhaps mysterious people whose gods may have been absorbed into the existing category of jinn. But getting back to questions of feasibility, how did the camel come to be domesticated in the Hadhramaut? What was the motivation? What people was responsible? The last question, unfortunately, cannot be answered at all. The earliest Semites, in the sense of people speaking known south Semitic languages, seem not to have reached southern Arabia until around the sixteenth century B.C., and who was there before them is a mystery.[54]

The archaeological record as presently known is blank be-   **49**
tween that time and about 5000 B.C.,[55] but unusual physical
types isolated in just such places as Socotra would appear to
be remnants of some pre-Semitic population.[56]

Presumably these earlier people inhabited coastal enclaves
or river valleys such as the Wadi Hadhramaut proper that
afforded a suitable climate and took their living from hunting
and the sea. A reasonably contemporary refuse dump exca-
vated on the Arabian coast of the Persian Gulf indicates that
there wild camels were eaten but the more important food
animal was the dugong or sea cow.[57] If man was ever to grow
away from the sea and his environmental limitations, some
kind of subsistence animal was necessary, particularly given
the extreme barrenness, perhaps somewhat less then, of most
of southern Arabia. Examples of domesticated animal life
were doubtless well known from sailing to other lands, but
sheep, goats, and cattle could not live well enough to sustain
human populations in the arid hills and the desert beyond.
Therefore, since the sea afforded adequate sustenance, there
was both motivation and time to try to tame the large, ungainly looking animal that ran wild in the hinterland, perhaps
already half tame by virtue of living in a predator free environment.

The intermediate steps between hunting and taming can
only be guessed at. Probably the scarcity of water facilitated
capture of wild camels at water points, and it is also possible
that food was used as a lure since even today dried shark and
sardines are used in this area as camel fodder as they are nowhere else in the world.[58] Whatever the means utilized, however, the primary object of this initial domestication is fairly
certain. It was milk.[59] The pattern of camel use surviving today
in the Hadhramaut reinforces this conclusion already indicated
from Somali camel use. While the south Arabs are more advanced than the Somalis insofar as they use camels for bearing
burdens to a greater extent and also for riding, they share with
the Somalis the use of camel milk as a staple of life and to
maximize usable milk production they kill at birth all but a few
male animals.[60]

Imagining a society of coastal fishermen and sailors aug-
menting their diet with camel milk and subsequently giving

rise to a subsociety concentrating its full efforts on the rearing of camels and production of milk, it is easy to see that questions of riding or loading would not automatically arise. Not only was the Hadhramaut virtually cut off by the great sand sea of the Rubᶜ al-Khali, or Empty Quarter, from direct land contact with the rising civilizations to the north, with their animal-drawn plows and wagons and their pack asses, but the sea going dhow, the sailing vessel characteristic of the Indian Ocean, provided them with a more obvious and more efficient means of transporting what meager trade goods they may have had. The only reason to put a load on a camel in such an environment would be to take the load off one's own back, and the only loads requiring such relief would be those entailed by changing camp. However, as long as tame camels were a mere adjunct to more or less settled community life along the coast or in the Wadi Hadhramaut, such changes in campsite were not a routine feature of existence. Changes in campsite come into being only when people give up settled life for a semi-nomadic or nomadic life following the grazing calendar. Therefore the impetus to use the camel for carrying a burden already betokens the evolution of a subsociety dedicated entirely or almost entirely to herding.

This is a point that must have been reached before the introduction of the camel into Socotra and the horn of Africa. Fisher folk or coastal traders could have had little reason to transport camels as part of their cargo; only camel herders on the move for one reason or another could wish to bring such a cumbersome piece of property along with them. Just as today the Hadhrami Arab is naturally inclined toward the sea and tribal groups show no reluctance to pack themselves into dhows and ride before the northeast monsoon,[61] so 4,000 years ago some camel herding group must have decided to migrate to a better land that they had heard about from the dhow masters, a better land whose main attraction was probably frankincense and myrrh which were beginning to find their way by sea to Egypt.

The technological level of the first camel users in Socotra and Somalia thus explains the peculiarities of the camel culture of those two areas at the present time. Relatively little is known about Socotran camels, beyond the fact that they seem to be

very fine animals,[62] or about Socotran camel usage; but there is
a basic similarity between the types of pack saddle used in the
two places which is all the more remarkable since in virtually
every other respect including language Socotra is an offshoot of
south Arabian culture and unrelated to the culture of Somalia.

The Somali saddle is described by the British army camel
veterinarian A. S. Leese as follows:

> In fact, it is not a saddle at all, but merely a number of
> mats, generally three, thrown over the back and hump, one
> on top of another, and secured there, bunched up, by a long
> rope (30 feet by 1-1/2 inches) passing under the belly and
> tail. In Jubaland [the area of the Juba river in southern
> Somalia] a pair of sticks crossing above the withers to repre-
> sent the arch or tree of the saddle are bound in position by
> the rope; the Sambur use two pairs of sticks, one pair cross-
> ing in front of the hump, one pair behind.[63]

With this may be compared descriptions of Socotran saddles by
J. R. Wellsted and then James Theodore Bent:

> I could not but remark the singular mode in which our
> baggage was placed; instead of allowing it to be suspended
> on each side, as is customary in Egypt and Arabia, they pile a
> succession of thick hair mats over the hump and along the
> back, which they bind up by cords into a ridge, and then
> stow the several articles in long baskets on either side; on the
> top of these were placed our beds, serving us, at an elevation
> of thirteen feet from the ground, as saddles.[64]

> A Sokotran camel-man is a most dexterous packer. He must
> first obliterate his camel's hump by placing against it three
> or four thick felt mats or *nummuds*, and on this raised
> surface he builds all his luggage, carefully secured in his
> baskets, ... The camels are very fine specimens of their
> race, standing considerably higher than the Arabian animal,
> and when mounted on the top of our baggage, above the
> hump thus unnaturally raised, we felt at first disagreeably
> elevated.[65]

Quite clearly the same basic saddle is in use both in Somalia
and on Socotra with local variations in the use of a sort of
frame made of long sticks in the former place and baskets in

11 Four-stick Somali camel saddles in northern Kenya.

12 Two-stick Somali camel saddle from southern Ethiopia. Use of carved boards and leather thongs in place of sticks and rope is unusual.

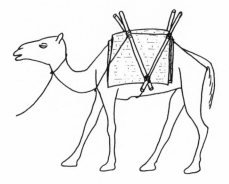

13 Schematic drawing of four-stick Somali saddle.

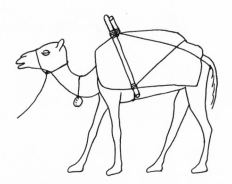

14 Schematic drawing of two-stick Somali saddle.

15 Schematic drawing of Socotran camel saddle

the latter. Plaited baskets, incidentally, are also used for loading in the Hadhramaut but in conjunction with a more advanced pack saddle.[66] It may also be noted that there is no
specific riding saddle on Socotra. Whether the Socotrans
themselves ride on their animals or only perch visiting Europeans on them atop their baggage is not indicated.

What lends importance to these observations about camel
saddles is the fact that the type of saddle involved is very
inefficient and ill designed for carrying very heavy weights. It
survived in these two areas because they were geographically
out of touch with other camel areas and developed no caravan
trade and hence no need for an efficient pack saddle. Leese puts
down the objections to the Somali saddle under five points:

1. Its great weight. The camel carries from 90 or 100
lb. upwards (much more after rain) before he is loaded, i.e.,
he carries about 50 lb. of load less than if he wears the Indian
or Arab pattern.

2. It cannot "fit," and there is pressure on the top of the
withers. With hired attendants it is almost impossible to
prevent sore withers.

3. Saddling previous to loading takes up much time and
requires extra care and skill.

4. The load rides too far forwards and is not by balance,
so that sores on the sides of the top of the withers are liable
to occur if one side of the load is heavier than the other.

5. Crupper-galls are frequent.[67]

A similar analysis of the Socotran saddle is unavailable, but
there is evidence that Socotran camel drivers seek out loads
that would be very light by Arabian standards and that a load
that could hardly have exceeded two hundred pounds (£ 500 in
one shilling pieces in a strong box) proved to be almost too
much for a Socotran camel although anywhere else such a
weight would be well within the camel's normal load limit.[68]

Thus saddle design adds another brick to the edifice of
deduction that comprises the argument for southern Arabia
being the original home of the domestic one-humped camel.
Whether the structure can stand with as many gaps in it as still
exist is not overly important since these gaps may well be
filled in by future archaeological investigation. What is impor-

tant is that it accounts for the origin and primitive state of camel breeding in Somalia and Socotra and lays the groundwork for the discussion to be taken up in the next chapter of the expansion of camel breeding outside the Arabian peninsula. As far as hard dates go, the 2500–1500 B.C. suggested earlier for the introduction of the camel into Somalia is the best that can be done from available data. Given the stage domestication had reached by the time the camels and their owners crossed the sea, some additional time must be allowed for earlier stages. Taking this into consideration, it is easily conceivable that the domestication process first got under way between 3000 and 2500 B.C.

3 The Spread of Camel Domestication and the Incense Trade

The early stages of camel domestication in southern Arabia were not inherently conducive to broad dissemination of the practice. Just as the yak has never been used as a domestic animal outside of the Tibetan highlands because it is not as well suited to other areas as competing species of domestic animal are, so it should not be surprising that the camel remained for many centuries a peculiarly south Arabian domestic animal spreading only to Somalia and Socotra because of the integration of those areas into the seaborne incense trade. Obviously, the camel was as well suited to being exploited economically in the deserts of central and northern Arabia and of Syria as it was to the deserts of southern Arabia, but more than geographical suitability is needed to foster the adoption of a new domestic animal, as the enterprising souls who tried to transplant the camel to other dry parts of the world in the

57

nineteenth century and earlier found out to their disappointment.[1] There must also be a recognized need for the new animal, some economic or military function which it clearly performs in a manner far superior to that of any other available animal. And there must be people willing to learn how to care for it and breed it. Among the people of northern Arabia and Syria no such impetus to adopt the camel into their herding pattern seems to have been felt for a very long time after they actually came to know of the animal. The impetus only began to be felt with the rise of the overland incense trade.

The debate mentioned in the last chapter over whether or not Abraham could have possessed camels was shown to be irrelevant to the question of the actual origin of camel domestication, but it goes to the heart of the matter when we turn our attention to the spread of camel domestication into northern Arabia. Those who have challenged W. F. Albright's dictum that "in the thirteenth century B.C. the domestication of the camel had not yet progressed to a point where it could have any decisive effect upon nomadism"[2] have done so by collecting depictions or other evidence that camels were known in incontestably earlier periods.[3] In so doing they have had to fight an uphill battle, for the weight of textual and archaeological evidence supporting Albright's thesis is overwhelming. Aside from the few bits of evidence mustered by the challengers, there is complete silence concerning camels in early sources, both written and pictorial, that yield an abundance of information about cattle, asses, sheep, and so forth.

Added to the challengers' dilemma is the apparent inability of early artists to fashion a recognizable camel, although it must be observed that in general the camel's neck has as often been considered its distinctive feature as its hump, which impresses most the Western visual sense. Scarcely one of the depictions offered as evidence of early camel use can be identified unequivocally as a camel. It seems odd that one of the most distinctive looking animals in the world should have so defied representation and come out looking instead like a donkey or a sheep, but it is certainly possible that unfamiliarity had precisely this effect. On the whole, therefore, while it is tempting indeed to agree with Albright in dating camel use in Palestine and Syria to the last two centuries of the second

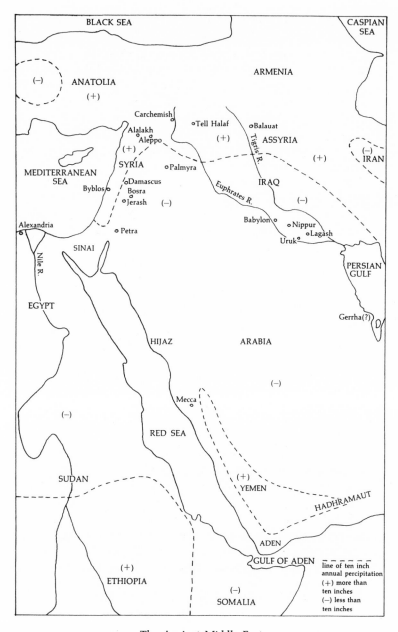

The Ancient Middle East

millenium, the items put forward as physical refutations of his argument cannot be casually brushed aside.

Aside from the textual evidence from the Old Testament cited earlier, five pieces of evidence stand out in particular as being too significant to overlook. The first of these is a cord three and a half feet long discovered by Gertrude Caton-Thompson in excavating an Egyptian gypsum works dating back to around 2500 B.C.[4] This cord was compared with camel, ox, sheep, goat, horse, ass, human, and other kinds of hair and incontestably identified as being braided from camel hair. This does not prove, of course, that camels were in use in Egypt at that time, nor does it prove that the source of the cord was a domestic animal since the wool of a camel may be picked up from the ground after the animal molts. It seems probable, following the discussion in the last chapter, that the cord ultimately derives from the land of Punt, perhaps the possession of a slave or captive, and from a domestic camel.

The second piece of evidence is a tiny bronze figurine included in the foundation deposit of a temple at Byblos in Lebanon.[5] The entire foundation deposit shows strong Egyptian influence and has been determined to date from before the end of the sixth Egyptian dynasty, that is to say, before 2182 B.C. Although on zoological characteristics alone the figurine might be taken to represent a sheep, its accoutrements strongly suggest a camel. Four lines are incised around the muzzle indicating a double strap, a strap around the muzzle being the characteristic way of haltering a camel in early Arabia;[6] thrown over the animal's back is a blanket, presumably a saddle blanket, with scalloped edges; and there is a hole in the back that may once have held a diminutive burden, which would explain the absence of a hump. It is difficult to imagine a sheep with these utilitarian adornments, and it is doubly so in light of the fact that unmistakable sheep figurines from the same foundation deposit do not display them. The local seller of votive figurines, one may surmise, came up with a variation on his usual sheep when asked for a figurine of a camel, an animal he was probably rather unfamiliar with, and then altered it to show that the beast was really a pack animal.

The third and fourth pieces of evidence, unlike the first two, say nothing as to whether the animals depicted were domestic

16 Votive figurine in the form of a camel from temple at Byblos. Note scalloped edge of saddle blanket, rectangular hole on back, and evidence of halter.

17 Camel's head from Uruk showing evidence of halter.

or not, but their places of origin, mainland Greece and Crete, are not only themselves outside the geographical range of the camel but also very far removed from the center of early camel domestication in southern Arabia. Hence they would appear to indicate the existence of the camel in intermediate areas with which Crete and Greece were in communication. One of the items is a small pot discovered in a tomb at Mycenae in Greece which bears as part of its decoration a frieze of animals including an excellently drawn camel and a passable representation of a cat.[7] The pot has been dated to the late Helladic II period 1500–1400 B.C. when Mycenaean art was subject to great Cretan influence. The cat suggests that the inspiration for the piece was ultimately Egyptian since the cat was an object of veneration in that country. A third figure can be interpreted as a dog with its slender head lowered and its tail curved slightly upward; this, too, would suggest Egypt, since a greyhound-type dog also figures prominently in Egyptian life at that period. Thus the frieze may be viewed altogether as a procession of typically Egyptian animals among which the camel is numbered.

The item from Crete is a steatite seal of the Minoan period which shows, if correctly drawn from the original, a most peculiar looking but indisputable camel.[8] The neck and head are well drawn, but the hump is placed too far forward on the shoulders. Overshadowing everything else, however, are the legs which bend forward at what looks to be the knee and terminate in two pincerlike toes. There is little indicated as to the exact dating and provenance of this seal, but a great deal of light is shed upon it by a cylinder seal of apparent northern Mesopotamian origin. This seal is datable stylistically between 1800 and 1400 B.C. and shows, among other things, two human figures seated facing one another on the humps of a two-humped camel.[9] The animal's head and neck facing left are strangely snaky but discernibly camelline and its legs bend forward at what appears to be the ankle and terminate in two pincerlike toes. The grotesque legs on the Minoan seal thus appear to be a poor interpretation of a Mesopotamian artistic formula for representing the camel's large, double toed foot, and the range of dates of the Mesopotamian model can reasonably be applied to it. The crucial difference between the two

18 Mycenaean pot from Late Helladic period. Animals represented are probably greyhound, cat, and camel.

19 Minoan seal showing camel. Compare foot with figure 20.

20 Mesopotamian cylinder seal showing two human figures facing each other on the humps of a two-humped camel.

seals, of course, is that the Minoan one depicts a one-humped camel and not a two-humped one. It therefore testifies to the presence of the one-humped camel in Mesopotamia or Syria at that period.

The fifth piece of evidence, unlike the first four, is textual, a list of rations written in Old Babylonian found in excavating the northern Syrian site of Alalakh and datable to the eighteenth century B.C. Although it is only a single entry on one of several long lists, it is a significant one: "one [measure] as fodder for the camel."[10] Not only does this attest the existence of camels in northern Syria at this time, but the animal involved is clearly domestic. Fodder is being allocated for it, and other animals on the list are all domestic. The second word of the two word phrase used for camel, *anše gam.mal*, literally "ass-camel," is one of the most common words for the animal in later Semitic languages. The location of Alalakh is also noteworthy. Well outside the border of the Syrian desert, it does not seem to have been so much a city of nomads as a well-established urban principality akin to nearby Aleppo, Ugarit, and Byblos.

These five pieces of evidence, needless to say, may not convince everyone that the domestic camel was known in Egypt and the Middle East on an occasional basis between 2500 and 1400 B.C. Other early depictions, alleged to be of camels, which look to my eyes like dogs, donkeys, horses, dragons or even pelicans, might be more convincing to some than the examples described above.[11] Yet it is very difficult to explain away all of the evidence pointing to the camel's presence outside the Arabian peninsula prior to the year 1400 B.C. The effort is better spent looking into the reasons why the evidence from this early period is so very scarce.

The archaeological record, as Albright affirms, shows no indication of camel use in the Syrian area during the period in question, 2500–1400 B.C., and this conclusion is corroborated by a thorough study of nomadism in Mesopotamia in the eighteenth century B.C. made from the records of the kings of Mari, a ctiy located on the Euphrates astride what was later to become the primary caravan route from Iraq to Syria.[12] If camels were present, then, as they appear to have been, they must have been present in very small numbers. Indeed, they must have played little or no part in the ordinary herding economy of the time.

The most satisfactory explanation of this circumstance is that the camel was known because it was brought into the area by traders carrying goods from southern Arabia but that it was not bred or herded in the area. It is worthy of note that whereas the citations from the Bible associating camels with Abraham and his immediate descendants seem to fit the generalized pattern of later camel use in the area, they could also fit a pattern in which camels were very uncommon. The largest number of animals mentioned in those episodes is ten, and those ten are probably most of what Abraham had since they were sent with his servant with the apparent intention of creating a sufficiently wealthy impression to entice the father of a woman of good family into letting his daughter cross the desert to marry Isaac. No man, incidentally, is described as riding a camel, only women, who seem to have perched atop camp goods instead of riding in an enclosed woman's traveling compartment as was later to be the norm.

This does not mean, necessarily, that Abraham or his descendants were mixed up in the Arabian incense trade, although they lived in such great proximity to the main route from Syria to Arabia that such involvement might have been possible. It means simply that in the nineteenth and eighteenth centuries B.C. when Abraham and his immediate descendants appear to have lived, camels were already known in small numbers in the northwestern corner of the Arabian desert where the western Arabian trade route branched out to go to Egypt or further into Syria. Local tribes in the area may have owned a few of the animals, perhaps as articles of prestige, without being heavily involved in breeding them.

Turning to the incense trade itself, the absence of any early sources from the incense producing area makes any reconstruction largely conjectural.[13] Incense was already in use in Egypt in the predynastic period, or mid-fourth millennium B.C. By the middle of the third millennium expeditions were undertaken by sea to the land of Punt. The Deir al-Bahri expedition mentioned in the last chapter is much later but of the same type. Sailing in the Red Sea, however, is a difficult business both because of shifting underwater hazards near the shores and because of the peculiar wind regime.[14] The southern half of the sea from approximately the twentieth parallel southward, roughly the level of the present day cities of Jidda and Port Sudan, is governed by the monsoons, so favorable southerly winds are available during part of the year. The northern half, on the other hand, is the abode of strong, year-round northerly winds and is too narrow to allow easy beating against the wind even in modern sailing vessels, not to mention the primitive ships of the third millennium B.C. Consequently, it is a feasible proposition to sail south from the Gulf of Suez to the Gulf of Aden, but going the other direction ships bound for Egypt were compelled until fairly recent times to land at a port on the western side of the sea and off-load their cargoes for shipment by pack animal to the Nile and then by boat down the Nile to the metropolitan centers in the north.

The need for an overland route for exporting incense was thus minimal. The main consumers of the products were in Egypt and Iraq, and both markets could be reached by water except for the brief trek from the Red Sea to the Nile. The only consuming area not directly served by sea routes was Syria. To be sure, ships could put in at a port on the east side of the Red Sea as well as on the west side, but there was no Nile River in Arabia to facilitate transportation from that point northward. There is every reason to assume, therefore, that the original route of the overland trade in incense and other south Arabian products was along the western coast of Arabia, or rather just inland on the inside of the coastal mountain range, either all the way from Yemen or possibly from some point halfway up the seacoast.

The beginning of this overland route has been dated as early as the beginning of the third millennium B.C., but there is no concrete evidence for this.[15] However, the migration of Semitic speaking peoples to southern Arabia has been analyzed as taking place in two waves, one arriving before 1500 B.C. and the other before 1200 B.C.[16] Given the immense hardship of the trek from northern Arabia to southern Arabia, especially if undertaken without the aid of camels, it is difficult to imagine what could have motivated these Semitic migrations if it was not the incense trade. The probable sequence of events seems to have been that by 2000 B.C. incense was reaching Syria with

some regularity along the western Arabian land route. Some
Semitic speaking tribes saw the potential benefits of this trade
and became interested in it at its northern extremity. In Biblical
parlance these would be the Ishmaelites who appear in the
story of Joseph as traders in incense. Other tribes, probably
later, undertook to follow the trade back to its source and thus
became the nucleus of Semitic settlement in southern Arabia.
Again, in Biblical parlance these would seem to be the children
of Abraham's son Jokshan (Arabic Yuqtān progenitor of the
south Arabian tribes).[17] When the Semites had arrived in
sufficient numbers, they overwhelmed the indigenous inhabitants of southern Arabia and became themselves masters of the
land and the incense trade.

This entire process, it has been argued, took place without
the benefit of camel transport, the camels making their appearance only at a much later date from parts unknown.[18] But it
has been demonstrated that the camel was already in use
during the period in question and that its probable homeland
was southern Arabia. It is much more reasonable, therefore, to
assume that the camel was the main carrier on the incense
route from the very beginning, or nearly so, and that the
Semitic tribes of the north came to know the camel in this way
in very small numbers. In other words, the presence of camels
in the Abraham story can be defended and the story treated
as primary evidence of camel use without disputing Albright's
contention that camel-breeding nomads did not exist in Syria
and northern Arabia at that time.

What remains now to be explained is why camel breeding
did finally take root in the north on a significant scale around
the twelfth century B.C. and what kind of camel breeding it was.
For an answer to this question we must turn our attention
again to the pattern of camel use in southern Arabia and in
particular to the question of saddle design. The first camel-
breeding society of southern Arabia and later of Socotra and
the horn of Africa was, as already described, a society that
valued the camel most as a milk animal and as a form of
wealth. It had little use for the camel as a pack animal and
none at all as a riding animal. The camel-breeding group that
first thought of using its animals as beasts of burden for carrying incense northward departed from this earlier pattern, and

in order to do so necessarily developed new types of camel saddles to increase the animal's carrying capacity and thus the profitability of the venture. The impetus for this new departure in camel use probably came from the incense exporters rather than the camel breeders themselves, but there is no way of knowing this for certain.

In developing a new and more efficient saddle, something both lighter and more effective than a pile of mats tied on however possible with a long rope, the central problem of putting a weight on a camel had to be faced: What do you do about the hump? A camel's hump is not exactly soft and squishy, but it is nonetheless a structurally unsupported mound of fat which is subject to deformation if a heavy weight is put on top of it. This cannot be too uncomfortable for the camel or the completely structureless Socotran saddle would be an impossibility, but it makes securing a heavy load very difficult, especially in view of the fact that during a long journey the size of the hump diminishes as the fat is used for energy. The most primitive answer to the problem was obviously to cover the hump up and forget about it, but all serious efforts to solve it have seen the need to transmit by one means or another the weight of the load to the camel's skeleton.

The three basic ways to obviate the hump difficulty are and always have been to place the weight directly over the shoulders in front of the hump, to place it directly over the haunches behind the hump, or to attach it to a framework that bears upon the animal's rib cage on either side of the hump. All three solutions, as well as some combination solutions, are in use in different parts of the world at the present day, but the first of the three chronologically seems to have been the behind-the-hump solution.

The theory of the chronological priority of the behind-the-hump saddle has been propounded before by Walter Dostal, an anthropologist, and has met with a chilly reception.[19] In part this is due to the fact that some parts of his supporting argument are much weaker than others. It is unfortunate, however, whatever the reason, that Dostal's views on the evolution of saddle design have not been followed up, for they contain important insights into the history of camel use and Arabian society in general. The discussion of saddles in this and the

following chapter relies to a significant extent upon ideas
originated by Dostal though by no means do I wish to endorse
all of his theories or supporting arguments.

The motivation for putting the weight behind the hump
would appear to be that riding bareback this is usually the only
place that affords a secure, if very hard, seat.[20] Herders
occasionally ride this way for short distances. Essentially, the
saddle consists of a cushion over the hindquarters and some
method of tying it securely in place. Direct evidence of this
type of saddle does not extend back to the earliest period of
the overland incense trade, but it is indicated on a number of
clay statuettes recovered from burials in Yemen dating back
possibly into the second millenium B.C.[21] and on others un-

21 Arab riding camel bareback behind hump.

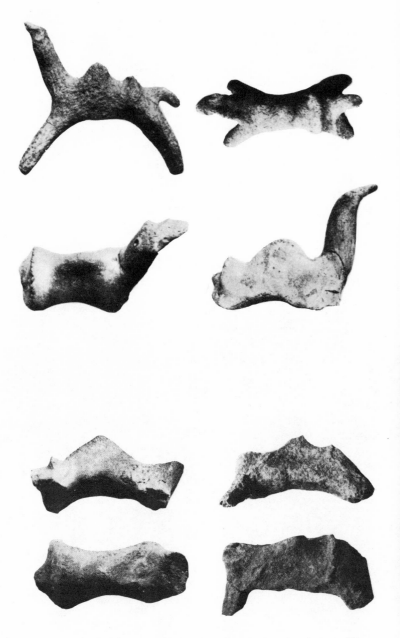

22 Figurines from Yemen showing traces of South Arabian saddles.

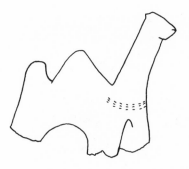

23 Camel figurine from Uruk showing trace of South Arabian saddle.

covered at Uruk in Iraq dating between 1000 and 500 B.C.[22] The figurines from the two areas are quite similar and look indeed to be closely related, presumably because the saddle was commonly used in carrying incense from Yemen to Iraq. The saddle is represented by a ridge or hump over the hindquarters and in some cases extending down the animal's sides.[23] Carl Rathjens who has written about the Yemeni figurines feels that they represent riding animals.[24] He notes, incidentally, that the camel, unlike other animals, was never used to represent a deity in Semiticized southern Arabia, which supports the contention already made that the camel was originally associated in the Semitic mind with an alien people with alien gods. As for the Iraqi figures, the sex of the animals is always female which suggests that they, too, are intended to represent riding animals since female camels are preferred for that role and the stronger male for pack work.[25]

What is interesting about this early evidence is that the camels are riding animals and that there is no indication of an arch or other support in front of the hump to which the cushion in back could be tied. The former observation may only indicate that camel riding developed, quite plausibly, at the same time as caravan trading and probably as an offshoot of it, but the latter observation is puzzling. How was the cushion attached to the camel so that it and the rider did not fall off backwards? Modern versions of this type of saddle, which is called *ḥawlānī* in southern Arabia, *hadāja* in northern Arabia, and *hawiya* in the Sahara and which will henceforward be referred to in this book as the South Arabian saddle, consist of two principal parts, a double (sometimes single) saddle bow made out of wood and a U-shaped fabric casing

24 South Arabian riding saddle in southern Arabia.

25 South Arabian baggage saddle in Tunisia.

26 South Arabian baggage saddle in Turkey.

27 Schematic drawing of South Arabian riding saddle.

stuffed with a cushioning material to form a pad. The pad fits around the back of the animal's hump and reaches forward along either side of it. The wooden bow is placed in front of the hump and rests either upon the U-shaped pad or upon a separate smaller pad. It serves to transmit the pressure of the load to the camel's rib cage when the saddle is used for baggage, but in riding it simply keeps the cushion from sliding backwards.[26] The saddle is secured in place primarily by a girth strap that goes over and between the two parts of the saddle bow and around the animal's chest just behind the great callus between its front legs which bears its weight when it is lying down. Additional straps may go around the neck and under the tail, but these are of secondary importance.

Perhaps originally the saddle bow was not part of the South Arabian saddle. Perhaps the cushion on the rump was held in place simply by a rope such as is indicated around the chest of two of the Iraqi specimens. On the other hand, the saddle bow may simply not have been represented because it fit too closely to the front of the hump to make a separate bulge. Whatever the case may be with the figurines, a distinct bump caused by the saddle bow is readily discernible on the camels figured on the bronze gates of Balawat which date from the reign of the Assyrian king Shalmaneser III (858–824 B.C.).[27] So the fully formed saddle can be affirmed to date from the first half of the first millenium B.C. and is very probably earlier. This does not mean, however, that the South Arabian saddle immediately supplanted the earlier mattress type. Indeed, the mattress seems to have evolved into a cushion (or two) going around

28 Assyrian bronze gates of Balawat. Camels are poorly drawn but pad behind hump and bulge on shoulders indicate a South Arabian saddle.

the hump. This type can still be found today in the Sahara, but it is still far from efficient.[28] It appears most likely that the new South Arabian saddle gradually replaced the old mattress saddle because it was a superior pack saddle and that the old type remained in use, as shall be seen shortly, in the form of a cushion saddle for riding purposes.

Of course, all of these technological changes are only a physical reflection of what must have been, for some tribes, a significant change in their notion of herding. Previously male animals had been little valued because they did not supply milk; now they could be rented or sold to caravan traders. Previously there was not much reason to ride a camel; now journeys of many days' distance made riding necessary. Previously camel breeding had been a self-contained activity; now it was integrated to some degree with the incense trade operated by non-nomads.

To what extent this new pattern of camel use had become widespread by the time of the Semitic migrations southward cannot be determined, and areas such as Oman which were never closely connected with the incense trade have preserved to this day the earlier pattern. Yet the Semites took over the

29 Cushion saddle in Sahara made of two skin bags.

land and the trade both and must have played an active role in
the evolution of camel nomadism in southern Arabia as users of
camels even if to begin with they did not breed them themselves. When eventually they did begin to herd camels, it could
only have been a matter of time before ethnically related tribes
farther north along the trade routes took up the practice. In
other words, the domestic camel itself became known in the
lands north of the Arabian desert because it figured in the
overland trade in incense before that trade was taken over by
the Semites; the camel as a herd animal, however, only became
known in the north after control of the trade had passed to the
Semites who now had a use for the animal. The pattern of
camel use adopted by the northern herders, naturally, was the
new one in which utilization as a pack animal played a major
role rather than the entirely subsistence related older pattern.

As one would anticipate from the primary incense route
being situated in western Arabia, the camel appears as a herd
animal earlier on the western side of the Syrian desert than on
the eastern side. Around 1100 B.C. the Midianites and Amalekites caused the Israelites to suffer by camping with their
animals on sown land until subdued by Gideon. "Both they and
their camels," according to the book of Judges, "were without
number."[29] It is noteworthy here that while the animal itself
does not seem to have struck the writer as being extraordinary, its large numbers do.

On the other side of the desert in Iraq and Mesopotamia
connection with Yemen and hence with the incense trade has
already been demonstrated from clay figurines dated 1000–500
B.C. The cuneiform records of the Assyrian empire tell a great
deal more about camel culture in this area, however. There is
silence about one-humped camels in these records for some two
hundred years after the Midianites and Amalekites had appeared in the western Syrian desert. During this period, however, two-humped camels are mentioned, as will be discussed
further in chapter six, and the incense trade in the west continued to flourish as is indicated by the story of King Solomon
(circa 955–935 B.C.) and the Queen of Sheba.[30] For a long time
camels in the east seem to have remained relatively few. During
the reign of the Assyrian king Tukulti-Ninurta II (890–884
B.C.) the city of Hindanu in Mesopotamia delivered tribute that

included 30 camels, 50 cattle, 30 asses, 200 lambs, and one talent of myrrh.[31] Camels clearly do not dominate the list, although their presence on it explains the source of the myrrh, which is a south Arabian product. Half a century later in the reign of Shalmaneser III (858–824 B.C.) it is recorded that 1,000 camel riders of Gindibu the Arabian fought against the Assyrians in the battle of Karkar, but this battle took place in western Syria and the number represents only a tiny fraction of a force that mustered over 50,000 infantry, some 4,000 chariots, and 1,400 cavalry.[32] All of the Akkadian (the language of the Assyrian empire) words for one-humped camels, incidentally, are loanwords from Arabic.[33]

Not until the reign of Tiglath-Pileser III (745–727 B.C.) are camels mentioned in really large quantities. The booty taken from the Arab queen Samsi, for example, consisted of 30,000 camels, 20,000 cattle, and 5,000 bundles or loads of spices.[34] Somewhat later in the reign of Esarhaddon (680–669 B.C.) the connection between camels and incense is again underscored in the annual tribute of Iata', the son of Hazael king of the Arabs, which consists of gold, precious stones, 50 camels, and 1,000 loads of herbs.[35] Altogether, this and other evidence from the Assyrian chronicles testifies to several things: a substantial expansion of camel breeding in the Syrian desert during the Assyrian period, a close correlation between camel owning or camel breeding and the incense trade, a slow increase in the use of camels for military purposes including their use as a baggage animal in the Assyrian army by the reign of Sargon II (721–705 B.C.),[36] and a very slow penetration of camel use into nondesert areas. The main substantiation for this last point is the absence of camels being mentioned in lists of spoil and tribute pertaining to exclusively agricultural areas.

The Assyrian period also affords important pictorial information about the prevalent mode of camel utilization. The problems of saddling a camel have already been discussed and the emergence of two types of saddle from the original pile of mats proposed. One was a pad secured behind the hump by means of being tied to a wooden saddle bow in front of the hump. This is the South Arabian saddle. The other was simply a cushion, probably doughnut or horseshoe shaped, surrounding the hump but unsupported by any rigid framework.

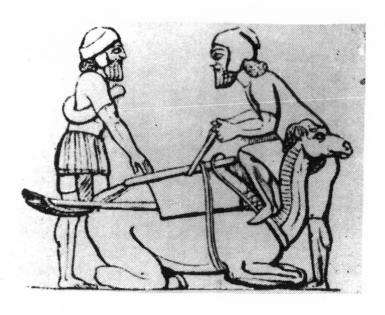

30 (A) Drawing from Assyrian relief showing camel being loaded. (B) Corrected drawing showing probable details of saddle design.

As already pointed out, the South Arabian saddle was used for both riding and loading. The clay figurines seem to be riding animals, and the camels on the bronze gates of Balawat have on them pack saddles. There is also evidence of an advance made at this time in using the South Arabian saddle for carrying loads. A badly drawn Assyrian relief shows a South Arabian saddle being fitted with horizontal wooden poles tied to the saddle bow in front, extending along the sides of the hump, and probably tied to each other in back.[37] This gives the camel driver an additional rigid support to tie the load to, and the variant is used today in India (the *palan* saddle),[38] although the South Arabian saddle is normally used elsewhere without the additional sticks.

The more interesting saddle is actually the seemingly more primitive cushion saddle. Its use as a pack saddle is attested by an Assyrian relief portraying refugees from Sennacherib's sack of the Palestinian city of Lachish in 701 B.C.[39] What is interesting, however, is its use as a riding saddle. Despite the figurines showing the South Arabian saddle apparently being used for riding, there are four separate depictions of a cushion saddle incontestably being used for this purpose. The oldest is a crudely carved stone relief found at Tell Halaf in northern Syria and dated approximately to 900 B.C.[40] The rider is shown sitting on a cushion with crossed straps on its side which is held onto the camel by crossed girths. There is no evidence of

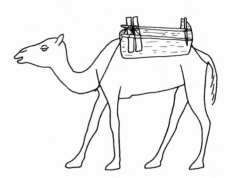

31 Schematic drawing of Indian *palan* saddle, a modified South Arabian saddle. Horizontal sticks are added for greater convenience in loading.

32 Cushion saddle used for baggage on Assyrian relief of refugees fleeing city of Lachish.

82 33 Earliest known depiction of camel rider on orthostat from Tell Halaf. Note use of cushion saddle.

a saddle bow, nor does the rider's posture suggest one. The
saddle differs from that shown in the flight from Lachish only
in having crossed girths, which may well have given it greater
stability.

   The next depiction is part of a series of well-carved scenes
from the reign of Assurbanipal (668–631 B.C.).[41] They all
show Assyrian cavalry triumphing over Arab camelry, but
oddly enough, considering the quality of the work, the camel
saddle is usually not shown. Yet there must have been a saddle because its girths are always shown, and even though they

34 Arabs fleeing Assyrians on Assyrian relief. Saddle girths and
   blanket are shown but not saddle itself.

disappear beneath a saddle blanket, they appear to be crossed girths like those at Tell Halaf. Fortunately, on one animal a distinct cushion saddle appears which must represent what is hidden in the other pictures.[42] These reliefs are also interesting in that they show two men riding on each animal, something that could imply that the tribe had only a small number of animals,[43] and that they are shown using the bow and arrow as their sole weapon and not the long lance and sword that eventually became associated with camel warfare.

The last two examples come from non-Assyrian sources. One is an Achaemenid (sixth to fourth century B.C.) cylinder seal showing the same motif as Assurbanipal's reliefs, a horseman with a lance pursuing a camel rider.[44] The cushion saddle is here clearly depicted but without the crossed girths. The other is a small bronze figurine found on the island of Rhodes but probably an import from the mainland showing very clearly a man mounted on a cushion saddle. It is dated 600–700 B.C.[45]

Given the tenor of these depictions, it might be surmised that the cushion saddle came to be used in particular for military purposes. The South Arabian saddle may have suited quite adequately a trader on route from the incense lands, but the distance of the rider from the camel's head would reduce his control and force him for guidance to use a camel stick which could well become an inconvenience in battle.[46] Moreover, the only advantage that riding a camel in battle affords to offset the many advantages of a horseman is its greater height, and this advantage would tend to be reduced by a seat behind the hump instead of atop it. Thus the surmise that the cushion saddle became the primary riding saddle and the South Arabian saddle the primary pack saddle in the borderlands of the Syrian desert can easily be supported by argument.

Nevertheless, the camel made a poor fighting vehicle. The Assyrians adopted it militarily only as a beast of burden. For the Arabs it was an insecure platform to fire arrows from and, faced with a regular army, probably served most effectively as a vehicle for flight. Once in the reign of Assurbanipal a group of Arabs fled into the desert but were cut off from water and forced to slit the camels' bellies and drink the water in

35 Assyrians plundering Arab encampment. Note cushion saddle.

36 Assyrian theme on Achaemenid cylinder seal. Note cushion saddle.

their stomachs, this being perhaps the earliest example of a semimyth about camels and water that persists to this day.[47]

The camel breeders of Syria and Mesopotamia were still of little military significance during the Assyrian period. The caravan trade relied upon their animals, but there is no evidence that they controlled the trade and reaped its profits. Indeed, Assyrian depictions of Arabs and Arab encampments suggest a very basic level of subsistence. What the camel-breeding Arabs lacked was a means of converting their potential control of the caravan trade into real control. Until they obtained a meaningful military capability, they had no choice but to remain despised desert tribesmen more preyed upon by the agents of settled civilization than preying upon.

37 Cushion saddle on bronze figure of camel rider from island of Rhodes.

4 The North Arabian Saddle and the Rise of the Arabs

Sometime between 500 and 100 B.C. a camel saddle was invented that transformed the economic, political, and social history of the Middle East. This type of saddle is known by various names but will be called here the North Arabian saddle after its apparent place of invention. It is composed basically of two large arches or saddle bows shaped like inverted V's, one situated upon a pad in front of the hump and the other upon the same or a different pad behind the hump. These two saddle bows are connected along the sides either by crossed sticks or by straight sticks, the entire assemblage forming a rigid, square frame converging toward the top with the hump in the middle. Over this frame and above the hump is placed a pad of some sort upon which the rider sits, his weight bearing not upon the hump but distributed by the framework to the camel's rib cage. When it is used as a pack saddle, the load is divided into two parts of equal weight and tied to each side of the saddle.

87

38 North Arabian saddle in Sahara.

39 North Arabian saddle in Darfur, Sudan.

40 North Arabian saddle in southern Iran.

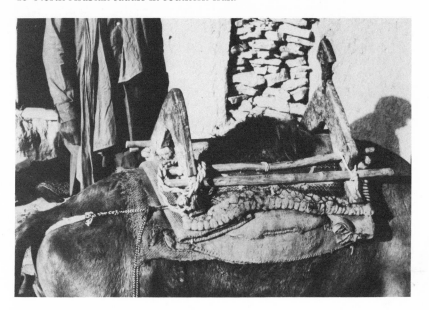

In claiming great historical influence for a technological development there is no escaping the charge of grossly over-simplifying historical reality and introducing a monocausal interpretation of events. The stirrup, the horseshoe, the horse collar, all these and many more have enjoyed their moment of historiographical prominence before being leveled to a greater or lesser degree by the obvious truth that such things as these can never be more than one factor among many in the complex process of historical change. Yet being aware of this vulnerability does not necessarily arm the historian for countering the charge of overemphasis, for the effort to eluci-date all the factors contributing to a development would not only require a much longer work but would also risk burying in a mass of other data the single factor that, rightly or wrongly, has struck the historian as being previously over-looked or in some way more important than the others.

The case at hand involves, at last, the specific answer for at least part of the region involved to the question posed in the first chapter: Why did the camel supplant the wheel at the particular point in Middle Eastern history that it did? The availability of the camel in quantity in the deserts bordering the settled lands of Syria and Mesopotamia by the seventh century B.C. has already been demonstrated, yet the wheel con-tinued to dominate the transport economy for an additional eight or nine hundred years before slowly giving way. The explanation for this long delay is that the camel could only be-come available as an efficient means of transport competitive with the wheel in settled areas when the camel breeder—the nomad—had become fully integrated into the society and economy of the Middle East. This latter development was not simply an automatic process. Although the notion of eternal hostility between the desert and the sown, between nomad and farmer, has been greatly overemphasized in the past as a motive force in history, it is demonstrable nonetheless that agriculturists and city dwellers tend to have an antipathy toward nomads and tend to resist receiving them into their society.

What happened between 500 B.C. and the period when camels became dominant in the transport economy was that camel-breeding nomads acquired unprecedented military, political, and economic power and were enabled thereby to achieve a degree of social and economic integration with the settled lands that their predecessors had never dreamed of. Clearly, this comparatively sudden access to power on the part of camel-breeding nomads must have stemmed from a variety of factors, some involving nomadic society and others specific to the sedentary society upon which it was impinging. However, without an effective means of applying force, it is difficult to see how this broad social transformation could have taken place. The means that was used was the camel-borne warrior mounted upon a North Arabian saddle.

Substantiation of this scheme of development must involve several distinct correlations. First, the invention of the North Arabian saddle must be shown to be significant in the rise of camel-breeding nomads as a political force. Second, it must be shown that an alteration in the balance of political power in favor of the nomads did, in fact, occur. Third, the connection between the political rise of the nomads and their integration with settled society on the social and economic level must be demonstrated. And fourth, this social and economic integration must be linked to the availability of camels as an efficient means of transport in settled areas that had previously used wheeled vehicles.

On the first point, demonstration of the connection between the North Arabian saddle and Arab political power, the evidence is circumstantial but persuasive. The earliest representations presently known of a North Arabian saddle are on Roman coins dated between 58 and 54 B.C. depicting the surrender of Aretas, king of the Nabataeans, the first politically significant Arab kingdom.[1] Several specimens are preserved, including some with the name of an unknown chieftain named Bachhius instead of Aretas, and the saddle is represented in different ways. Possibly the cushion saddle, which seems to be depicted on some, was still in use; or possibly the die-cutter simply summarized the more complicated North Arabian saddle. But some specimens definitely show the saddle bows that prove the identity of the new design. The saddle was surely invented some time before that date, and there is reason to suppose that it was already in use in the second century B.C. when the Nabataeans, with their capital at the desert city

41 Roman coins showing Arab chieftain surrendering. Note indications of North Arabian saddles on (A) and (B).

of Petra, began to become politically and economically important. Although the Nabataeans became unusually skillful in utilizing marginal and desert land for agricultural purposes, their great period of prosperity was based upon their dominance of the overland trade from the Arabian peninsula to Syria and the Mediterranean coast. Petra's importance, in particular, was as a caravan city.[2]

The trade in exotic products from southern Arabia, of course, had been going on for some two millennia at that time; yet never before this does it appear that the profits from the trade found their way back into the desert and into the hands of the people who supplied the transportation, the camel breeders. Before the rise of Petra, the first of the great caravan cities, control of the Arabian trade lay in the hands of the buyers and producers of the products traded.

The story of King Solomon and the Queen of Sheba is a good indicator of this fact going back to the middle of the tenth century B.C. The Queen of Sheba was a ruler in southern Arabia who came to Solomon, who was not, of course, a ruler over camel breeders, "with a very great train, with camels that bare spices, and very much gold, and precious stones." She gave Solomon the spices, the gold, and the precious stones, and Solomon gave in return unspecified goods. In addition, Solomon is said to have received money from "the merchantmen, and of the traffick of the spice merchants, and of all the kings of Arabia."[3] No later ruler of the incense lands ever seems to have come north to check on conditions in the marketing area.

At a much later date the same conditions of trade are noted by the geographer Artemidorus who flourished around 100 B.C. As quoted by the later geographer Strabo (died around 25 A.D.), Artemidorus describes the Sabaeans, the people of Sabaea or Sheba, as having "aromatics in such abundance that they use cinnamon and cassia and the others instead of sticks and firewood . . . From their trafficking both the Sabaeans and the Gerrhaeans have become richest of all."[4] The town of Gerrha was the entrepot of the incense trade on the Persian Gulf in the vicinity of Bahrain whence the goods were trans-shipped to Iraq, but it was not a settlement of Arab camel breeders as Petra was, at least to some degree. Strabo says that Gerrha was "inhabited by Chaldaeans, exiles from Baby-lon."[5] As was the case in Solomon's time, the major parties in the trade did not include the people who supplied the means of transport.

Since the profits from the caravan trade were substantial and the pattern of trade favoring the retention of profits at the termini of the trade routes was well established, there is no reason to suppose that the diversion of those profits into the desert for the benefit of the carriers of the trade, a development that started with the rise of Petra and continued until the Is-lamic invasions of the seventh century A.D., was accomplished without resistance from those parties which had previously been in control. Once dominance of the trade had passed to the desert dwellers, the attempts of Romans, Persians, and south Arabians to regain control of it by military or diplomatic means are numerous enough to show that the change in the trading pattern was worth fighting about.[6] In view of this, the initial change in dominance of the trade calls for explanation.

At the close of the Assyrian period and, if the cylinder seal in the British Museum is not based on an archaic motif, at the beginning of the Achaemenid period in roughly 500 B.C., the camel-breeding nomads of the Syrian-Arabian desert were still at the mercy of the superior military force of the settled lands. They rode camels primarily to escape into the desert. Their weapon was still the bow and arrow. Camels were used in imperial armies solely as pack animals. The first recorded appearance of camelry in an imperial army, aside from Cyrus the Persian's experiment in mounting non-Arab soldiers on baggage camels to frighten the horses of King Croesus,[7] is the Arab contingent in the host of Xerxes that invaded Greece in 481 B.C., and it is significant that their characteristic weapon was still the bow.[8]

A caravan on the trail probably had little to fear from these nomads. If a large enough number of merchants participated, the potential fighting force of a caravan could be sure of outnumbering most forces that could be brought against them in the sparsely populated desert; and if it came to a fight, the advantage lay with the caravan. Both sides might have bowmen, but the caravan men or possibly their armed escort would undoubtedly have an advantage in weapons of iron, swords and spears. Such items are costly in the desert, and Arab tribesmen up until modern times have left the forging of iron implements to a special caste of people or else have purchased them from settled peoples.[9] As long as the advantage of metal weapons lay with the caravan, the camel breeders had no way of profiting from the trade except by selling or renting their animals to the traders on the latter's terms.

Strabo's information on this matter is not devoid of ambiguity since he was gathering his information in the first century B.C. and first century A.D. when the status of the Arab tribesmen was already changing; but while he describes the Scenitae (tent-dwelling) Arabs of the Syrian desert as brigands and shepherds, meaning by this, apparently, that they harassed the farming populations near whom they pastured their flocks, he adds that "the Scenitae are peaceful, and moderate towards travelers in the exaction of tribute, and on this account merchants avoid the land along the river and risk a journey through the desert . . . For the chieftains who live along the river on both sides . . . are each invested with their own particular domains and exact a tribute of no moderate amount."[10] In other words, the Arabs could annoy the inhabitants of farming villages just as they had been able to do in the days of Gideon, but they could not exact as much tribute, that is, charge as much for transit rights from caravans, as the people along the river could. Nevertheless, they were exacting tribute.

Elsewhere Strabo reports that when the Roman general Aelius Gallus was sent by the emperor Augustus to explore Arabia, he got as far as northern Yemen where a battle was

fought in which 10,000 Arabs are alleged to have fallen and
only two Romans. The reason for the Romans' lopsided victory
was that the Arabs "used their weapons in an inexperienced
manner, being utterly unfit for war, using bows and spears and
swords and slings, though most of them used a double-edged
axe."[11] Obviously, the rise in Arab military prowess had not
yet had much effect that far south. Of the Nabataeans themselves, on the other hand, Strabo states that "they are not very
good warriors even on land, rather being hucksters and merchants."[12] This is in contrast with the Scenitae Arabs of
Mesopotamia who allowed merchants to pass through their territory but were not themselves merchants.

Strabo thus reflects a middle stage in the rise to economic
and political prominence of the desert tribes. Some tribes, the
Scenitae, had begun to make their power felt to the extent of
levying tolls on trade passing through their territory; others,
the Nabataeans, had gone a step further and become merchants themselves; while others still, such as those in the northern Yemen, were remote from these developments and still
at the mercy of any trained military force. There is no explicit
statement that the first two groups had adopted the North
Arabian saddle and in so doing acquired the ability to fight
effectively from camel-back with sword and spear, but the
military history of the northern desert peoples indicates that
such was the case. Livy writes that Arabs in the army of An-
tiochus III at the battle of Magnesia in 190 B.C. had swords
four cubits long to be able to reach the enemy from their great
height atop their camels.[13] Similar tactics are indicated by
Herodian who says that the Arabs in the army of the Persian
Artabanus when he fought the Roman emperor Macrinus in
218 A.D. "forced their way by jabbing from above with their
long spears."[14] And Diodorus the Sicilian in paraphrasing
Ctesias of Cnidus's account of the legends surrounding the
name of the Assyrian princess Semiramis seems to be adding
details from his own time, the first century B.C., when he puts
swords four cubits long into the hands of Arabs in her army.[15]
Assyrian artistic representations of Arabs never show them
using swords.

Sitting upon a doughnut shaped pad of uncertain stability,
a camel rider could not be expected to use such weapons. Any
effort to lunge with a spear or swipe with a sword would have

been as likely to unseat the rider as it would to wound the enemy. Although the new weapons probably were first used with a cushion saddle, they must have quickly prompted the invention of the North Arabian saddle, called *shadād* in Arabic from *shadīd* meaning hard or firm,[16] for stability is necessary for such weapons. The conclusion is inescapable that the development of the North Arabian saddle was motivated by military considerations since the South Arabian and cushion saddles were adequate for all peaceful purposes.

The specific impetus for these linked developments in weaponry and saddlery was surely contact with or, as in the army of Xerxes, participation in armies whose striking force consisted of cavalry armed with spears and swords. Walter Dostal maintains that the saddle bow of the North Arabian saddle is borrowed from that of the horse saddle, but he dates the invention of the latter to the end of the first century B.C. and finds no evidence that the former was in use prior to the second century A.D.[17] The North Arabian saddle was evidently in use in the second century B.C., however, as has already been demonstrated; and, in any case, the saddle bow concept was present in the South Arabian saddle as early as its depiction in the ninth century B.C. on the bronze gates of Balawat. What seems most logical is that the double arch of the South Arabian saddle was separated so that one arch went in front of the hump and the other behind and the whole thing placed on top of a cushion saddle to keep it from abrading the camel's back. Thus although the new weapons were undoubtedly patterned on those of cavalry, whatever borrowing may have gone on in the field of saddle design probably went from camel saddle to horse saddle and not vice versa.

Outside the area of direct contact with cavalry, of course, the militarily inspired technological developments were adopted more slowly. In the first century B.C., depending upon how one interprets the saddle on a poorly carved funerary relief,[18] the South Arabian saddle seems still to have been ridden in Yemen, but later reliefs from the area show the new saddle and the long lance.[19] As for Oman and the Hadhramaut, they were so far removed from economic and political changes taking place in the north that they never adopted the North Arabian saddle and to this day ride the South Arabian saddle.[20]

42 Tombstone from Yemen. Pad rising vertically in front of tail suggests South Arabian saddle.

43 Tombstones from Yemen testifying to adoption of warhorse, long lance, and North Arabian saddle.

The effect of the new developments, therefore, was to give **99**
the tribes that first utilized them, those on the northern fringes
of the desert, a singular capacity to control desert trade. On
the one hand, they enjoyed a military advantage over tribes
deeper in the desert who were still armed with bow and arrow,
and thus they were able to give genuine protection to any
caravans that desired it. On the other hand, any caravans which
were unwise enough not to ask for protection would be subject to raiding by the northern tribes themselves. At an earlier
period the merchants could realistically anticipate fighting
off such raids since arrows alone had little chance of halting
their march and at close quarters their better weapons would
give them the advantage. But under the new circumstances the
advantage lay with Arab tribes. With a skill at riding camels
that the sedentary merchants could not hope to match, tribal
warriors armed with swords and spears could close with the
caravan and take advantage of their superior height, seated as
they were above the animal's hump, to strike down any un-
mounted defenders. Needless to say, it was logistically out of
the question to defend a caravan crossing the desert with a
force of horsemen.

Yet if new saddles and weapons put desert tribes in a position to coerce caravans into buying their protection, they did
not by any means make a camel rider the equal of a similarly
armed horseman. The gallop is an unusual pace for the camel
and one that requires both a well-trained animal and an expert
rider.[21] Yet even with the gallop there is no parallel in camel
warfare to the cavalry charge; the camel simply cannot produce
the momentum and impact of the warhorse. There can be no
mistaking the realization on the part of camel warriors of this
comparative inferiority. It shows up in Arabic poetry in which
the lance is considered to be ideally a horseman's weapon
despite the fact that it became a characteristic weapon of camel
riders.[22] It shows up again in Arab tactics against cavalry
which have always dictated dismounting and fighting as infantry or, if possible, changing mounts to a warhorse which has
been brought along solely for combat.[23]

Above all, however, the camel's inferiority as an animal of
war is revealed by the Arab tribesman's obsession with
horses, an obsession that goes so far as to hold horses in higher

esteem than camels.[24] In the desert areas of Syria and northern Arabia from the period under discussion until the twentieth century an unmistakable sign of wealth among tribesmen has been possession of horses. Contrary to the firmly held belief of horselovers, this cannot be explained simply as the natural preference of any rational people. The camel-breeding Tuaregs of the central Sahara are every bit as proud, warlike, and admiring of fine mounts as the Arab tribesman, but they have no great interest in horses.[25] Furthermore, in Somalia horses have virtually disappeared in recent times since their military usefulness has diminished.[26] Nor do the Assyrian records mention horses as part of the booty or tribute coming to the king from camel-breeding tribes.[27]

The association of Arabs with fine riding horses goes hand in hand, then, with the adoption of the sword, the spear, and the North Arabian saddle. As was the case with metal weapons, horse breeding implies a higher degree of economic integration with settled society than is indicated by the pattern of camel culture in the Assyrian period. Metal must be acquired by purchase or by force from settled peoples as must the grain necessary to sustain horses in the desert. Whether it was force or money in any given area that made this change in the nomad's material culture possible is beside the point; either way the development of horse breeding in the desert makes it clear that the camel nomad was becoming increasingly able to control his economic life as it impinged upon settled society.

It is difficult to demonstrate from textual sources exactly when and how the camel breeders took over the incense trade. The process was a gradual one, as has already been pointed out. The Nabataeans of Petra, Strabo's "hucksters and merchants," had definitely become an important factor in the trade by the first century B.C., and by the first century A.D. they probably controlled the desert route as far north as Damascus.[28] Another entrepot, Gerrha, which was not peopled by camel herders, transshipped incense northward to Babylonia by sea in the fourth century B.C., according to Aristobulus who should have been in a good position to know having accompanied Alexander on his campaigns.[29] But some two centuries later in the time of Diodorus, Gerrha's trade had become redirected overland to Petra.[30]

Influence in the field of trade did not make Petra a military power by any means. She could certainly muster enough force to intimidate the less sophisticated Arab tribes along the route southward, for there is inscriptional evidence that specific individuals were charged with maintaining road security,[31] but against a serious expedition like that of Aelius Gallus she had to resort to giving misleading advice and guidance to frustrate the Roman purpose of exploring the way south.[32] Later caravan cities, notably Palmyra and Mecca, were to emerge as important military powers. Time was not given to Petra to do the same, however. In 105 A.D. the city lost her independence and was absorbed into the Roman Empire by the emperor Trajan. Much of Petra's trade became relocated at Bosra (Bostra) farther to the north which had been a Nabataean city of secondary importance but now flourished as a caravan city under Roman control.[33] A coin of Antoninus Pius (138–161 A.D.) with a camel on the reverse testifies to the continued importance of camel caravans at Bosra.[34]

The example of Petra shows that the new economic configuration of the incense trade was politically precarious. Rome was too powerful to tolerate a wealthy, independent minor state on her frontier. Yet this political instability does not imply economic instability. Rome did not conquer the Nabataeans so that the trade could once again come under the control of the centers of consumption along the coast. After the conquest the trade continued to be centered in caravan cities such as Bosra and Jerash; these cities were simply situated closer to Roman power centers. There is every reason to believe that the

44 Roman coin from caravan city of Bosra.

actual merchants continued to be Arabs with contacts among the camel-breeding tribes, and archaeological investigation has proved that great wealth became centered in these newer cities just as it had in Petra.

Still further to the north in the middle of the Syrian desert the city of Palmyra began to become known as a significant caravan city in the first century B.C. but did not become truly wealthy until the following century. Too far north to be involved with the incense trade, Palmyra's profits came from caravans crossing the desert from the Euphrates to the Mediterranean. Strabo's description of the Scenitae Arabs of Mesopotamia has already been cited to show that in the first century B.C. the desert route was beginning to receive heavier use even though the merchants do not seem at that time to have been the Arabs themselves. Palmyra's rise marks the Arabs' transition from charging tolls for crossing their land to being themselves in control of the trade. The profits from the desert trade continued to pour into Palmyra even after she came under Roman tutelage in the reign of Trajan.

The role of the camel caravan in Palmyra's prosperity has already been noted in chapter one where evidence was brought forward to indicate that legal steps were taken by the Palmyrene merchants to suppress competing forms of transport, and it is also evident in Palmyrene art where Arsu, the god of the caravans, is usually depicted either upon or standing next to a camel and where several reliefs show in great detail the accoutrements of the camel troops who guarded the desert track.[35] Needless to say, they are mounted upon North Arabian saddles and armed with swords and long spears. Due in large part to her situation on the frontier between Rome and the Persian empire, Palmyra enjoyed in the third century A.D. a brief period of military and political glory much greater than any Petra had ever known. But the ultimate result was the sack of the city in the year 272 by a Roman army, a sack from which it never recovered. It is interesting to note that the great queen of Palmyra's period of glory, Zenobia, is said to have disdained the use of a covered carriage and to have usually ridden on horseback. When Palmyra was defeated, she attempted to flee on a fast riding camel but was captured by the Roman cavalry and eventually forced to march in golden

45 Relief from Palmyra showing equipment of Palmyrene camel corps.

chains through Rome in the triumphal procession of the emperor Aurelian.[36]

When the Nabataeans were first rising to prominence on the strength of their trade, both the Ptolemys of Egypt and the Seleucids of Syria had tried to bring them under their control. What these Hellenistic kingdoms failed to do, Rome accomplished; and Rome proved to be Palmyra's nemesis, as well. Petra and Palmyra were situated too near their powerful rivals to survive indefinitely as independent political entities. Yet it was natural that the desert lords of the caravan trade should have first appeared where they did, barely on the outskirts of settled country. It was there that the lessons of cavalry warfare would first have been learned and hence where the new developments in weaponry and saddlery would logically have taken place. As the new technology gradually spread further into the desert along the caravan routes, however, control of distant tribes must have become almost as vexing a problem as political relations with Rome.

Werner Caskel has propounded the theory that the bedouinization of Arabia and Syria took place as a direct result of the decline of the Nabataean kingdom and related states that had previously maintained some degree of order in the desert.[37] Trade declined; tribal warfare increased. Another way of looking at the same phenomenon is to say that the technological changes that originally made it possible for desert tribes bordering settled empires to gain control of the trade passing through their lands eventually raised the military capacity of all the Arab tribes to such a level that anarchy replaced the control exercised by the first trading states.

Another factor, however, was the decline of the incense trade because of lessened demand. Palmyra, after all, which did not depend upon the incense trade remained prosperous. The cause of the decline in demand for incense seems to have been Christianity. To be sure, incense eventually found a place in Christian ceremonies, but it never came into use in anything like the quantities consumed by earlier religions in the area. For the time period in question, writings of the church fathers Tertullian, Athenagoras, Arnobius, and Lactantius can be cited condemning its use. Presumably it had too intimate associations with Jewish and pagan ritual to be found tolerable at that early date.[38]

For a complex of reasons, therefore, from the second century A.D. onward conditions in the Arabian desert became
increasingly chaotic while the incense trade declined causing
serious economic problems in the incense producing states of
southern Arabia. The caravan cities in Syria continued to
flourish, however, because they did not depend solely upon the
sale of incense.

The force that eventually ordered the chaos in Arabia and
changed permanently the historical role of the Arabs was the
city of Mecca, the last of the great caravan cities. Mecca is
situated on the main trade route paralleling the Red Sea coast
of Arabia halfway between the incense producing lands of
the south and the incense consuming lands of the north.
Its location is often described as being a natural one for the
growth of a commercial center, but nothing could be farther
from the truth.[39] It is situated in a barren valley incapable
of sustaining a large population without substantial importation
of goods, and only by the most tortured map reading can it be
described as a natural crossroads between a north-south
route and an east-west one.[40] It is, of course, a halfway point
on the long route from Yemen to Syria, and this has been
adduced as an explanation of its growth. Yet on a journey of
some two months duration the concept of a halfway point as a
natural resting place is rather strained, nor does it explain why
as much wealth accumulated in Mecca as is indicated by descriptions of the city in the time of Muhammad.

In the economy of the ancient and medieval world trading
wealth gravitated toward four types of commercial centers:
producing centers, consuming centers, transshipment points
including crossroads, and points of coercion such as customs
stations. Mecca produced nothing; it consumed only negligible quantities of the incense and spices that were the staple of
the trade; and there was no natural feature such as a river
to require transshipment. The only reason for Mecca to grow
into a great trading center was that it was able somehow to
force the trade under its control. Mecca probably began as a
tribal shrine with, perhaps, a surrounding encampment.[41] Its
rise as a trade center began only with its being taken over
about the end of the fifth century A.D. by the tribe of Quraish,
led by a shaikh named Quṣayy, which emanated from northern
Arabia and had close relations with Arab tribes on the fringes

of Byzantine territory. In the relatively short space of time between the coming of the Quraish to Mecca and the birth of Muhammad, traditionally put in 570 A.D., the entire north-south trade of Arabia, which was still substantial although diminished from what it had been several centuries earlier, came under Meccan domination, and its profits flowed into Mecca. The Qur'an complains numerous times about the Meccans' pride in their wealth.[42]

Mecca gained control of the trade by organizing under her suzerainty the surrounding camel-breeding tribes which, on the one hand, supplied transportation and, on the other, were capable of raiding caravans. The Meccans were able to organize the trade so that each tribe gained more from co-operating with caravans traversing its territory than it stood to gain from raiding the caravans and thereby depressing the total volume of trade. To do this, however, Mecca had to fight the Fijār war with an important neighboring tribe. That all of this should have been accomplished in such a short space of time clearly indicates that control of trade was a specific goal of the Quraish. Their selection of Mecca as the site for their settlement, while influenced, certainly, by the religious shrine there which afforded the would-be traders a useful sacred month of truce, was primarily dictated by the need to be located in the midst of the tribes they had to dominate and as far as possible from potential sources of imperial interference in Syria and Yemen. As it was, there was both an abortive attempt during the period of Mecca's rise to make Mecca into a client state of the Byzantine empire and another to invade Mecca from Yemen.[43] The failure of these two efforts shows the wisdom of the Quraish in selecting an intermediate point as a trade center.

Volume of trade, even after Mecca achieved her hegemony, appears to have been lower than in the heyday of Petra, and it languished yet further after the rise of Islam.[44] Still, it was undoubtedly the main force calling the city of Mecca into existence, and the rise of Mecca cannot be separated from the earlier history of Petra and Palmyra. It simply marks a further step in the entire process by which the camel-breeding Arabs first found the means of controlling their greatest potential source of wealth and then jeopardized that source through failure to organize adequately among themselves, a failure that surely owes as much to the vast and barren distances involved as it does to an inclination toward political fragmentation.

Of the four desiderata put forward early in this chapter, two have now been satisfied. The invention and spread of the North Arabian camel saddle has been shown to be integrally related to the rise of the camel-breeding nomads as a political force, and the reality of that rise has been demonstrated in various stages. What remains is to link this political ascendancy with social and economic integration between desert and sown and to show that thereby camels became available in such quantity and at such price in settled country that they could compete successfully with wheeled transport and eventually drive it out of existence.

The reality of the social and economic integration of Arabs and settled folk is revealed in a thousand different ways. Once the Arab tribes had military and financial power, there was no way to keep them isolated in the desert. Both Roman and Persian governments subsidized Arab tribes on their borders to guard the desert frontier and, no doubt, to assure that the subsidized tribes themselves did not harass defenseless villagers. This put more money into Arab hands and integrated Arab warriors into the imperial military organization. Under the emperors Trajan and Hadrian (117–138 A.D.) camel corps are known to have been part of the Roman army in Syria and Egypt respectively.[45] Recruits for these new units most likely came from experienced camel people.

Military influence in the opposite direction, as was pointed out earlier, took the form of horse breeding by the Arabs for military purposes. Whenever the money was available to sustain horses, the Arabs acquired them. The army of Palmyra was predominantly a cavalry force although there was also a camelry for protection of the caravans. It is noteworthy that at the battle of Badr in 624, the opening act of warfare between the fledgling Muslim community in Medina and the merchants of Mecca, their erstwhile fellow townsmen, there were only two horses available to the Muslim combatants as opposed to one hundred available to the Meccans. In the second battle, the battle of Uhud in 625, the Muslims had no horses and the Meccans two hundred.[46] This obsession of the commercially wealthy Arabs with horses inevitably tied them into the economy of the settled lands for fodder if not for breeding stock, but it also afforded the armies of Islam with knowledgeable cavalry leaders when the conquests began in 633. When the armies came to be put on a sound administrative basis a few years later, a cavalryman was paid more than an infantryman, and the category of camel rider was not recognized.[47]

On the civilian side Arab traders became common in the Roman empire alongside the earlier traders of the settled areas of the Levant. Camel figurines were sacrificed to Nabataean gods in Italy itself.[48] Under the emperor Elagabalus (218–222), himself a Syrian although not from a desert region and reputed to be a fancier of camel's-foot stew, the dignity of senator was conferred upon the Arab rulers of Palmyra; and in 244 Philip, an Arab from the caravan city of Bosra, actually ascended the imperial throne for a brief reign.[49] All of this was merely part of a much broader integration of the peoples of the Middle East into the fabric of the Roman Empire, but it served to break down almost completely the earlier pattern of rigid exclusion of desert peoples from settled areas. Some desert peoples were still excluded, but the policing of the frontiers was either done by other camel breeders or by camel corps dependent on camel breeders. These camel people themselves were fully part of the Roman world.

Again in the artistic and cultural sphere there is an abundance of evidence to show that the desert dwellers, having been accepted into Roman society, aped the fashions of the settled lands. Petra and Palmyra in their days of prosperity were decorated completely in accordance with prevailing styles in the nondesert parts of Syria. Temples, colonnades, monumental arches, all reflect the cosmopolitan taste of the sown and testify to yet another economic link between desert and sown in the form of employment of artists and craftsmen from older cosmopolitan centers to turn these caravan cities into showplaces of Hellenistic art. Strabo says that "the Nabataeans are a sensible people, and are so much inclined to acquire possessions that they publicly fine anyone who has diminished his possessions and also confer honours on anyone who has increased them . . . Some things are imported wholly from other countries, but others not altogether so, especially in the case

of those that are native products, as, for example, gold and
silver and most of the aromatics, whereas brass and iron, as
also purple garb, styrax, crocus, costaria, embossed works,
paintings, and moulded works are not produced in their
country."[50]

Yet if the cultured Arabs of Petra and Palmyra came to be
accepted under the Roman empire as the equals of their distant
kinsmen of the cosmopolitan lands nearer the Mediterranean,
still they did not cease to be simply the top stratum of a tribal
desert society based upon camel breeding and caravan trading. Through them a bridge was built between the desert and
the sown. Camel-breeding tribes that had formerly been considered inherently opposed to settled life became through the
agency of these cosmopolitanized Arabs an integral part of
Middle Eastern society. There was a natural limit to how many
camels could be utilized in long distance caravan trade and
how much money earned, but there was virtually no limit to
the economic potential of using the camel for humbler transport duties once the nomad and his animal became acceptable
to settled society.

The Arab merchant found himself with the means at hand,
through his tribal contacts, to compete directly in the entire
transport industry from hauling stone from quarries to bringing
in the harvest from the fields. In this light the economic data
presented in chapter one takes on fuller meaning. The merchants of Palmyra levied an exorbitant duty upon merchandise
transported by wagon because they saw the competitiveness
of the two modes of transport. It did not take much more
vision to see that the camel could compete with the wheel on
a more extensive basis than just the caravan trade. Consciously
or not, the Palmyrenes were acting not only for themselves
as the middlemen between camel breeder and shipper but for
their tribal kinsmen on the fringes of settled land and even
deep in the desert who became by their actions still further integrated into the economy of the region. Even in the twentieth
century camels have been collected for sale from all over the
Arabian peninsula, a special caste of camel buyers having come
into being for the purpose.[51]

The indication in Diocletian's edict on prices that camel
transport was 20 percent cheaper than wagon transport is en-

tirely explicable on practical grounds alone—cost of fodder, cost of wood to build a wagon, and so on—assuming there is a ready supply of camels. Since 600 B.C. at the very latest camels had been present in the deserts bordering the settled land of Syria and the Tigris-Euphrates valley in sufficient quantity to compete successfully with wagon transport. Between camel and farmer, however, was a cultural gulf far broader than the few miles that separated them geographically. That gulf had to be bridged before significant competition could occur, and a number of intricately interrelated elements went into building the bridge.

In schematic summary, the North Arabian saddle made possible new weaponry, which made possible a shift in the balance of military power in the desert, which made possible the seizure of control of the caravan trade by the camel breeders, which made possible the social and economic integration of camel-breeding tribes into settled Middle Eastern society, which made possible the replacement of the wheel by the pack camel. But, of course, in reality this neat schematic development becomes much too complex to be followed with precision. Different stages in the process were reached in different areas at different times. The process in locations situated upon major caravan routes was different from that in more remote areas. While some tribes ultimately became primarily suppliers of camels for the general transport market,[52] others, such as those in southern Arabia, continued throughout the centuries to use their camels primarily for milk. Yet however confusing the process appears, it did lead in the end, after perhaps five hundred years of gradual change, to the disappearance of the wheel in the Middle East. The impact of the process on different camel-breeding tribes was very uneven, but its impact upon settled society was uniform and its effects far-reaching.

5 The Camel in North Africa

If the rise of the Arabs caused indirectly the disappearance of the wheel, then there would seem to be no reason to expect the latter phenomenon to be spread beyond the region in which the Arabs lived. Yet it has already been demonstrated that the society in which pack camels served in the place of carts and wagons extended throughout North Africa and the Iranian plateau, regions where Arab tribes certainly were not present until after the Islamic conquests. Moreover, evidence has been brought forward indicating that in these areas, as in the Middle East proper, the replacement of the wheel by the camel substantially antedated the coming of Islam. Therefore, it is necessary to ask whether the disappearance of the wheel in these non-Arab areas proceeded from separate but coincidentally contemporary causes or whether the developments described in the last two chapters did in some indirect fashion affect the transportation economy in lands beyond the reach of Arab influence.

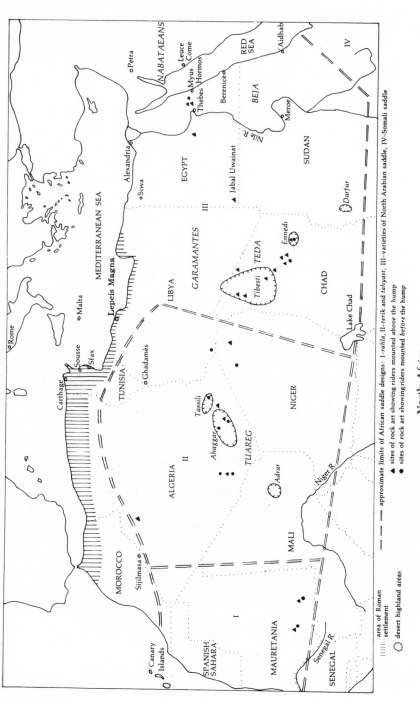

North Africa

I–*rahla*, II–*terik* and *tahyast*, III–varieties of North Arabian saddle, IV–Somali saddle — approximate limits of African saddle designs: ▲ sites of rock art showing riders mounted *above* the hump ● sites of rock art showing riders mounted *before* the hump

○ desert highland areas

⫲⫲⫲ area of Roman settlement

The task of resolving these questions for North Africa is greatly simplified by the existence of an excellent study by Emilienne Demougeot entitled "Le Chameau et l'Afrique du Nord romaine."[1] This study is part of the debate of long standing on the date of the introduction of the camel to North Africa, a debate which has given rise to three schools of thought. Some writers with great bonds of sentiment and affection for North African camels, notably that most thorough compiler of camel lore Commandant Cauvet, maintain that the North African camel of purest lineage, the *méhari*, a slender, graceful riding camel prized by the Tuaregs and other desert tribes, is a separate species descended from the pre-historic camel that is known from fossil evidence to have roamed the then grassy Sahara in the pleistocene age.[2]

The second theory has had wider acceptance, largely because it appears to be so firmly based upon textual evidence. This theory holds that the introduction of the camel into North Africa and the Sahara occurred during the Roman period and, in all probability, was the work of Romans who were familiar with the animal from Syria.[3] It is pointed out that the first literary mention of the camel in Africa comes in the account of Caesar's campaign against Juba in 46 B.C.[4] He captured from the Numidian king twenty-two camels, a small enough number to suggest that the animal was then relatively rare. Later Roman writers of the first century A.D., notably the naturalist Pliny, fail to mention camels in North Africa. Then in the third and fourth centuries the literature indicates an abundance of camels. Ammianus Marcellinus, as a prime example, speaks of a requisition of 4,000 camels imposed upon the city of Lepcis Magna in Tripolitania in the year 363 A.D.[5]

It is with regard to this second school of thought that Demougeot's study is most conclusive. By a meticulous mustering of both textual and archaeological evidence she shows clearly that the Romans *encountered* camels in Tripolitania (western Libya) and southern Tunisia from the first century B.C. onward but did not *introduce* them to the area. Instead she postulates two routes of introduction, one along the Mediterranean coast from Ptolemaic and then Roman Egypt and the other across the desert from the south side of the Sahara.[6] These conclusions put her squarely into the third school of thought which considers the camel in North Africa to be an immigrant from somewhere in Egypt or the Sudan.

This third viewpoint, it should be pointed out, is not necessarily incompatible with the first one. The camel could have been domesticated in one part of Africa and have spread at a later date to other parts. But there are other and insurmountable objections to the theory of African domestication. Physically, African and Asian camels cannot be considered separate species. It has been alleged and disproven that they differ in number of teeth, and the only other distinctive characteristics that have been mentioned for the African species are piebald coloration and a longer distance between neck and hump.[7] The first characteristic, however, is more likely to be an indication of selective inbreeding than of a separate species.[8] As for the second, hump size and placement differ noticeably from one breed or individual to another, and camels can be found in Arabia with as much room over the shoulders as those in the Sahara.

Once these biological arguments are put aside, the case for the independent domestication of indigenous camels in North Africa has little supporting it and much going against it. The most overwhelming opposing testimony comes from the vast corpus of Saharan rock paintings and engravings.[9] Although no one has yet discovered a way to date these pictures absolutely, relative dating can be achieved by stylistic analysis, by noting which paintings overlap others, and by the relative degree of patination or formation of a tinted mineral coating over the picture. This latter phenomenon is a natural function of time and the desert climate, but the rate of patination has not been established nor whether the rate is regular under all conditions. Yet even without absolute dating, there is no doubt but that camels are absent in the earliest periods of Saharan rock art. To explain this the argument has been put forward for the Sahara as it has for Egypt that some sort of religious taboo forbade the representation of camels in early times, but there is no evidence for this being the case beyond the fact that in Egypt there is a Coptic prohibition on eating camel flesh which may possibly be related to the similar dietary restriction in Judaism.[10] Unfortunately for his argument, Cauvet himself draws attention to pictures of camels on Coptic fabrics.[11] Thus

even though the Copts could not eat a camel, they could draw
one, just as the Tuaregs of today do not eat camels but are not
adverse to representing them.[12] Therefore there is no possibility
of basing a pictorial ban on Coptic dietary law. The case for
the indigenous camel must, consequently, be rejected on the
basis of its absence in rock art. As has already been stated, the
Saharan camel died out in prehistoric times and was reintroduced at a later date from the east.

Going back to the basic question of why the development
of the transportation economy in North Africa seems to
synchronize so well with that in the Middle East, it becomes
apparent that whether the causal factors in North Africa are
independent of those at play in the Middle East or indirectly
related to them can only be determined by looking at conditions
in Egypt, Sudan, and the southern Sahara since it is from those
areas that the camel reached the Roman colonies in the north.
As in the Middle East, determination must be made of the
animal's availability, its value or utility in the eyes of potential
users, and the patterns of use that developed in the area.

Geographically the camel may be found today throughout
the arid belt of northern Africa from the Atlantic Ocean to the
Red Sea. Some well-watered mountainous areas of Algeria,
Tunisia, and Morocco are beyond its range, and it is not bred
in certain farming areas where it is worked, notably the Nile
delta and the Tunisian coastal plain north of Sfax. The
Ethiopian highlands also serve to cut off the camel country of
the horn of Africa from that of the Sudan as has previously
been discussed. But on the whole, the Sahara and its borderlands constitute a truly vast territory in which camel herding
may take place; and great ethnic, cultural, and linguistic
variety presently exists among the different camel-herding
peoples who inhabit that territory.

In the eastern part of this arid belt an additional geographical
factor is the Nile river valley which is essentially a long ribbon
of oasis parting the desert from the southern Sudan to
Alexandria. To a camel the river is no obstacle since camels are
good swimmers,[13] yet it could nevertheless have acted as a
serious obstacle to the spread of camel breeding if strong
animosity existed between the farming population of the valley
and the camel herders who wanted to make their way to the

lands on the other side. On a strictly geographical basis a
stronger barrier is the desert country west of the Nile. The
Sahara is by no means a uniform desert area; it encompasses
rugged mountains, sand seas, stony plateaus, salt flats, and
many other types of country. The most barren and waterless
parts of the Sahara, however, are located toward its eastern
end, the sand seas of eastern Libya, western Egypt, and
northwestern Sudan.[14] Caravan trails pass through this area,
to be sure, but it is far from being attractive pasture land even
for camels. Thus the routes by which camel breeding could
have reached the peoples of the central and western Sahara
are basically the two suggested by Demougeot, either along
the Mediterranean coast in the north or through the western
Sudan south of the forbidding deserts. However, given the fact
that the northern route adjoins the intensively cultivated Nile
delta where camels die of fly borne diseases and camel-breeding
nomads are held in low esteem,[15] the southern route must be
considered the more feasible of the two.

Historically, the earliest explicit indications of camel use in
northeastern Africa date back to the sixth and seventh centuries B.C. and are related to Assyrian and Persian invasions
of Egypt across the Sinai peninsula.[16] Since it has already been
demonstrated, however, that camel herders at that time were
still poor, despised desert dwellers, it is unlikely that the
services they rendered in the Assyrian and Persian supply
trains would have led to their permanent settlement in the Nile
valley any more than the occasional presence of camels
carrying incense had at even earlier dates. Of much greater
importance are references of the second and first centuries B.C.
to camelborne trade along the desert routes between the Nile
and the Red Sea some 500 miles south of the river's mouth.[17]
Whether the merchants involved were themselves from camel-
breeding tribes is not specified, but there can be no doubt that
such tribes were native to the eastern desert of Egypt at that
time. An adequate supply of animals at reasonable prices
could be obtained in no other way. Yet it is also clear that the
camel had still not made itself felt in the Egyptian economy
overall.[18] A camel-post existed in the second century B.C., but
wheeled vehicles were still used not uncommonly after the
Romans brought the dynasty of Ptolemy to an end in

30 B.C., and Strabo himself traveled through upper Egypt in
a carriage.[19]

From that time on the presence and power of camel nomads
in the Egyptian desert increased steadily. Numerous figurines
of camels carrying loads have been found in Egypt dating to the
Roman period.[20] These, along with the textual evidence mentioned in chapter one, testify to the increasing impact of camel
breeding upon the tranportation economy of the irrigated area
of the Nile valley and go hand in hand with the growing
military and political power of such camel-breeding nomads as
the Blemmyes or Beja in northeastern Sudan. By the third
century A.D. Beja raids were a serious threat to order in the
upper Nile valley, and after the Arab conquest of the seventh
century the Beja remained largely outside the Islamic orbit and
continued to dominate the southerly trade route between the
Red Sea port of ᶜAidhab and the Nile.[21]

As increasingly the desert east of the Nile became the home
of camel breeders, obvious questions arise as to who these
camel breeders were and where their knowledge of camel
breeding came from. Since there is no good reason to question
the commercial impetus of the first camel use in the eastern
desert, and since the Nabataeans during the same period
operated caravans between Petra and Leuce Come, a port
on the Red Sea just opposite the Egyptian port of Myus
Hormos, it seems more than likely that both animals and
experience migrated across the sea rather than across the Sinai
peninsula and then southward.[22] This is reinforced by the fact
that there is little to indicate that the camel herders of the
eastern desert were predominantly Arabs.[23] Skills and livestock
immigrated but not any appreciable number of people.
Instead, indigenous desert dwellers must gradually have been
encouraged by traders to produce the camels necessary for
the trade.

In the course of time the new animal spread southward,
possibly because of trade in that direction, since cataracts interfere with river boat traffic in northern Sudan, or possibly
because the new animal held out to the nomads of the eastern
desert the same promise it held out to the Arabs of Syria and
Mesopotamia, the promise of military power. Sources, of
course, are scanty; but there is evidence, in the form of a

118 figurine of a saddled camel, that the camel was used as a pack animal at Meroe, an ancient capital on the Nile in northern Sudan, in the first century B.C.;[24] and there is inscriptional evidence by early in the second century A.D. of warfare against camel-owning tribes in southern Egypt not long before the Blemmyes began to be a serious problem further south.[25] In sum, it would appear that the practice of camel breeding began in Egypt in the desert east of Thebes (modern Luxor) for purposes of trade, developed in a military as well as a commercial direction, and spread southward in this dual form into the eastern desert of the Sudan. Yet there is no evidence of any significant movement of peoples from the eastern side of the Red Sea to the western.

The proposal that the impetus for the introduction of the camel to the eastern desert trade route came from the Nabataeans or from merchants familiar with the Nabataean caravan route from Leuce Come already links the camel's arrival in northeastern Africa with the rise of the Arabs as a significant economic and political power, and the pattern of

46 Camel figurine from Meroe. Compare saddle with figure 15.

camel culture adopted in Africa makes the linkage even clearer. However, one commonly adduced similarity between the African and Middle Eastern camel cultures actually proves the opposite. Rock drawings and engravings from northwestern Arabia have been linked in style with those found in the Sahara from Mauretania to Egypt, a circumstance that would tend to indicate a movement of people rather than simply a movement of ideas and techniques.[26] In point of fact, however, the depictions of camels in the two areas differ greatly in that many of the Arabian examples show camel stallions with erect penises—this is very obvious since the camel's penis normally points backward between its legs and changes direction only when erect—and camel mares with upward curling tails, which is a sign of pregnancy, while Saharan art rarely shows either posture.[27] The Arabian artists clearly were using their skill to affect or symbolize the fertility of their herds, while the Saharan artists had other motives.

The truly telling indications that camel skills were borrowed from the Arabs around the second or first century B.C. lie in the area of saddle design and weaponry. Thanks to the meticulous work of Theodore Monod, the basic geography of saddle design in the Sahara is known.[28] It is very important to grasp this geography because unlike the Middle East, where variants of the North Arabian and the South Arabian saddle constitute the entire range of saddle design, the Sahara contains a broad diversity of saddles. Most notably, it is the home of three quite distinct saddles which rest upon the camel's shoulders in front of the hump. As mentioned earlier, the camel offers a rider a selection of seats: behind the hump, above the hump, and before the hump. The South Arabian saddle takes advantage of the first position which is also the least efficient in terms of control of the animal and use of weapons. The North Arabian saddle, evolved in response to the challenge of cavalry warfare, seats the rider firmly above the hump in closer proximity to the animal's head and high enough off the ground to make up in part for the inherent inferiority of the camel to the horse in warfare. Only along the southern side of the Sahara, in isolation from Roman or other cavalry forces across the desert to the north, did saddle designers take advantage of the position in front of the hump.[29]

47 Rock carvings from Jordan.

48 Rock carvings from Sahara.

49 Typical posture of rider on South Arabian saddle. Note long camel stick used to guide animal.

50 Typical posture of rider on North Arabian saddle.

51 Typical posture of rider on Saharan shoulder saddle. Note use of feet on neck to control animal.

The advantages of riding in front of the hump are several. **123** Greater control is one. Not only does the rider sit closer to the animal's head, but on the two types of saddle used by the Tuareg nomads of the central Sahara, the *terik* and the *tahyast*, he sits with his legs resting on the camel's neck thus making it possible for him to direct the camel with his toes. The *rahla* saddle of Mauretania and the western Sahara, which also

52 Tuareg *terik* saddle. See figure 9 for depiction of saddle in place on camel.

53 Tuareg *tahyast* saddle.

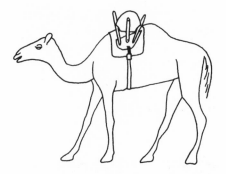

54 Schematic drawing of Mauretanian *rahla* saddle.

seats the rider before the hump, does not facilitate this kind of action, but this saddle may have been developed only after contact with the Arabs at a much later date.[30] Other advantages besides control are lighter weight, a simple, single-girth attachment to the animal, lessened need to adjust the padding under the saddle to accommodate changes in hump size, and positioning of the rider's weight directly over the animal's strong shoulders and front legs instead of over the weak hind quarters or in the middle of the back. All in all, as European military men concerned with camel corps in North Africa have several times pointed out, the position before the hump is markedly superior for riding to that on top of the hump.[31]

Given this superiority of the shoulder saddle over the North Arabian saddle, the question arises how the shoulder saddle developed and why it did so uniquely in the Sahara. The first of these two questions can be answered with some assurance: the shoulder saddle developed from the North Arabian saddle although possibly the idea originated in Yemen where some tombstones from the same period seem to show riders seated bareback before the hump.[32] The evidence for this lineage is three-fold. First, throughout the Sahara, whatever pack saddle or riding saddle is in use among a particular people, the riding saddle for women is constructed on the basic framework of the North Arabian saddle.[33] This conservatism in design of women's saddles is precisely parallel to that of the Arab tribes of northern Arabia whose women's saddles are based upon the South Arabian saddle instead of the North Arabian.[34]

55 Altar from Yemen apparently depicting man riding bareback in front of hump.

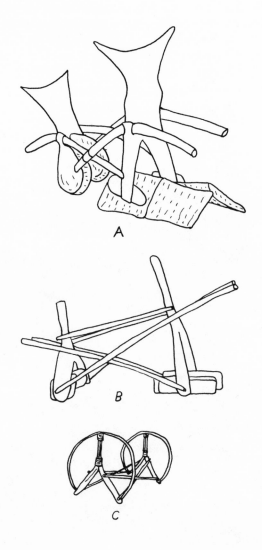

56 Schematic drawings of Saharan women's saddles. (A-B) Maure-tanian, (C) Teda.

Second, some of the shoulder saddle designs preserve a **127**
structural feature pointing to their descent from the North
Arabian saddle. In the shoulder saddle, pommel and cantle are
inclined toward each other at the bottom and away from each
other at the top. They are also, of course, much closer to each
other than the two analogous saddle bows of the North
Arabian saddle since there is less room for a saddle in front of
the hump than on top of it. In all designs a single girth is
attachable to the convergent bottom parts of the pommel and
cantle, and in some designs the bottom parts actually touch.
Despite the fact that pommel and cantle are quite close together, however, they are not structurally braced by horizontal
side bars as are the two closely spaced arches that make up
the front part of the South Arabian saddle as it is used
for baggage in the same area; instead they are often braced by
diagonal crossbars just like a North Arabian saddle.[35] This is
true even when the convergence of pommel and cantle is so
great as to minimize the effectiveness of the crossed supports.

An intermediate stage between the North Arabian saddle
and the Tuareg shoulder saddle can be seen in the *terke* saddle
commonly in use among the Teda people of the Tibesti and
Ennedi highlands in the southern Sahara between the Tuareg
country and the Nile. The *terke* is like the North Arabian
saddle in its essential design, but where the front and rear
arches of the North Arabian saddle are identical, the rear arch
of the *terke* slants backward like the cantle of the Tuareg
shoulder saddle. The horizontal side bars that support the
rider's seat are, as a result, attached higher and thus closer
together on the rear arch than on the front arch. The effect is to
make the front part of the seat broad and low and the back
high and narrow. The rider is forced to sit forward in the
saddle over the very front of the hump or even before it. From
this design to the Tuareg saddle is only a matter of moving the
whole apparatus forward and shortening the distance between
pommel and cantle. The principle of sitting low and in front
of the hump is already present.

The third evidence of descent from the North Arabian
saddle is the extensive corpus of Saharan rock art already mentioned. Attempts at setting up a relative chronology for the
various styles represented in this corpus have tended to lump

57 Tuareg *kantarki* saddles. Note crossed supports characteristic of North Arabian saddle.

58 South Arabian pack saddle in Sahara.

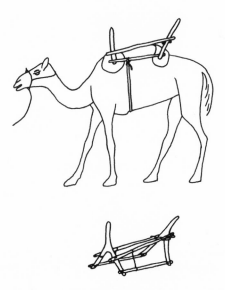

59 Schematic drawing of Teda *terke* saddle.

together all pictures of camels in a hypothetical "latest" or
"camelline" period. This is not always done, but when chronological differentiation among camel pictures is attempted,
saddle design is not usually thought of as a criterion.[36] Unfortunately, the result is that no competent specialist has
compared the relative chronology of saddle designs appearing
in the art of one area with that of other areas. Consequently,
no one but Demougeot, who comes to no conclusion,[37] has
commented upon the intriguing fact that from Mauretania to
the eastern desert of Egypt, across the entire breadth of the
southern Sahara, wherever pictures are found of riders
mounted on top of the hump as if on a North Arabian saddle,
in the same region (with only minor exceptions such as Jebel
Uwainat in southwestern Egypt)[38] there can be found pictures
showing riders mounted before the hump. For example, in the
Adrar district of Mauretania where today only the *rahla*
shoulder saddle is used, pictures of top mounted riders are
found;[39] and in the Tuareg highlands of Ahaggar and the
Tassili where only the *terik* and *tahyast* shoulder saddle are
used for riding, riders are likewise found depicted sitting above
the hump.[40] On the other hand, in the Ennedi, where the Teda
variant of the North Arabian saddle is presently supreme,

60 Riding postures on Saharan rock carvings.

pictures of shoulder saddles exist[41] just as they do in the Egyptian desert east of the Nile,[42] almost 2,000 miles from the eastern limit suggested by Monod for the distribution of shoulder saddles at the present time.[43] The conclusion seems inescapable that at some time in history the North Arabian saddle or variants of it were used in areas that are today the exclusive territory of the shoulder saddle while the reverse is true in areas presently using the North Arabian saddle, with one crucial exception: depictions of riders mounted before the hump are not found in the cosmopolitan areas north of the desert.

It has been maintained by Cauvet and others following him that the shoulder saddle is an invention stemming from the independent domestication of wild Saharan camels by indigenous Berber tribesmen, and this argument has been buttressed by the fact that the present day stronghold of the shoulder saddle is among the Tuaregs in the most solidly Berber part of the desert.[44] Yet the testimony of women's saddles, of the structural likeness between the shoulder saddle and the North Arabian saddle, and of rock pictures showing top mounted riders in this same Berber heartland makes this argument impossible to maintain. These non-Arabized Berber tribesmen clearly at one time used North Arabian saddles and abandoned them for shoulder saddles.

A more satisfactory hypothesis is that the family resemblance among saddles found on the south side of the Sahara and the apparent evolution over much of the same region from North Arabian to shoulder designs reflects a pattern of dissemination of camel breeding from upper Egypt and the Sudan in the east all the way across the southern Sahara to Mauretania.[45] It has already been stated that the southern Sahara is a more logical route for the spread of camel breeding than the Mediterranean coast because of the obstacle to nomadic movement posed by the Nile delta, and the evidence of saddle design appears to bear this out. A succession of rugged highland areas starting with Darfur in western Sudan and going from Ennedi to Tibesti to Tassili to Ahaggar to Adrar of the Ifoghas marks a feasible route linking the major centers of southern Saharan rock art with the region of the upper Nile valley. Even today this is the most important route of east-west

61 Riding postures on rock carvings from upper Egypt.

communication in the southern Sahara.[46] Once the camel had spread south from eastern Egypt to the Beja country of eastern Sudan, there was no major geographical or agricultural obstacle preventing it from spreading naturally from tribe to tribe all the way to Mauretania. All that would have been needed is motivation, and since the rock pictures suggest that the camel gradually supplanted the horse[47] and it has already been established that at the time of its introduction into Africa the camel had evolved into a military mount, there is every reason to suppose that the camel was welcomed as a riding animal superior to the horse because of its desert capability.

In this light, the development of the shoulder saddle becomes more meaningful. The shoulder saddle cannot be used as a pack saddle, unlike both the South and North Arabian designs, but it is a superior riding saddle, obviously the invention of a people whose primary interest was in riding. Moreover, the long lance that appears in some Saharan camel pictures affords additional support for the contention that the camel reached the Sahara only after its emergence as a military animal. There are also depictions of camel riders leading horses which suggest the Arab practice of switching to a horse for battle. Earlier weapons remained in use in the Sahara, however, and the nomads of the Sudan who confronted the Arabs at the time of the Islamic conquests were particularly expert with the bow.[48]

It would seem, then, that the shoulder saddle evolved from the North Arabian saddle in the southern Sahara because of the desire for a superior riding saddle. The *terke* saddle in use in the Tibesti and Ennedi would represent an intermediate design still in use among a particularly primitive people, and pictures of shoulder saddles in that area probably represent inroads of the Tuareg enemies of the Teda. The rock art, naturally, followed changes in design, although the exact chronology in different areas undoubtedly differs. In Egypt and the Sudan the chronology is further complicated by the later reintroduction of the North Arabian saddle by the conquering Arabs, but representations of riders mounted before the hump and armed with long lances show that the shoulder saddle came into use in the area before the present-day designs became known.[49]

62 Riding postures on rock paintings from Tibesti region.

63 Sudanese saddle.

136 To return to the question of the arrival and utilization of the camel in the cosmopolitan areas of Roman North Africa on the opposite side of the desert, the relative importance of camels coming along the coast from Egypt and others coming north across the Sahara must still be determined. Once again, the technology of camel utilization holds the key to the situation, and the conclusions that it suggests do not coincide with any of the previous theories regarding North African camel culture. Camel technology in Roman North Africa shows features that are entirely unique and clearly not derivative from Egypt or Syria or even from the technology of the Berber tribes. Of course, other features are not unique. The use of the North Arabian saddle can be confirmed from several figurines of camel riders, but this could be a borrowing from either Egypt

64 Figurines from Roman Tunisia showing riders mounted above hump.

or the Berbers since the Berbers may not by that time have switched to using the shoulder saddle.[50] In addition, the use of plaited baskets suspended like saddle bags on either side of the hump without any additional saddle is known today in Tunisia and exhibited on Roman figurines from Egypt.[51]

The unique features, however, are more impressive than these indications of technological borrowing. Camels were used in Roman Tripolitania and southern Tunisia for plowing and for pulling carts,[52] and they were used militarily in the sixth century to form laagers or defensive circles of couched animals behind which soldiers fought on foot.[53] None of these practices is attested for Syria, Egypt, or the Sahara. They are so far different from camel techniques used in these other areas, in fact, that independent innovation appears more than likely.

65 Basketry saddle used in Tunisia.

It is hard to imagine that the camel could have come to be used in such an innovative manner if its initial route of introduction was along the Mediterranean coast from Egypt. Techniques should have moved freely between these two imperial provinces, and a similarity in methods of camel utilization should have developed, presumably upon the Egyptian model.[54] In this regard, it should be noted that Demougeot presents little evidence that caravan traffic along this route was substantial. Indeed, she cites evidence that the camel was still unknown on this route at almost exactly the same time that Caesar was capturing Juba's camels in southern Tunisia.[55] Even a thousand years later under Arab rule travelers and traders along the Libyan coast much preferred to travel the route by sea than by caravan.[56]

Roman relations with the Berbers of the desert, on the other hand, were of an entirely different character. Prior to the introduction of the camel there was little trade across the Sahara and much hostility between the peoples of the coast and those of the desert, notably the Garamantes of southern Libya. As time went on and Roman rule penetrated further inland in arable regions, the peoples of the desert, who were gradually becoming predominantly camel nomads, remained a hostile threat; and elaborate *limes* or chains of fortified frontier posts had to be built to keep them out of settled territories.[57] In other words, the Berbers did not become integrated with settled society in the way that the Arabs did at the same point in time. Although the Berbers did possess the military potential to dominate a trans-Saharan caravan trade and siphon the profits into the desert, there was very little trade to dominate. Large-scale trading with black Africa does not seem to have gotten underway until the Islamic conquests, after which such desert caravan cities as Sijilmasa in Algeria became economically and politically important.[58]

Obviously, the Romans obtained camels from the desert tribes they were in contact with once those tribes had picked up the practice from other tribes further south. But camel herding probably worked its way north much more slowly than it worked its way west, not only because the center of the desert is a more inhospitable area than its northern fringes or southern highlands but also because the different rainfall regime in north and south, lands of winter and summer rains (if any at all) respectively, may have interfered with the camel's breeding cycle and made acclimation difficult.[59] The Garamantes, in particular, may have been slow in adopting the camel since their homeland was somewhat isolated geographically from camel-breeding areas further south.[60] There should be no cause for wonder, therefore, that the camel did not reach Roman territory from the south in significant numbers until several centuries after its introduction into the eastern desert of Egypt.

When the Romans finally did obtain access to camels in some quantity, probably beginning in the first or second century A.D., they had to decide what, if anything, to do with them. There was little to be learned from the Berber tribes on this score, even if the Romans had been willing to learn, since their main use for the animal was as a source of milk and a mount for riding.[61] Ideas gleaned from Egypt and Syria may have been influential in adopting the animal as a beast of burden, and the South Arabian saddle was probably introduced along with the North Arabian saddle to facilitate this. Both types are used for carrying loads in North Africa and the Sahara at the present time. The absence of a major caravan trade must have limited this utilization somewhat, however.

What the Romans really needed was animal traction to turn semidesert lands in southern Tunisia and Tripolitania into farmlands, and it was to this purpose that they adapted the new animal. The economy of upkeep that helped the pack camel replace the wheel further east recommended it as a plow animal alongside the ox. As for its impact on wheeled transport, the harnessing methods devised to attach the camel to a plow appear to have led, in a limited area at least, to the camel's being harnessed to carts. This unusual development will be discussed at length in chapter seven, but the fact that the camel was used at all for pulling carts makes it unclear whether or not the camel actually did supplant the wheel in North Africa. It seems likely that it did do so and that its utility as a pack animal proved greater, in the long run, than its utility as a draught animal, especially after the expansion of the desert caravan trade; but there is too little information about the extent to which wheeled vehicles were in use in North Africa at that time to be sure.

66 Harness of Tunisian camel cart.

Overall, the scheme of development in North Africa is very unlike that in the Middle East, but it is indirectly linked with it nevertheless. The Berbers did not play the same role as the Arabs, but had it not been for the emergence of the Arabs as an economic and political power, the introduction of camel breeding into Africa might not have taken place when it did. In the Middle East the camel was known long before it was used by settled peoples; in North Africa it was used almost as soon as it became known. There had been a great gulf between the camel breeder and the farmer in the Middle East which had to be bridged if the camel was to come into general use. Bridging it meant accepting the camel herders as an integral part of the economy and society of the region. Since acceptance of the camel had already been achieved in the Middle East, however, it did not have to be achieved all over again in the Roman African colonies. It was already generally known to be a useful animal. As a result, the Berbers' camels were adopted by Roman farmers for their own uses, which entailed entirely new techniques, but the camel-breeding Berber nomad remained alien to settled society. Only later when trans-Saharan caravan trading developed on the initiative, surely, of merchants in the north did the camel nomads of the Sahara experience a change in their status vis-à-vis settled society analogous to that which the Arabs had experienced centuries earlier.

6 Iran: One Hump or Two?

The two-humped camel has been little discussed in this book up to this point, but it comes into the very center of the picture when attention is shifted to the Iranian plateau. Historically, the most important seat of Persian political power has as often been centered in the Tigris-Euphrates basin, which has never been ethnically an Iranian area, as it has been in the mountain and plateau regions of present day Iran, Afghanistan, and Turkmenistan, which have been the homelands of the Iranian languages ever since the speakers of those languages arrived in the Middle East. These latter areas would also appear to encompass the original homeland of the domesticated two-humped camel, a homeland from which the practice of breeding that animal spread until it was known not only throughout the entire Iranian plateau area but in neighboring parts of Iraq, Mesopotamia, Anatolia, India, and Central Asia as well. Yet at some point in time this process of dissemination was reversed, and the range of the domestic two-humped camel receded to such an extent that at the present time the two-humped camel is virtually unknown west of northeastern Afghanistan and the Oxus River (Amu Darya) in Central Asia.

This amazing spread and subsequent retraction has never before been investigated nor, apparently, even recognized. The literature that provides such extensive discussion of problems pertaining to camels in North Africa and which covers to some degree the camel problems of the Middle East gives way almost entirely when one moves eastward.[1] It has already been pointed out that the extent to which wheeled transportation was in use in Iran in ancient times is difficult to determine, and the same thing must be said for the status of camel breeding. Thus while it seems quite likely that the changes in the transportation economy that took place in Roman territory on the western side of the Syrian desert took place in Persian governed territory on the eastern side of the desert in roughly the same fashion—and some data will be presented later in this chapter to lend substance to this presumption—it is impossible to say with the same degree of likelihood that the pack camel replaced the cart on the Iranian plateau. What can be affirmed and to some extent explained is that the one-humped camel replaced the two-humped camel in Iran roughly during the same period that it was elsewhere replacing the wheel. The wheel may actually have been supplanted in Iran at an earlier date by the two-humped camel itself, but this is far from certain since, as will be seen, the two-humped camel unlike the one-humped camel was used from a very early date to pull vehicles.

Clearly, the place to start in trying to unravel these various riddles is with the origin of the domestic two-humped camel, but first it is important to establish what happens when camels of these two species are mated with one another. Much of what is reported in camel books on this subject is incorrect, particularly regarding the alleged infertility of the hybrid. The source generally quoted is a letter from H. Pognon, French consul at Aleppo, dated January 8, 1899, and it is little realized that scientific experimentation on this matter has been carried out in the Soviet Union where one-humped camels are bred by the Turkmen tribes of Turkmenistan and two-humped camels by the Kirghiz tribes of Kirghiziya.[2] This is very unfortunate

because the hybrid camel plays an important role in the history
of camels in Iran and Anatolia.[3] The accompanying chart of
terminology relating to hybridization in various languages has
been compiled from this modern research done in the Soviet
Union and from earlier sources mostly dating back to the medieval period when camel hybridization was well understood and
deemed a subject worth writing about.[4]

This chart will be referred to later in other contexts, but it
should be noted at this point that the two species do mate; that
their hybrid offspring (class 4) shows what is called hybrid
vigor, meaning that it is larger and stronger than either parent;
and that successive generations either revert to the characteristics of one of the pure species if one of the parents is pure bred
(classes 8, 9), or become degenerate and economically useless if
hybrids are mated with other hybrids (classes 7, 10, 11). The
first generation hybrid, incidentally, has either a single, rather
long hump or a single long hump with a noticeable indentation
in it some 4–12 centimeters deep which makes the fore part
substantially smaller than the rear.[5] Later generations resume
the hump type of whichever parent is pure bred.

The two locations most commonly hypothesized as the
homeland of the domestic two-humped camel are Bactria, the
classical name for the valley of the Oxus River in northern
Afghanistan, and Mongolia or northwestern China. The first
area has little to recommend it other than the fact that the
Greeks called the animal Bactrian, the Greeks, of course, coming into contact with it only many centuries after it had been
domesticated.[6] As for the other location, it is today the only
refuge of the so-called wild camel about which travelers and
scholars have debated for decades.[7] The crux of the debate is
whether the wild camel is truly a wild species or merely a feral
beast descended from domestic camels that at some time or
other escaped into the desert. Scientific examination appears
finally to have settled this debate in favor of there being at
least some truly wild characteristics present in these wild
camels even though escaped domestic stock may have interbred
with them from time to time.[8] The most persuasive evidence
for this is the absence in the wild camel of the large chest callus
which bears much of the weight of the recumbent animal. In
the domestic species this callus, as well as others on the leg

144   Camel Hybridization Terminology

Classification	Arabic	Persian	Turkish: Anatolian
1. Generic term	ibil	shotor	deve
2. One-humped	jamal (m.) baʿīr (m.) nāqa (f.) and others	lūk (m.) arvāna (f.)	
3. Two-humped	fālij yaʿlūl duhānij	dokūhānī bughur (m.)	bughur
4. First generation hybrid: cross between 2 and 3	bukht jammāza (f.)	bughdī bukht bīsarāk jammāza (f.)	māya bishsharak beserīk
5. Second generation hybrid: cross between 2 and 4	bahwaniya ṣarṣarāniya	bughdī lūk (m.) arvāna (f.)	kufūrud
6. Second generation hybrid: cross between 3 and 4	[useless runt]	guhurd (inferior animal)	tāūs (very small)
7. Second generation hybrid: cross between 4 and 4	[short neck, runt]	bughdī	deli (bad temper)
8. Third generation hybrid: cross between 2 and 5			
9. Third generation hybrid: cross between 3 and 6			
10. Third generation hybrid: cross between 4 and 6			
11. Third generation hybrid: cross between 6 and 6			

Source: al-Jāḥiẓ, *al-Ḥayawān*, I, 138; II, 240; III, 145, 162; V, 459; VI, 216, VII, 169, 242; ʿAllāmī, *Āʾīn-i Akbarī*, I, 146–147; Burckhardt, *Bedouins and Wahābys*, p. 110; Kolpakow, "Ueber Kamelkreuzungen"; Roux, "Le chameau en Asie Centrale," pp. 37–43; Raymond, "Afghanistan," p. 9.

ᵃ Bracketed words indicate hybrid categories that are described in the literature but not labeled with a specific term.

Turkish: Turkmen	Turkish: Kirghiz	Mongolian
teve	tüö	tämägän
arvana lök (m.)	arvana (f.) lök (m.)	
irkek azhrī	buwra air-bura īngän (f.)	bughura inigän
boghī iner ner	nar bertuar brtugan	
	kurt (m.) arvana half- breed (f.) (poor breed)	
	kospak (sound and useful)	
	charbai (runt)	
	lök (m.) arvana (f.) (good one- humped camel)	
	[good two- humped camel]	
	kiyssik-töss (degenerate)	
	taskarin (degenerate)	

67 Hybrid camel breeding in northwestern Iran. Second animal from left has hump pattern characteristic of hybrids.

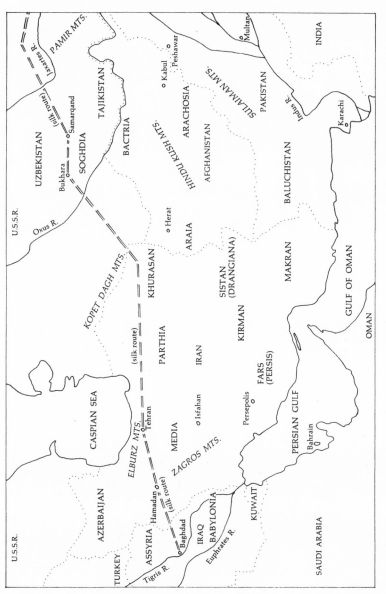

Iran and Central Asia

joints, appears in the foetus. Since the leg calluses do appear on the wild camel, the absence of the chest callus is unmistakably a significant genetic difference.[9] Yet this does not by any means prove that the Gobi desert or Lop Nor basin are the homeland of the domestic two-humped camel. It merely shows that the wild species still survives in these remote regions long after it has disappeared from other areas where it once roamed freely. Since Chinese records indicate no knowledge of the camel before the fourth or third century B.C., these areas must be ruled out along with Bactria.

In the light of recent archaeological discoveries it is becoming increasingly apparent that the two-humped camel was actually domesticated in what is today the border region between the northeastern Iranian province of Khurasan and Soviet Turkmenistan.[10] The earliest evidence is a potsherd from Siyalk, an archaeological site south of Tehran, which shows what may be a two-humped camel.[11] This sherd is dated

68 Model wagon with camel's head from excavation in Turkmenistan.

between 3000 and 2500 B.C., and there is no suggestion that **149** the animal shown is domestic. More important, several archaeological sites in Turkmenistan have yielded camel bones and clay models of wagons with a camel's long neck and head rising from the wagon floor in contexts dated 2500–2000 B.C. and 2000–1600 B.C.[12] Other excavations in the eastern Iranian province of Sistan have turned up a clay jar filled with camel dung and fragments of camel's hair fabric from the same period.[13] Since there are marked similarities between artifacts from the Turkmenistan sites and those from sites in southern Iran, it may be assumed that the domestic camel was known over a fairly large area at that time.[14] Traces of camels datable to before 1500 B.C. have not been found elsewhere in Soviet Central Asia, so there is no indication that domestication reached Turkmenistan from the north or east; but the association of camels with wagons suggests a rather advanced stage of domestication. It is entirely possible, therefore, that the date of domestication may reach back several centuries before 2500 B.C.

But were the camels indicated by these archaeological finds indeed of the two-humped variety? This is an assumption which the available evidence does not unequivocally bear out. Somewhat later evidence makes this identification appear very likely, but a few early bits of information cast some doubt. One source of uncertainty is the close connection between cultural deposits discovered on the east coast of Arabia in the vicinity of the Qatar peninsula and others found in southeastern Iran.[15] A movement of people originating in Iran across the narrow straits separating Iran and Arabia appears certain. Rock drawings found on the Arabian site show that these people encountered the one-humped camel in their new home. There is at present no way of telling, however, whether they encountered domestic or wild animals, whether they took some back with them to southern Iran, or whether it might have been by this improbable route that the idea of camel domestication reached Arabia from Iran or vice versa. Even if the idea of domestication moved by this route, however, the difference between the methods of controlling the animal in Arabia and in Iran is so basic as to preclude the idea that there might have been some exchange of technology at that time. The two-humped camel is always controlled by a nose peg while all early evidence shows that the Arabian camel was controlled by a strap around the muzzle.[16] The former practice indicates, perhaps, the influence of cattle-herding techniques in Iran and the latter the influence of ass breeding.

One further complication stems from an ambiguous piece of data in the form of a bronze ax head with its blunt end modeled in the form of a kneeling camel. This ax head was discovered in a grave in southeastern Iran by Sir Aurel Stein and can be dated only by stylistic means. On this basis its date has been estimated at 2600–2400 B.C.[17] The ambiguity of the figure arises from the fact that while it is unquestionably a camel, the modeling of the head and neck being particularly realistic, it has only one hump, and that one is situated directly over the hind quarters much too far back to be a realistic representation of a one-humped camel. Does it, then, represent a one-humped camel whose hump has been badly misplaced, a two-humped camel with the second hump missing, or, as F. E. Zeuner has rather improbably suggested,[18] a separate camelline species otherwise unknown? The first alternative would strongly indicate transmission of camels or cultural traits associated with camels across the Persian Gulf from Arabia. However, there is evidence against this identification other than the misplaced hump. The head and neck of the figure indicate a very heavy coat of wool such as is common for camels of either variety in northern Iran and Central Asia, but in hot climates such as Arabia and southern Iran this heavy growth of wool does not occur. As for the notion of a separate species, without a shred of additional evidence it cannot be maintained.

On the other hand, if it is actually a representation of a two-humped camel, what became of the second hump? The answer to this appears to lie in a bulge on the upper left side of the animal which has been determined metallurgically to be part of the original figure.[19] This bulge can only be the corroded remnant of the second hump which was originally portrayed flopped over on the animal's side rather than upright. Such flaccidity is quite common and is one of the noticeable differences between one-humped and two-humped camels. In this case it must have been rather exaggerated, but it was made artistically necessary by the too short length of the figure's

69 Two-humped camel on pick-ax found at Khurab in southern Iran. Second hump has corroded away.

back which practically rules out a realistic depiction of one hump directly behind the other. In substantiation of this interpretation it may be observed that the sole remaining hump is definitely inclined toward the right to counterbalance the flaccid hump, a situation that commonly occurs among living camels. The proper identification of the figure therefore is with the two-humped camel, which strengthens the view that early Iranian camel culture was roughly homogeneous from northeastern to southeastern Iran and was without influence from Arabia.[20]

How the camel fitted into the overall herding economy during this earliest period of domestication is an open question. Just as the Semitic migrations to southern Arabia submerged the earlier cultures of that area, so the proto-urban culture of northeastern Iran, from which the earliest evidence of two-humped camel domestication emanates, declined by 1800 B.C., and the entire area became so much under the dominance of the culture of the Indo-Iranian peoples who migrated there from the north during the following centuries that the identity of the earlier peoples is entirely lost. As already mentioned, archaeological finds prove that camel dung was collected for fuel and camel hair woven into cloth; but since both products are obtainable from the wild animal, the only solid indication of domestication is the appearance of camels' heads on model wagons. And even here there exists some ambiguity since the sole photograph of a camel wagon that has found its way into print shows an animal that is not unquestionably a camel.[21] Presumably, since many specimens have been discovered, the identification is clearer on other examples.

All of this amounts to more material evidence than is extant from southern Arabia from a similar period, of course, but whereas in the latter area there still exists a tradition of camel breeding that might preserve ancient practices, in northeastern Iran the two-humped camel is no longer herded and hence no clues can be sifted from modern anthropological data. However, one final source of information raises the possibility that two-humped camel herding in northeastern Iran never did exist on more than a minor scale. This is the evidence of bones discovered in archaeological excavations. At Shahr-i Sukhta, the site in Sistan which yielded the pot of camel dung and the

fragment of camel's hair cloth, no camel bones have been
identified among the close to one million bones discovered.[22]
At Anau in Turkmenistan only 5 percent of the bones uncov-
ered in contexts dating to 2700–2000 B.C. were camel bones.[23]
At Harappa in the Indus valley, a pre-Indo-Iranian metropolis
which had cultural contacts with the contemporary Turkmenistan culture, only three camel bones have been discovered.[24] In short, the people who domesticated the two-humped
camel may never have herded more than a small number of
them. It has already been argued in chapter two that the two-
humped camel by the time of its domestication was a rare
animal on the brink of extinction dwelling in desolate areas.[25]
Since it was big and strong, it may have seemed like a reasonable beast to use as the ox was used for pulling plows and
wagons; this would explain why the nose ring was adopted for
control purposes and why the only concrete evidence of
domestication relates to wagons. But since the people involved
in its domestication already had cattle, sheep, goats, and increasingly horses, there is good reason to doubt that the camel
played more than a minor role in their herding economy.
Unlike the early inhabitants of southern Arabia, these pre-
Iranians did not really need the camel for subsistence and
certainly did not develop a nomadic economy based primarily
upon camel herding.

With the coming of the Indo-Iranian peoples to the Iranian
plateau, information on the two-humped camel becomes more
substantial. The date of this momentous migration is much
debated, but few plausible estimates much antedate 1700 B.C.
It is equally difficult to date the earliest literary works of the
Indo-Iranians, the Rig Veda and the older parts of the Avesta,
religious texts of Indians and Iranians respectively; but the
culture that gave them form was that of the people who made
the first migrations. What makes the question of dating important is the appearance in both the Rig Veda and the Avesta of
references to camels, the word *ushtra* being used in both
sources.[26] This word for camel is the source for most later
words for camel in Iran and India (modern Persian: *shotor;*
Hindi: *ūṭ;* Assamese, Bengali, Oriya: *ut;* Dardic: *tor;* Baluchi:
ushtir), but it is completely unrelated to any Indo-European
words for camel north and west of the area of Indo-Iranian

linguistic influence (Gothic: *ulbandus*; Old Norse: *ulfalde*; Old High German: *olbento*; Russian: *verbliud*; Polish: *wielbłąd*).[27] Our word "camel" itself, of course, is a borrowing through Greek from the Semitic languages. This split between the basic word used by the Indo-Iranian branch of the Indo-European language family and that used by the western branches of the family suggests quite strongly that the word *ushtra* was coined by the Indo-Iranians when they first encountered the animal during their migrations. Archaeologically this conclusion is buttressed by the fact that camel bones (one animal out of fifty-three) are first found in Russia in remains of the Andronovo culture which occupied the southern Urals and northern Kazakhstan between 1700 and 1200 B.C. and which has been identified with the Indo-Iranian peoples.[28] Other Indo-European peoples encountered it at other times in other cultural contexts and hit upon a different word to describe it.

What, then, is the meaning of this word that was chosen to designate the camel? It could, naturally, be a loanword from some language in the area the Indo-Iranians were moving into;[29] but there is every indication that it is actually derived from an Indo-European root. The most commonly repeated view is that the word means buffalo as well as camel, the former meaning being the original one, and that the root meaning is "the shining one" (Sanskrit root: *vas*; Avestan root: *vah* = "to shine").[30] However, there are several reasons for rejecting this interpretation. Most persuasive intuitively is the fact that neither a camel nor a buffalo fits very well the epithet "shining one." But beyond that, use of the word to mean buffalo is not unequivocally attested,[31] and all of the words derived from *ushtra* in modern languages mean camel exclusively. Furthermore, *ushtra* appears meaning camel in an Old Persian (a language different from Avestan) inscription of the sixth century B.C.; and *udru* or *uduru*, an apparent Indo-Iranian loanword, is used in Akkadian for two-humped camel starting in the eleventh century B.C.[32] Thus the proposed connection between *ushtra* and buffalo must be rejected.

A much more plausible derivation of the word is from a hypothetical Indo-European root *vegh* (Latin: *vexo*; Sanskrit: *váhati*) meaning "to carry."[33] By ordinary phonological rules

the Sanskrit form from this root should be *uḍhra* rather than
ushtra, but this anomaly can be explained by the influence of
semantically related words from the same root (Sanskrit: *voḍhṛ*
and Avestan: *važdra* = "that which brings forward"; Avestan: *vaštar* and Rig Veda: *uṣṭŕ-* = "draught animal"). Support for this derivation may possibly be found both in the
Akkadian word already cited, which could hardly be derived
from the root *vah*, and in the word for two-humped camels
used by the Turkmen tribes of Turkmenistan and shown on
the chart of camel terminology. This word is *azhrī*, and it is
obvious from the chart that it bears no relation to any properly
Turkish word for camel nor is it derived from modern Persian.[34] In all likelihood it is a Turkmen borrowing from an
earlier Indo-Iranian language of Turkmenistan such as Khwa-
rizmian.

The obvious conclusion to be drawn from the Indo-European
linguistic evidence, therefore, is that when the Indo-Iranians
entered camel-breeding country, and before the Indian language group and the Iranian diverged, they adopted a word
for camel that implies a pattern of domestication characterized
by the animal being used for hauling. This conclusion serves to
corroborate the inference made by Soviet archaeologists from
their discovery of camel-headed wagons that as early as the
first half of the third millennium B.C. two-humped camels were
used in Turkmenistan for drawing wagons, and it suggests that
the Indo-Iranians simply took over the usage pattern of the
people they supplanted.

Further corroboration is afforded by some of the earliest
appearances of the word *ushtra* in surviving literary sources.
In the Rig Veda (8.6.46) there appears the phrase "granting
four pairs (yokes) of camels" (*úṣṭrān catur-yújo dádat*). It is
improbable that the word *yújo*, meaning both pair and yoke,
would have been used for enumerating an animal that was not
customarily thought of in terms of pairs, for example for
sheep; hence the pairing of camels must have been commonplace, which would strongly indicate the use of camels under
a yoke for draught purposes. The sole appearance of the word
ushtra in Old Persian referred to earlier has the animal being
used for carrying loads. Cyrus had it recorded that he put
some of his men on camels for transport, not combat, pur-

poses.[35] Presumably baggage camels already in the army's train were used on this particular occasion. Later Cyrus experimented with putting warriors on baggage camels to frighten the enemy's horses.[36] Whether one- or two-humped camels were used the second time cannot be determined. Back on the Indian side, both the *Laws of Manu* compiled several centuries before the beginning of the Christian era and the writings of the grammarian Patanjali, who lived in the second century B.C., specifically mention carts drawn by camels.[37] Moreover, Strabo quotes Nearchus, an officer of Alexander the Great, to the effect that in the fourth century B.C. elephants in India were "driven under the yoke like camels."[38] Thus there is altogether good reason to believe that the pattern of camel utilization suggested by archaeological discoveries in Turkmenistan and Sistan remained basically unchanged after the arrival of the Indo-Iranians.

Now it is necessary to return to the questions raised at the beginning of this chapter. The practice of using domestic two-humped camels spread in all directions from its original homeland. To the northeast, camel bones have been found in remains of the Karasuk culture which flourished in the ninth and tenth centuries B.C. in the Minusinsk basin in western Siberia, and by 200 B.C. it was known in China.[39] To the northwest, the bones of a single camel have been found near the Don River in western Russia among remains of the late Srubnaya culture which is dated to the eighth and ninth centuries B.C.[40] Evidence of the camel's spread eastward into western India has already been presented. Finally, to the west there is an abundance of evidence starting with the second millenium B.C. Mesopotamian cylinder seal mentioned in chapter three. The Akkadian word *udru* is first used in the reign of the Assyrian king Assurbelkala (1074–1057 B.C.) who bought some two-humped camels from merchants with dealings in the east.[41] Which Indo-Iranian people the word may have been borrowed from is unknown. From that time on *udru* appears not infrequently in royal records, sometimes, as the one-humped camel came gradually to be known, with the specific added notation that the animal had two humps.[42] In most instances it is mentioned as part of booty or tribute coming from the mountainous lands east and northeast of Assyria, that is, from the Iranian plateau.[43] Pictorially, there are two depictions of two-humped camels from the reign of Shalmaneser III (858–824 B.C.). On a black obelisk commemorating his victories two tribute delegations are shown leading two-humped camels, and on the bronze gates of Balawat another such delegation appears.[44] All of these animals are led, oddly enough, by ropes around the neck rather than nose pegs. Finally, there is an eighth century B.C. report of an Urartian king named Sardur capturing a number of two-humped camels in what is now Armenia. The number is 115 out of 55,959 animals of all sorts.[45]

As for the Iranian plateau itself, as opposed to the lands surrounding it, there is evidence to verify that the two-humped camel was known throughout virtually the entire area. A few Luristan bronzes datable to roughly the seventh or eighth century B.C. confirm the Assyrian reports of camels in the Zagros mountains which form the demarcation between the Iranian plateau and the Tigris-Euphrates valley,[46] and a piece of decorative gold appliqué work found at Hamadan testifies to the animal still being known in the area in the reign of Artaxerxes II (404–359 B.C.), although the artist could not have been too familiar with it since he gave it a horse's head and portrayed it in the most atypical posture of rearing on its hind legs.[47] Strabo, finally, mentions that camel breeders are to be found in the most northerly part of Fars (Persis) province on the borders of Media.[48]

The camel's presence elsewhere in Iran is confirmed by the processions of national delegations bearing tribute carved in the fifth or sixth century B.C. on the walls of the Achaemenid palaces at Persepolis. One-humped camels led by a muzzle strap are portrayed solely with the Arabian delegation, but five separate peoples are shown leading two-humped camels by nose pegs: the Parthians, the Arachosians, the Arians, the Bactrians, and the Drangianans.[49] Geographically, this locates the camel in northern Afghanistan (Bactria), northeastern Iran (Parthia), eastern Afghanistan south of the Hindu Kush (Arachosia), western Afghanistan around the city of Herat (Araia), and in Sistan province in eastern Iran (Drangiana). Putting this evidence together with that pertaining to western Iran, the only habitable parts of the country for which there is no indication that the two-humped camel was known in the

70 Two-humped camels on black stele of Shalmaneser.

71 Two-humped camels on bronze gates of Balawat.

72 Two-humped camel on bronze belt buckle from Luristan.

73 Achaemenid period gold appliqué camel found at Hamadan in western Iran.

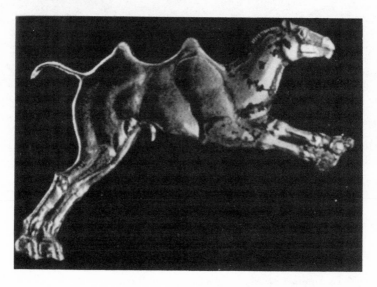

first millenium B.C. are the subtropical coast of the Caspian Sea
north of the Elburz Mountains and the torrid southern provinces along the Indian Ocean.

Thus the herding of two-humped camels spread very far
indeed from its original point of domestication. In some of the
areas to which the practice spread it remains vigorously alive
to the present day, notably in Central Asia and Mongolia. But
in other areas it has totally disappeared. Anatolia, whence the
Assyrians received camels as tribute, had by the nineteenth
century only a few male animals imported from north of the
Black Sea for breeding purposes.[50] The Indus valley had two-
humped camels well into the Muslim period but has none
today. They are very seldom seen also anywhere in Iran or
Turkmenistan, and in Afghanistan few are known apart from
those bred by Kirghiz tribesmen in the extreme northeast.[51]
What is most striking about this pattern of disappearance is
that in all those regions from which the two-humped camel has
disappeared the one-humped camel has become common, and
in those regions where the two-humped camel is still bred the
one-humped camel is only rarely seen.

Why did the one-humped camel replace the two-humped
camel? This question can be only tentatively answered because information on the subject is difficult to find, but what
seems to be at the heart of the answer is the great difference in
patterns of usage between the breeders of the two animals. The
one-humped camel was herded on a very large scale in the
Syrian-Arabian desert. It provided the economic base for an
entire nomadic society. The people who bred it valued both it
and the products it provided. The two-humped camel, on the
other hand, was domesticated by peoples who were already
familiar with the cow, the sheep, and the goat and who were
becoming familiar with the horse. The camel was never a
necessity of life for them, nor was it valued as much for its
products as it was for its work potential. There were, after
all, plentiful alternative sources of milk and meat. This does
not mean that the camel was not valued at all; quite the contrary, in the oldest portion of the Avesta a recompense of one
camel, one stallion, and ten mares is mentioned, while in the
Vendīdād, the youngest portion of the Avesta put in final form

74 Arabs leading one-humped camel in procession of tribute bearers at Persepolis. Note halter.

75 Tribute bearers with two-humped camel from Persepolis. Note use of nose-peg.

at the very latest in the fourth century A.D., the order of importance of sacrifices is a male camel, then a stallion, then a bull, and finally a cow with calf.[52] It does mean, however, that the two-humped camel was always herded in small numbers and utilized primarily for labor.

When these two herding regimes came into contact, the circumstances of the contact were such as to make the Arab pattern dominant. Those circumstances appear to have arisen in connection with the growth of the overland caravan trade through Central Asia to China, the famous Silk Route. It is impossible here to go into the reasons for the opening up of this trade route since they involve not only the political and economic history of China and Persia but also the very complex history of tribal movements in Central Asia.[53] It must suffice instead to observe that traffic along the Silk Route began to become important around the first century A.D. when China was under the rule of the later Han dynasty and Persia under the rule of the Parthians, an originally nomadic people from northeastern Iran who had gradually encroached upon the Hellenistic state set up by Alexander's general Seleucus until by the second half of the second century B.C. they had reached the Tigris River.[54] Parthia, it may be remembered, was one of the areas presenting tribute camels to the Achaemenid king in the Persepolis friezes.

There is no question but that the caravan trade that developed under the Parthians initially used two-humped camels. Figurines of loaded camels found with Parthian remains at Seleucia and Uruk in Iraq bear too close a resemblance to later camel figures from China for it to be a matter of coincidence, particularly since the figures bear no resemblance to contemporary representations of one-humped camels.[55] What makes the resemblance striking is the shape of the load on the camel's back. It is round and almost hemispherical, as if it were a leather or fabric container filled with some kind of liquid or granular substance. On many of the Chinese figures this round load is decorated with the face of a fantastic dog, but more sober examples show that a definite container of some sort is intended.[56] Without trying to guess what the product being traded might have been, it is nevertheless evident that under the Parthians the same type of camel load was reaching Iraq that was later reaching China—and on the same type of animal.

76 Parthian period two-humped camel found at Seleucia on the
Tigris. Note hemispherical load.

77 Parthian period two-humped camel from Uruk in southern Iraq.
Note broken hemispherical load.

78 Sui dynasty camel figurine from China with characteristic hemispherical load.

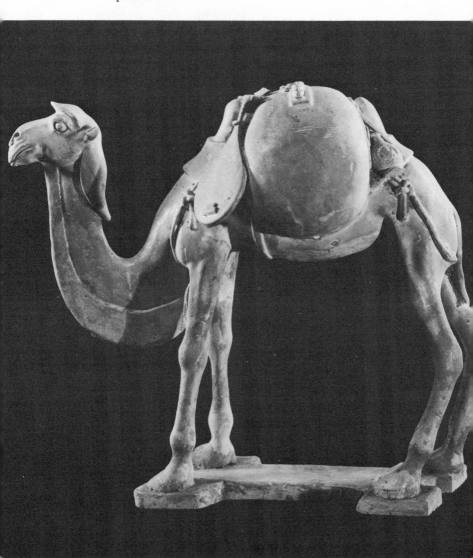

79 Graffito from Dura-Europus showing caravan of two-humped camels.

In further substantiation of this point a graffito showing a
caravan of two-humped camels was found at Dura-Europus on
the Euphrates frontier between the Parthians and the Romans,[57] and Diodorus the Sicilian reports that in a part of
Arabia which borders the ocean, is swampy, and is traversed
by great rivers, different types of camels are bred including
"both the hairless and the shaggy, and those which have two
humps, one behind the other, along their spines and hence are
called *dituloi* [double knobbed]."[58] It has been suggested that
this account indicates that the two-humped camel was in use at
one time in southern Arabia,[59] but surely a more plausible
reading is to understand the area being described to be northeastern Arabia adjoining Iraq and bordering the Persian Gulf
where the lower courses of the Tigris and Euphrates create
enormous swamps. Here would be the pasture lands servicing
the western terminus of the Central Asian caravan route, and
the reference to three distinct types of camel would imply that
Arabian and Persian camels were being crossbred in this area
to produce a powerful, one-humped hybrid specifically for
caravan work—Diodorus's "shaggy" camel. It should be noted
in this respect that the Greek *dituloi* is simply a translation of
Persian *dokūhānī*, the common term for two-humped camel
given on the terminology chart. Still further in this regard, one
figurine found at Seleucia on the Tigris and dating to the Parthian period is unlike the ones previously mentioned in that it
shows an animal with one long hump with only a small dip in the
middle of it.[60] This corresponds very closely to the profile of the
first generation hybrid camel described earlier in this chapter.

80 Parthian period camel figurine from Seleucia on the Tigris. Note shallow dip in hump indicative of hybridization.

The first logical step in the confrontation of the one-humped and the two-humped camel seems, therefore, to have taken place during the Parthian period in the Tigris-Euphrates valley. Someone—most likely merchants connected with Arab camel breeders—thought to cross the two species and discovered that the hybrid was an ideal pack animal. Some of them, if Diodorus is not exaggerating, could carry as much as 900 pounds of wheat.[61] An animal so obviously superior to either of its parents could not help but be in demand by all merchants involved in the trade. Its spread along the caravan route was inevitable. In 128 B.C. it is reported in a Chinese source that the Yüeh-chi, an Indo-Iranian people then living north of the Oxus River in Soghdia, had one-humped camels; but the same source simply says that "camels" are bred in the Kabul area well south of Soghdia.[62] Although it is unlikely that many purebred one-humped camels actually lived beyond the Oxus at that time, especially since the area has cold winters and is not today one-humped camel territory, it is nevertheless evident that the Yüeh-chi had some hybrids and possibly some one-humped breeding stock. The fact that the Chinese observer commented specifically on the single hump testifies to

81 Two-humped camel on Kushan coin of the ruler Kadphises.

the animal being unusual and indicates that in other areas for which the word camel is used without modification the two-humped species was herded, including areas to the south of the Yüeh-chi.

Later evidence confirms this intrusion of hybrid camels along the caravan route. The Yüeh-chi themselves moved south into Bactria, evolved into the Kushan empire, and returned to breeding two-humped camels either because their source of one-humped breeding stock was cut off or because the two-humped animal was better suited to plying the route over the Hindu Kush mountains into India. Numerous coins of the Kushan king Kadphises I who reigned in the first century A.D. bear the image of a two-humped camel.[63] In the fourth century two-humped camels were still used south of the Hindu Kush where their depictions are found on Buddhist religious sculpture from Hadda and Peshawar.[64] Since the sculptures depict riding camels whose masters are shown bearing sacred relics, the artist's intent could conceivably have been to show pilgrims from Central Asia riding typically Central Asian animals. Earlier in this century two-humped camels were still seen at Peshawar in caravans coming from the north.[65] An Arab geographer writing around the year 900 proves, however, that two-humped camels were still actually being bred in India. His account of the Budha people who lived in the mountains of Pakistan west of the Multan district reads: "They are camel people, and their camel is the *fālij* which is transported to all corners, to Khurasan, Fars and the rest of the countries where there are *bukhtī* camels."[66] A later Arab geographer expanding upon this account explains further: "[The *fālij*] possesses two humps. The male is mated wth Arab females, and the *bukhtī* is born from them. [The *fālij*] is imported only from their country."[67]

This last statement may not have been entirely accurate since an Arab writer of the ninth century speaks of the *fālij* of Kirmān, a province in south-central Iran, being used for cross-breeding.[68] But it is certain that through the first few centuries of the Islamic period two-humped camels continued to be bred in territories south of the main axis of trade through northern Iran to Central Asia, and they were bred primarily to provide breeding stock for producing hybrids. The *bukhtī* hybrid was found according to these and other sources in Khurasan, Fars, Kirman, Samarqand, and Kabul.[69] It might also be noted that the people who today inhabit the territory of the Budha people are a Baluchi tribe called the Bugti.

The development of hybridization that began under the Parthians in perhaps the second century B.C., therefore, grew increasingly important as traffic along the Silk Route increased until by the early Islamic period the sole use of two-humped camels in Iran and Afghanistan was as breeding stock. The dominance between the two species could theoretically have gone the other way, however. In the nineteenth century, for example, while a few two-humped camels were imported into Anatolia to provide studs for Syrian one-humped camels, among the Kirghiz in Central Asia a few Turkmen one-humped stallions were kept for the opposite purpose.[70] No one, it should be pointed out, would regularly herd both species together since continued free interbreeding of hybrids produces degenerate, useless animals. Why, then, to repeat an earlier question, did the one-humped camel become dominant in Iran?

Two separate factors appear to be involved: differing usage patterns and the rise of the Arabs as a political and economic force. The differences between the usage patterns of Iranian two-humped camel breeders and Arab one-humped camel breeders have already been discussed. For the former the camel was an auxiliary work animal kept in relatively small numbers; for the latter the camel was a major subsistence animal and a vital economic resource to be herded in as large numbers as possible. In terms of the caravan trade this meant that a few male two-humped camels could be introduced among the herds of the Arabs to produce a great many hybrid camels, but the reverse situation could not arise as long as two-humped camels were kept only in small numbers. And in Iran there was little impetus to herd them in much greater numbers since the hybrids could be produced more easily in the Tigris-Euphrates valley where a nomadic society devoted to camel breeding already existed. Only in Central Asia proper, among such peoples as the Kirghiz, did truly extensive two-humped camel breeding develop to service that portion of the caravan route that was climatically too harsh even for the hardy hybrids. Among people such as these who evolved a society based primarily upon camel breeding, camel products, especially milk, became important subsistence items as they were among the Arabs; but in Iran the two-humped camel was not extensively used other than for labor, and when it was supplanted for this purpose, the rationale for herding it at all was severely diminished.

The other factor is the rise of the Arabs which has already been analyzed at some length, although with an emphasis on the western side of the Syrian desert. On the Persian side of the desert evidence is less abundant, but there is every reason to believe that the same stages of development were experienced at roughly the same time. Cooperation between settled society and Arab nomads must be assumed from the evidence of Diodorus that hybrid camels were being bred in the area. Traces of this cooperation can be seen as well in a few Arabic terms relating to camels that are borrowed from Persian. One such term is the word *duhānij*, a synonym of *fālij* meaning two-humped camel.[71] This word appears to come from a Middle Persian word *dohānak* meaning something like "possessing two" (cf. Greek *dituloi* = "double knobbed"; modern Persian *dokūhānī* = "double mounded"; Sanskrit *dvikakud* = "double humped"). An even more suggestive word is *dahdaha* meaning "a large herd of camels numbering over one hundred" which is an early borrowing from Persian *dah dah* meaning "ten ten"; the interest of the Persians in the large camel herds of the Arabs is here plainly indicated.[72]

To repeat the point that was made earlier with regard to the camel supplanting the wheel, the camels of the Arabs could not have been integrated into the commercial pattern of the Persian empire if the Arabs themselves had not enjoyed some degree of status and respect in the eyes of the Persians; and this status and respect was a product of the change in the balance of power along the trade routes of the Arabian and Syrian deserts. The fact that the Persians accepted and respected the Arabs is well borne out by the historical record. The Parthian dynasty itself is not known to have had too close relations with the tribes on their western frontier, but the Sasanian dynasty which defeated and replaced the Parthians early in the third century A.D. definitely had such relations. An Arab kingdom centered on the city of Ḥīra west of the Euphrates plays a very important part in the political history of the Sasanians, and the kingdom's ruling family was sometimes closely associated with the Sasanian family.[73] Moreover, depictions of two-humped camels from Iraq and western Iran virtually cease under the Sasanians. Instead, the Sasanian emperor is shown riding on a one-humped camel with a North Arabian saddle, and similarly equipped camels are shown carrying game from a royal hunt.[74] Most important of all, however, are the numerous seal impressions from the Sasanian period showing one-humped camels.[75] There are no similar impressions of two-humped animals. If, as is likely, these sealings are connected with trade, the dominance of the one-humped hybrid in the caravans would seem to be confirmed.

Possibly these two factors need not have resulted in the disappearance of the two-humped camel on the Iranian plateau. Even though it became obsolete as a pack animal, it still had a use as a breeding animal. Arab camel breeders did not actually occupy Iranian camel-breeding territory to a significant extent

82 Sasanian silver plate showing emperor Bahram Gur hunting from back of one-humped camel. Note North Arabian saddle.

83 One-humped camels carrying game from royal hunt on Sasanian relief at Taq-i Bustan. Note North Arabian saddles.

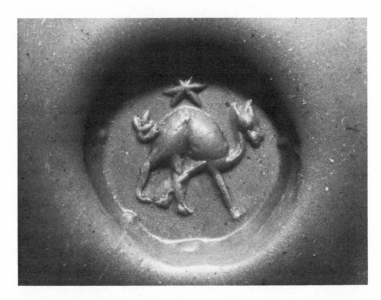

84 Impression of Sasanian seal with camel design.

even after the Islamic conquests. What sealed the fate of the
two-humped camel was actually a by-product of the experimentation with hybridization. At some point in time, apparently well into the Islamic period, a breed of one-humped
camel was developed that was perfectly adapted to the Iranian
plateau. This new long-haired, cold-resistant breed is presently
found in northern Iran, Turkmenistan, and northern Afghanistan and is definitely not a hybrid. At an earlier period when
two-humped camels were still readily available for breeding, a
new breed might not have been very successful since it would
not have provided the great strength of the hybrid. Once two-
humped stallions had to be imported from as far away as
eastern Afghanistan, however, as is testified to by the Arab
geographers, the value of having a purebred line of cold-
adapted one-humped camels increased; and once the new breed
had become established and the Central Asian caravan trade
declined as it did after the fifteenth century, there was no need
whatsoever for two-humped camels.

As for the wheel, the one-humped camel must have driven it out of use in the Tigris-Euphrates valley by the same process that was effective on the Roman side of the Syrian desert, but of the Iranian plateau there is little that can be said. The two-humped camel had originally been used for drawing wagons, but there is no evidence that this practice survived in Iran into the Parthian period. In any event, the camel as a draught animal will be dealt with in detail in the next chapter. It is worth observing, however, that the only parts of Iran that have retained the use of the wheel continuously from ancient times to the present day are the Caspian seacoast where the climate does not permit camels to live and western Azerbaijan in the far northwest where Armenian and Byzantine rule held sway until the time of the Muslim conquests. This alone makes it tempting to conclude that the one-humped camel replaced the wheel on the Iranian plateau just as it did further west, but more information is needed to confirm this conclusion.

7 The Camel as a Draft Animal

Discussion of the camel as a draft animal has already been deferred several times because it involves complex problems that must be dealt with at length. Yet the subject should not be considered separable from those treated in the preceding chapters because the entire course of events already described might have been entirely different if the camel had been used in the ancient Middle East to haul wagons and not just as a pack animal. Naturally, if the camel were absolutely hopeless as a draft animal, no explanation of its not being used for draft would be called for; but there is abundant evidence that the camel is as suitable for this purpose as an ox, its chief rival—if, that is, it is suitably harnessed. Hence the failure of the wheeled economy of the ancient Middle East to adapt the camel for draft is both significant and deserving of explanation.

At the present day the use of one-humped camels to pull carts and wagons is quite restricted. They are used extensively in the Indus valley and northern India, and also in the farming areas of the Cap Bon peninsula in northeastern Tunisia, around Mazagan (El-Jadida) on the Atlantic coast of Morocco, and in Aden at the southwestern tip of the Arabian peninsula. Elsewhere their use is only occasional and evidently of recent origin. Australia, where teams of camels were used in the desert to pull heavy wagons in the early part of the twentieth century, presents a special case.[1] The use there of camels for hauling arose from its being an imported animal that the European inhabitants knew little about. The "Afghan" (really Baluchi for the most part) drivers who were imported with the camels stuck to pack work, but the European teamsters experimented successfully with harnessing the animals for draft and created thereby an alternative to the horse and bullock wagon, all destined to be replaced soon by the coming of the automobile.

As for the two-humped camel, although major inroads have doubtless been made by motorized transport in the USSR and the People's Republic of China, it has traditionally been used on at least a small scale to pull carts or wagons throughout its geographical range from the Crimea to Peking. As has already been mentioned, this type of utilization goes back to the earliest known period of two-humped camel domestication in the third millenium B.C. Yet a major question is raised by this very fact. Were camels harnessed in the third millenium B.C. in the same manner as they are harnessed today, or has the technique of harnessing changed? What makes this a question of major importance is the likelihood that what barred the one-humped camel from entering the transport economy of the ancient world as a draft animal was the state of harnessing technology. Thus it is important to know what kind of harness was used for two-humped camels in ancient times, how efficient that harness was, and whether it was ever adapted for one-humped camels.

Broadly speaking there have been two main lines of technological development in the field of harnessing.[2] The yoke harness is unquestionably the earlier of the two. With the yoke harness the point of traction is designed to be above the animal, and this is very effective for bovine animals where the yoke can pull against the arch of vertebrae (seventh cervical, first to fifth thoracic) joining the neck to the body or, more rarely, be tied to the horns. For an equine animal the yoke harness is less effective because of the absence of a suitable point to pull against on the animal's neck or back.[3] The camel like the ox has a usable skeletal process in the long vertebrae joining the neck to the body (not, of course, in the hump which is without skeletal support).

To adapt the yoke harness to equine animals, the throat-and-girth harness was invented. Although the throat-and-girth harness is extremely ancient and continued in general use until about the third century B.C. in China[4] and until the early Middle Ages in the West—indeed, can still be found today in remote parts of the Middle East[5]—it is a poor adaptation.

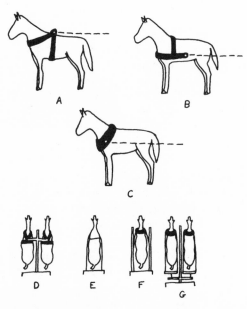

85 Basic types of equine harnessing: (A) ancient throat-and-girth harness, (B) modern breast-strap harness, (C) modern collar harness, (D) top view of throat-and-girth harness, (E) top view of breast-strap harness, (F) top view of collar harness, (G) top view of collar harness showing use of whippletree to attach two animals to a wagon.

To make up for the absence of a suitable point to pull against on top of the horse's body, a strap is put around the animal's throat and attached to the end of the yoke. A second strap, which appears to have little function in pulling, goes from the end of the yoke under the horse's breast. The primary point of traction thus becomes the horse's chest or throat, but the pulling force is still transmitted to the vehicle (horses were not used for plowing with this harness) through the yoke on its back. As a result, the yoke exerts constant upward pressure on the throat strap which causes it to press against the animal's trachea and strangle it if full force is applied. Therefore, while it was quite an effective harness for light weights, such as chariots, the throat-and-girth harness could not tap the full potential of the horse for hauling heavy loads or for plowing.

86 Ancient throat-and-girth harness in use in eastern Arabia.

A different problem arises in adapting the camel to a yoke harness. It is easy to see what the yoke pulls against, namely, the elongated vertebrae joining the neck to the body; but what holds it in place? In bovine animals the line of neck and back, except for the projecting vertebrae already mentioned, is fairly level, and the yoke stays in place by its own weight with some sort of downward projection or strap around the neck to keep it centered. On a camel there is nothing to prevent the yoke from sliding down the steep slope of the neck and ending up in the hollow at the bottom. Yet this is not necessarily an insuperable problem. A strap going back behind the hump, or behind the first hump in two-humped camels, might serve to secure the yoke in place. Straps of this sort are used for the withers-strap harness which will be described shortly. Unfortunately, I have been unable to find a satisfactory picture or description of the yoke harness used for two-humped camels so I cannot confirm the use of this solution with a yoke; but the one-humped camel would, in any case, appear to present a much greater problem than a two-humped camel.[6]

The second main line of harness development, which includes all modern harnesses for nonbovine animals, puts the point of traction low along the animal's sides. In order to do this equal pull must be exerted on both sides, and this in turn calls for a different vehicle design. Instead of having a central pole projecting from the front of the vehicle with the yoke as a cross piece, there must be two shafts going along the animal's sides. Complex harnesses provide for animals to be harnessed side by side with a wagon tongue between them and with the load still being distributed equally along each animal's sides by means of trace chains or ropes attached to a bar perpendicular to the wagon tongue behind each animal. This bar is known as a whippletree. In its most basic form, however, the development of efficient harnesses for nonbovine animals had to wait for the discovery that a vehicle with two shafts instead of a central pole afforded new lines of approach.

It should be noted that the yoke harness is as effective with a two-shafted vehicle as it is with a central pole.[7] There being but a single point of traction on the yoke, it makes no difference whether it is linked to the vehicle on both sides or only on one side. A single pole vehicle, naturally, requires an

animal on each side of the pole while the shafted vehicle could
be drawn by a single animal, but with bovine animals neither
system is more efficient than the other. Double shaft vehicles
represent an important step forward only in the harnessing of
nonbovine animals.

In terms of the history of wheeled vehicles, the single pole
vehicle and the two-shafted vehicle are both considered early
inventions;[8] and it would appear that in China harnesses
with points of traction on either side of the animal evolved
from a shafted cart using a single animal with a yoke.[9] The
West, however, seems to have thought only in terms of single
pole vehicles until Roman imperial times. Thus, even though
the existence of two-shafted vehicles does not by itself imply a
modern harness, the absence of such vehicles in the West
would seem to have greatly delayed the invention of such a
harness.

The modern harness for nonbovine animals made possible
by the two-shafted vehicle took two forms. The earlier form
both in China and the West was the breast-strap harness.[10]
Essentially, this is simply the throat-strap of the throat-and-
girth harness, but with attachment made to shafts (or traces)
along the animal's sides instead of to the yoke on its back. An
additional strap over the back holds the shafts up and may,
with a cart, bear a great deal of weight if the load is not care-
fully balanced over the two wheels. The effect of this harness is
to allow a horse to pull with its chest on a horizontal plane.
There is no pull from a yoke connection on the back and hence
no tendency for the breast-strap to ride up onto the horse's
throat and interfere with its breathing.

The second form of modern harness is the horse collar. The
horse collar consists of a cushioned rigid frame (cushion and
frame being either separable or combined) encircling the
horse's neck. The shafts (or traces) are attached to the frame
at shoulder level, and the animal pulls with its shoulders. The
horse collar is somewhat superior to the breast-strap harness
for very heavy loads, but it is more complicated and apparently
a later invention.

Like the yoke, the breast-strap harness and horse collar
require special adaptation for use on camels. Since the camel's
breast does not have any space for a strap because of the

182   low curve of the neck, the breast-strap must be placed over
the shoulders against the flat vertebrae mentioned before. It is
more appropriate in this case to call it a withers-strap. A strap
passing either between or around the humps or, supported
by a saddle, over a single hump is important for holding up the
shafts and keeping this withers-strap in place, but this
additional strap is less important for a plow harness than for a
cart harness since trace ropes are used instead of rigid shafts
and there is consequently less weight tending to pull the
withers-strap down onto the camel's neck. As for the horse
collar, it is awkward to use it on a camel for the same reason it
is awkward to use a yoke; it slips off the shoulders and down
the neck. In Australia this problem was solved by the use of
additional straps, called "spiders," anchored around the hump

87   Two-humped camel cart in Central Asia.

which held the trace chains up in back and held the collar in place in front.[11] Outside of Australia the horse collar has rarely been used on camels, and the most common camel harness in modern times has been the withers-strap harness.

To make this brief outline of the history of harnessing techniques meaningful in terms of the history of camel use we must go back to the earliest known two-humped camel culture, that which existed in Turkmenistan and eastern Iran in the third millenium B.C. The model wagons discovered by Soviet archaeologists at sites belonging to this culture sprout but a single camel's head, and from this it might possibly be concluded that a single animal harness was used.[12] It has already been pointed out, however, on the basis of the counting of camels in pairs or yokes in the Rig Veda and on the basis of

88 Camel wagon in northern India. Note use of North Arabian saddle.

184   Strabo's ambiguous reference to Indian camels being driven under the yoke, that a two-animal harness employing a yoke is more likely to have been in use at that time. Conceivably, the use of yoked camels in the Crimea in the nineteenth century was the last survival of this ancient practice. The type of vehicle they drew was a four-wheeled wagon called a *madgiar*, which name implies some connection with the Magyars of Hungary who moved west permanently from the Crimean area in the ninth century A.D.[13] An engraving made to illustrate the account of Friar Rubruquis's travels in Central Asia in the thirteenth century also shows camels (one-humped) harnessed in pairs to carts, but the details of this engraving do not inspire confidence in its accuracy.[14]

Regardless of how long the yoke harness survived in some particular area, however, it eventually disappeared. Today in Central Asia single two-humped camels are harnessed with a withers-strap for traction and another strap passing between the humps to support the weight of the shafts. In Pakistan and northern India, one-humped camels are now harnessed either by the same method, but with the supporting strap going over the hump borne by a North Arabian pack saddle, or simply by a strap bearing on a North Arabian saddle. It is apparent, then, that at some point in time an important change in harnessing technique took place in these areas that were originally part of the domain of the two-humped camel. It is important to determine insofar as possible when and how this change came about because it may hold implications for the entire evolution of the relationship between the camel and the wheel.

If the development of the efficient withers-strap harness came before the disappearance of the wheel and of the two-humped camel in Iran, why didn't the new harnessing concept revolutionize horse harnessing as well and prevent the wheel's disappearance? On the other hand, if the development came after the incursion of the one-humped camel, why did the idea of harnessing one-humped camels for draft catch on only in the Indus valley and northern India and not spread to other one-humped camel areas?[15] The timing of the development obviously is crucial, but whenever it took place, it raises questions. Pictorially the first appearance of a single two-

89 Rock drawing of camel cart from Minusinsk.

humped camel pulling a cart between shafts is a rock drawing
found near Minusinsk, a town in Siberia west of Lake Baikal
and not far north of the border between Mongolia and the
USSR.[16] The cart is enclosed, has a window in the side, and
rides upon spoked wheels; the harness itself is not depicted.
This drawing is described as being apparently contemporary
with the Karasuk culture which flourished luxuriantly in the
Minusinsk basin around the ninth to tenth century B.C.[17] If this
dating, which, as with that of most rock pictures, is probably
not susceptible of confirmation, is correct, this would be an extremely early example of shaft harnessing. Breast-strap and
shaft harnessing did not become common in China until the
fourth to second century B.C.[18] But even if it dates from a somewhat later period, it still shows that camels were used in single
harness at a very early date.

Between this first representation and the next that I have
been able to find reference to there is an enormous gap. The
next is from a Chinese cave painting about 600 A.D. and shows
a camel harnessed to a covered cart by what looks to be an
arch over its neck.[19] Currently accepted theory, it should be
pointed out, dates the introduction of breast-strap harnessing
to Europe either to the eighth century A.D. on pictorial grounds
or the fifth or sixth century A.D. on philological grounds and
the introduction of the horse collar to the ninth or tenth century
A.D.[20] Given the evidence for early use of camels with carts
and assuming for the moment the validity of the theory linking
the introduction of modern harnessing to Europe with a
migration of harnessing techniques westward across Central
Asia, the crucial question regarding the Indian practice of
harnessing one-humped camels to carts can be framed in the
following manner: Did modern harnessing of either the breast-
strap or horse collar variety reach northwestern India around

the fifth through eighth centuries by the same process of dissemination that brought those techniques to Europe, in which case the two-humped camel would still have been the species in common use; or did it arrive at a later date subsequent to the supplanting of the two-humped camel by the one-humped camel in the Indus valley?

Pictorial evidence dating the advent of modern harnessing of any type in India is surprisingly hard to find. Representations of wheeled vehicles usually show oxcarts, except for certain religious motifs which are extremely stylized and conservative and therefore unreliable as indications of contemporary usage. Nevertheless, one realistic miniature painting of the fifteenth century shows a carriage drawn by two horses which are harnessed by what can only be an inefficient throat-and-girth harness.[21] Thus, modern harnessing appears not to have arrived by 1400. But had the one-humped camel replaced the two-humped species by that time? It was concluded in the last chapter that hybrids became dominant in the

90 Camel cart in Chinese cave painting.

91 Earliest recognized representation of modern harness technique
in Europe, circa 800.

Central Asian trade before the rise of Islam and that one-humped camels slowly replaced the increasingly obsolete two-humped camel from that time onwards, but no conclusions were reached as to when the two-humped camel disappeared in specific areas not along the Silk Route. Such conclusions may, in fact, be unreachable for many areas because of lack of data; but some data is available for India.

In India as in Iran the word *ushtra* originally meant two-humped camel and came to mean one-humped camel. In western Iran the notice of Diodorus that the two-humped camels were called *dituloi* and the adoption into Arabic of the Persian word *duhānij* prove that an explicit terminological distinction between the two species existed in the pre-Islamic period and that the two-humped species, certainly the less numerous, was the one for which new terms were devised. In India the same type of distinction arose, but it first appears in the Sanskrit dictionary of Hemacandra, a Jain scholar from Gujarat who lived from 1088 to 1172. He singles out among camels the *dvikakud durgalanghanah* meaning "two-humped [camel] capable of crossing difficult passes."[22] In this connection it is also relevant that the Baluchi people, who inhabit the desert of western Pakistan and southeastern Iran, and who are probably the most important group of one-humped camel breeders east of Arabia, only moved into their present territory between roughly 1000 and 1200.[23] If the one-humped camel arrived in the Indus region only with the Baluchis, it would explain not only the late appearance of a clear distinction between one-humped and two-humped camels in Sanskrit but also the account of a fourteenth century Arab writer who says that in India "there are a few camels which only the Kings and his followers such as Khans, Amirs, Wazirs and other great people of the Government possess."[24] In addition, the Indian two-man riding saddle known as the *pakra*, which is descended structurally from the North Arabian saddle, could be taken as an indicator of scarcity at the time when one-humped camels were first being introduced as riding animals.[25]

Going back once again to the question of the use of one-humped camels in India for draft purposes, it seems more than likely that the one-humped camel became known in India in significant quantity only after the year 1000 but that modern

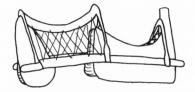

92 Indian *pakra* saddle, a two-man saddle derived from the North Arabian saddle. For example of this type of saddle in use see figure 121.

harnessing still was not known in 1400. Thus by the time modern harnessing became known, whenever it was, the two-humped camel had disappeared. Why, then, did the idea of harnessing one-humped camels to carts ever catch on if modern harnessing was not available? And why only in India? The only answer that can be suggested to this question is that the use of the two-humped camel for draft influenced the uses to which the one-humped camel was put when it finally became available. Since a yoke would have been particularly difficult to manage on a one-humped animal because holding the apparatus in place by a strap around one small forward hump is easier than doing so by a strap around a large hump centered on the back, the manner in which the new one-humped beast was harnessed was probably a simple rope or strap thrown over a North Arabian pack saddle. The North Arabian saddle, it will be remembered, is an integral part of present day Indian harnessing.

A report on the organization of the court of the Moghul emperor Akbar in or around the year 1590 affirms both that one-humped camels predominated in the emperor's camel stables and that camels were used for pulling vehicles.[26] Although it is possible that by that date modern harnessing had been introduced, it does not seem likely nor is the use of camels for draft treated as a recent innovation. Instead it would appear that just as the practice of using a nose peg was transferred in India from two-humped camels to one-humped camels, so was the practice of using camels to pull wagons. Only the technique of harnessing was changed from the inconvenient yoke to the North Arabian pack saddle, which could not have been terribly efficient either. Withers-strap harnessing was a later additional improvement. As for why the practice never spread, the answer must be that only people who had originally known the two-humped camel as a draft animal could conceive of its one-humped cousin being used for such, and these people were concentrated in India by the year 1000. In Iran, where two-humped camels had once been known as draft animals, the one-humped camel had triumphed completely through its dominance of the caravan trade for which vehicles were not suited.[27] Beyond the one-humped camel's range in Central Asia the two-humped camel continued to be used for draft.

Two conclusions that may usefully be drawn from this discussion of draft camels in Central Asia and India are, first, that the two-humped camel can be harnessed to a wagon by a yoke but not as efficiently as it can be by the withers-strap harness that supplanted the yoke and, second, that there is no evidence that the one-humped camel was ever harnessed by a yoke although it may conceivably, but not very probably, have happened in the Indus valley before the introduction of modern harnessing there. Looking toward the Middle East and the competition between camel and cart during the first five centuries of the Christian era, the weight of these conclusions is that with only yoke harnesses and single pole vehicles available it was probably impossible to harness one-humped camels to wagons with great enough efficiency, given such added costs as that of the wagon itself, for them to compete with their own abilities as pack animals.

As for light harnessing, there are several literary references to and even one depiction of chariot races in which the chariots were drawn by teams of camels, and camels were occasionally used to pull ceremonial vehicles for the same reason, that they lent the proceedings an air of novelty and exoticism.[28] Even in the Muslim period in the ninth century there is a report of someone who "made the pilgrimage from Basra on a cart drawn by camels; and the people wondered at that."[29] The only other reference to teams of camels drawing vehicles in the Middle East or North Africa that I have been able to find is mention in Isaiah 21:7 of a camel chariot, but modern translations of the Bible translate the "chariot" of the King James version as a "pair of riders."[30] In short, attempts were

93 Roman clay plaque from North Africa showing camel chariot race.

made to harness camels to vehicles, but the attempts were not of a serious nature, except in Tunisia and Tripolitania as will be discussed below. The reason for this lack of success must be deemed to be inadequate harnessing techniques based on the principle of the yoke.

Only three restricted areas where camels are used for draft remain to be accounted for: one in Tunisia, one in Morocco, and a final one in southwestern Arabia. Taking the last and least important case first, photographic evidence of camels being used to pull carts in Aden is not too difficult to find, and a description written in 1877 of the British settlement there mentions that "the municipal rubbish carts are drawn by camels."[31] The harnessing shown strongly resembles that in India. A single camel between shafts both pulls and bears the weight of the load by means of a strap passing over the front arches of a South Arabian saddle. An introduction of the practice from British India is thus suggested. However, primitive oxcarts do appear to be in use in at least some parts of Yemen.[32] No connection can be drawn between their ponderous yoke harness and the harness used for camels, but it is just conceivable that knowledge of the use of wheeled vehicles of any sort fostered a willingness to try camel carts once the idea was introduced.

Draft camels in Morocco present an even more obscure issue than those in Aden, but since the practice of using them there may be related to the similar practice in Tunisia, it is best to treat the two cases together. In Tunisia camels are used both for plowing and to pull two-wheeled carts. The former practice occurs both among bedouin in desert areas and in the relatively lush farming area along the eastern coast; the latter practice is limited approximately to Cap Bon, the northern part of the coastal farm area, and is unknown in the desert areas, although horse carts are used in the Saharan date-growing oases of Gafsa, Tozeur, and Nefta.[33] Needless to say, the camels are bred solely in the desert areas.

The type of harness used for both purposes is a withers-strap harness. As in India and Central Asia, the withers-strap goes over the camel's shoulders and bears upon the long vertebrae joining the neck to the back. Unlike the Indian harness, however, the weight of the cart shafts is carried by

94 Camel carts in Aden. Note use of South Arabian saddle.

95 Primitive oxcarts in use in Yemen.

two belts attached to the same ring on each shaft (see fig. 66). One belt crosses the animal's back just before the hump and the other just behind it. No saddle is used, although the double belt over the back is reminiscent of and probably related to the practice of suspending baskets on either side of the animal mentioned in chapter five. In India, as already described, a single belt joins the shafts and rests on the animal's back on a North Arabian saddle. When the camel is used for plowing, the traces of the plow being relatively light, a rope over the camel's rump is sufficient to hold them up and help keep the withers-strap in place.[34]

In Morocco the situation is quite different as far as plowing is concerned. The camel is used extensively for plowing but almost always in two animal teams, either two camels or more usually a camel and another animal. The yoke used for these teams is situated beneath the animals behind the front legs, and the tractive force is exerted through a belt going over the neck or attached sometimes to a wooden beam on top of the neck.[35] This subventral yoke allows animals of unequal size to be attached to the same plow, but a regular yoke can rather awkwardly be used with unlike animals also.[36] As for the cart harness, I have been unable to find out more than that the *araba sicilienne*, as the camel cart is called, is drawn by a single camel harnessed by means of a pack saddle.[37]

Clearly, separate but perhaps not unrelated harnessing traditions are involved in these two different parts of North Africa. The plow harnesses are totally different, and from the reference to a pack saddle with the Moroccan cart harness it would seem that the cart harness is more like that in Aden than that in Tunisia where no saddle at all is used. Unfortunately, there is no data available pertaining to the history of harnessing in Morocco except for an analysis of vocabulary which points to a probable Roman origin.[38] For Tunisia, on the other hand, there is pictorial evidence of great interest and importance, evidence, in fact, which suggests that the existing theory regarding the introduction of modern harnessing to Europe is incomplete if not substantially wrong.

Several stone reliefs dating from Roman times have been discovered in Tripolitania just east of the Tunisian border which depict plowing being done by a single camel.[39] The

96 Tunisian plow harness. Note rope over rump holding up traces and whippletree set perpendicular to beam of plow.

196 camel is clearly harnessed by a withers-strap across its
shoulders in precisely the same way that camels are harnessed
in Tunisia today. Yoke harnessed oxen, as would be expected,
are shown plowing in the same fields. Since these reliefs have
been dated between the late second or early third century A.D.
and the middle of the fourth century, they constitute the
earliest representations in the West of the efficient harnessing
of single animals.[40] If the identity of design between this
Roman camel harness and the modern Tunisian camel harness
is not in itself sufficient proof that camels have been used
continuously in Tunisia for plowing since Roman times, there
is corroborative evidence of continuity in the *History of the
Berbers* of Ibn Khaldun (d. 1382) where he notes that Arab
tribesmen in Tripolitania use the camel for plowing.[41]

Thus it appears that three inventions of the utmost importance in the history of harnessing can be traced to the
farmers of Roman Tripolitania. Tilling their fields in the hinterland of Lepcis Magna, the northern terminal of the cross
Saharan trade route, these farmers were the first plow-using
people in North Africa to come into contact with camels as
they made their appearance by slow infiltration from the

97 Roman relief from Libya showing single camel and team of oxen
plowing in same field. Note withers-strap and whippletree on
camel harness.

south.[42] The animal was unfamiliar, but it quickly became common enough to be easily purchased, and its economy of upkeep in comparison with an ox was obvious. Moreover, there was as yet no established pattern of camel utilization in the area since camel nomadism was only beginning in the north, and the camel had not yet achieved its predominant position in the camel-using areas to the east. Thus, innocent of preconceptions about the camel and its proper use, the farmers invented a way of harnessing it to a plow. In so doing they originated single animal harnessing, discovered in the withers-strap the principle of the breast-strap, and invented the whippletree, the wooden bar set perpendicular to the beam of the plow to keep the traces separate behind the animal.

The question to be asked is whatever became of these wonderful inventions? It has been generally accepted hitherto that single animal harnessing and the breast-strap originated in the Far East and reached Europe during the Merovingian period by way of movements of nomads across Central Asia.[43] The whippletree is of somewhat more debatable origin, but the French word for it, *palonnier*, has been traced to a Germanic root and the inference drawn that it, too, came from somewhere in the east.[44] Clearly, the existing theory cannot account for the Tunisian evidence. The most generous reading of history would be hard put to find a significant Central Asian influence in Roman North Africa in the third century A.D.

It might be possible to argue that Tunisian camel harnessing was never more than a local phenomenon were it not for a few additional pieces of information. Most important, because it is pictorial, is a Roman lamp in the museum at Sousse, once the Roman city of Hadrumetum on the eastern coast of Tunisia.[45] This lamp, dated between the first and third centuries A.D., bears the molded impression of a light, two-wheeled cart being drawn by a single horse harnessed between two shafts which are attached to what appears to be a horse collar. In functional terms, despite the lack of detail in the picture, it appears that every feature of a modern harness is present. Moreover, the horse's neck is shown extended, which is its appropriate position for efficient pulling. It is usually shown in Roman depictions abruptly raised to tighten the neck muscles against the pull of the throat-strap.

98 Roman lamp from museum in Sousse, Tunisia, with image of horse cart utilizing modern harnessing.

This is not the only known Roman portrayal of a modern or almost modern harness. Several single animal harnesses have been discovered previously in reliefs and mosaics.[46] In the interest of clinging to the theory of the Central Asian origin of modern harnessing, however, these depictions have either been labeled as anomalies or found wanting in some functional aspect.[47] Several of them do indeed show shafts or traces attached to rather insubstantial collars poorly situated on the horse's neck, but so do accepted representations of modern harnessing from medieval sources.[48] Accurate drawings of new devices by artists whose primary aim was not to duplicate reality are probably too much to expect. The lamp from Sousse can now confirm that an effective modern harness was in use in Roman imperial times and thereby rehabilitate the other depictions that have hitherto been given too little attention.

99 Apparent modern harness on Roman relief from Trier.

Is it possible that modern harnessing technique with all that it implies for improved agricultural efficiency actually reached Europe from the south as a final gift of Roman ingenuity instead of from the east several centuries later? Only a thorough study of the agricultural and transportation economy of southern Europe can decide the matter. However, data of several different types can be mustered in support of the following hypothesis: In Tripolitania and southern Tunisia the gradually increasing availability of camels from the first century B.C. onward challenged Roman colonists to adapt the animal for agricultural purposes. A new concept in harnessing emerged as a result. Experimentation resulted in animals other than camels being harnessed for plowing in the new manner, in camels being harnessed to carts with a withers-strap, and finally to horses being harnessed to carts with a breast-strap. Parallel developments involving the idea of the horse collar may have been underway in Europe as well as North Africa, but the fall of the empire led to an economic retrenchment from which Tunisia recovered sooner than most areas thanks to the Islamic conquests. Since the sharing of culture and interests between Tunisia, Sicily, and southern Italy had remained strong throughout the period of Roman decline and foreign invasion, and was reasserted in the ninth century with the Muslim conquest of Sicily, a route existed for the introduction or reintroduction of modern harnessing ideas from Tunisia into southern Europe; and Muslim Spain afforded an additional route, although the ideas are ultimately Tunisian. Consequently, the origin of modern harnessing in southern Europe can be traced to Tunisia even if a separate, eastern influence can be identified in northern Europe.

The first two points of this hypothesis have already been argued, but the single lamp from Sousse cannot be considered proof that a transfer in technique was made from camels plowing to horses drawing carts. Additional links in the chain of development are needed and are supplied by two relief

100 Roman relief from Libya showing single camel plowing with another animal also harnessed singly.

carvings and an inscription. One relief carving is one of those depicting a camel pulling a plow, but it also shows part of another single animal, possibly a horse, pulling a plow just before the camel. The other shows an indisputable horse harnessed to a plow by what is probably a breast-strap.[49] Thus the single animal technique first used for camels clearly was transferred to other animals. The inscription is a fragmentary list of tolls dating from the first half of the fourth century which sets a rate for a *camelus carricatus,* a camel pulling a cart.[50] Since the word *camelus* is singular, a single animal withers-strap harness of the type still used in Tunisia may be presumed. Thus the new technique was evidently tried on vehicles as well as plows. The next step to the lamp from Sousse with its horse-drawn cart is both logical and elementary.

For the remainder of the hypothesis regarding the dissemination of the new technique to be valid an anomaly must have existed in medieval Tunisia whereby the general disappearance of the wheel in the Middle East and North Africa did not occur. The reason for such an anomaly would obviously be that the economic efficiency of a pack camel was not

101 Roman relief from Libya showing single horse pulling plow with what appears to be a breast-strap harness.

sufficiently greater than that of a cart equipped with a modern harness to drive it off the road in direct competition; but if such an anomaly existed, there should be evidence of it in historical sources. In fact, such evidence does exist in the form of two late ninth century historical notices indicating that carts of some kind were still being used in significant numbers at that time. The first reference, dated 881–882, speaks of the Aghlabid emir of Ifriqiya (Tunisia) using carts (ᶜajal in Arabic) to carry the bodies of massacre victims to a trench for disposal.[51] This took place in Zab, a district in Algeria not far west of the border of southern Tunisia. If these carts were merely a part of the possessions of the slaughtered inhabitants of this not yet fully pacified region, their mention might be discounted as a remnant of a past era; but the other reference confirms that carts were still in use in the Arab capital of Ifriqiya itself, in Qairawan. In 894 the same ruler, Ibrahim II, suppressed a revolt in Tunis and sent carts there from Qairawan to bring back the spoils.[52] Since 1,200 captives are mentioned, it is certain that many carts were involved and that the vehicle was not uncommon at that time even in the Arab capital, which was not a pre-Islamic city but originally a military camp established by the invading Arabs in 670 just west of Sousse. Furthermore, there is a not unequivocal indication in a Greek text emanating from Sicily that wheeled vehicles were also in use on that island during the period of Muslim rule.[53] The Muslim conquest of the island was completed by the same Ibrahim II.

Considering, therefore, that wheeled transportation did not die out in Tunisia as it did elsewhere,[54] what remains to be established if the proposed hypothetical development is to be considered viable is the continuity of harnessing technique between Tunisia and southern Europe and its antiquity. In strictly material terms, it is observable that breast-strap harnessing is much more common in southern Europe than it is in northern Europe and that cart harnesses are identical in Tunisia, Malta, and Sicily.[55] This gives no indication, however, of how long this similarity of technique has been in existence. For an indication of age one must turn to a comparison of technical terminology.

102 Harness of Tunisian *kirrīta*.

103 Sicilian cart with same type harness as figure 102.

The chart of harnessing terminology in Arabic and the Romance languages shows clearly the close relationship between terms in Tunisian Arabic, Italian, Spanish, and Portuguese and the dissimilarity of those in French and Provençal, but several specific points should be made to illuminate the situation further. Looking at the Arabic terminology associated with Tunisian carts, the most startling discovery is that *ᶜaraba* is the word commonly used for cart in the coastal farming areas of Tunisia while the word used in the Saharan date-growing oases of the south is *kirrīta*. The former word is the modern Arabic term for cart and came into use only after the coming of the Turks to the Middle East in the eleventh century.[56] The latter word is obviously the same as *carretta*, the basic word for cart in all the Romance languages. Given the prevalance of *ᶜaraba* in the more cosmopolitan parts of the country and that of *carretta* in the remoter parts, the conclusion is hard to avoid that the former word replaced the latter, which would therefore date back at least to the thirteenth or fourteenth century. It is also attested, complete with Arabic plural and diminutive forms, in the Spanish-Arabic dictionary of Pedro of Alcala compiled in 1505.[57]

Particularly significant among the other terms cited are those for breast-strap, whippletree, and a connecting device that will be discussed presently. The word for breast-strap in Tunisian Arabic, Maltese, Italian, Spanish, and Portuguese is derived from the word for breast either in Arabic for the first two or in Latin. The English word is also derived from breast, for that matter, and the derivation seems perfectly natural. Yet French and Provençal have entirely different words apparently derived from an Italian word for a kind of catapult, a device that perhaps was drawn by a single animal using a breast-strap harness.[58] As for the antiquity of the terms derived from breast, Malta, where a highly Italianized Arabic is spoken, has not been under Arab rule since the year 1090. It is not surprising that the Maltese word is simply an Arabic translation of the Italian, but it is difficult to see how this word could have gained currency in Tunisia after the eleventh century.

Roughly the same situation applies to the words for whippletree. French and Provençal have words of apparent Germanic

origin while Italian, Spanish, Portuguese, and Tunisian Arabic **205**
all have words connoting balance or smoothness.[59] It seems
likely that both in this case and in that of the term for breast-
strap the Arab invaders of North Africa in the seventh century
translated existing Romance words into their semantic equivalent in Arabic. The whippletree, it is worth noting, is not
commonly used with plows, and the plow harness used in
Tunisia is unusual in this respect.[60] Hence, the device could in
no way be considered a recent importation from Europe even
if there was no Roman evidence in existence to prove its
antiquity in Tunisia.

The third term that suggests appreciable antiquity is that
applied to a strap that goes over the animal's back—a double
strap in the case of a camel—and connects the two shafts
whose weight is thus borne on the back, in the case of a horse
through the intermediary of a pack saddle. The Tunisian
Arabic word appears not to come from an Arabic root. It appears, rather, to be related to a confused group of terms in
Italian, Spanish, and Portuguese with meanings that involve
harnessing, yoking, connecting two things, and the shape of a
hook. Once again, French and Provençal are uninvolved. It
is hard to determine the exact etymological history of these
terms, but a picture of a *cangai* (provincial form of the word
cangalha) in use in Algarve province in southern Portugal
proves that the same basic device is intended even though the
Portuguese placement of it differs markedly from that in
Tunisia, Malta, and Sicily.[61] It is this substantial variation in
form combined with the great etymological uncertainty that
suggests that the term is a very old one in all of the countries
involved.

All of this evidence cannot be considered to prove conclusively the Roman and Tunisian origin of modern harnessing
in Europe, but it strongly suggests that such was the case.
Italy, Spain, and Portugal were in closest contact with Muslim
civilization and share with Tunisia a common technical
vocabulary of substantial antiquity. Southern France was more
remote from Muslim influence and belongs to a different
terminological sphere. Although the wellspring of invention
can be localized to southern Tunisia and Tripolitania, Muslim
Spain seems to have shared with Sicily the role of transmitter.

206

English	Classical Arabic	Tunisian Arabic	Andalusian Arabic ca. 1500	Spanish	Portuguese
cart	ᶜajala ᶜaraba	ᶜaraba kirrīta	aájéle carréta pl. carárit dim. coráyrata	carreta carro	carrêta carro
breast-strap	taṣdīr (girth for tying a saddle to a camel) ṣadr (breast) sadīl (pieces of cloth covering a woman's enclosed camel saddle)	ṣudra s°dāl (withers-strap)		petral pecho (breast)	peitoral peito (breast)
whipple-tree whiffle-tree single-tree swingle-tree swing-bar	sahala (to be smooth, level, easy)	sậhla		balancín	balancim
saddle	bardhaᶜa, bardaᶜa (donkey saddle) sarj (horse saddle) ḥarj (type of camel saddle)	barda harj	bardáa[a] çárg (horse saddle)	silla[b] albarda[a] basto[a]	sela[b]
device going over an animal's saddle to connect and hold up the shafts on either side		ghunj		enganche (coupling, connecting link) enganchar (to harness horses to a carriage)	cangalha canga (yoke of oxen) cangar (to put in yoke)

[a] Pack.
[b] Riding.

Italian	Maltese	Provençal	French
carretta	carrettun	carretto	charrette
carro		carri	char

Italian	Maltese	Provençal	French
pettorale	sidra	peitrino	poitrine
petto (breast)		(breast)	(breast)
briccola (catapult)		bricolo	bricole
bilancino		palounier	palonnier
		paloumeou	
		reinard	
sella[b]	sarġ	sello[b]	selle[b]
barda[a]		bast[a]	bât[b]
		bardo[a]	
gancio (hook)	ġanc (hook, hinge)	ganche (hook)	

208 In fact, camels were still in use pulling carts in Spain in the
nineteenth century, although no depiction of them has
survived.[62] A connection between Muslim Spain and Muslim
Sicily as transmitters may finally explain the Moroccan
enclave where the *araba sicilienne* camel cart is used.

Possibly it is extravagant to conclude that while the one-
humped camel drove the wheel out of existence in most areas
of contact, in one unique case it stimulated the invention of
modern harnessing and thereby triggered a fundamental change
in European agriculture and transportation. It is still hard to
explain why modern harnessing did not spread in North Africa
beyond the restricted parts of Tunisia. Perhaps it is simply
that the cosmopolitan population of Tunisia was so Romanized
and so northward looking that well into the Muslim period it
held to a culture that was fundamentally different from that in
other parts of the Maghreb. Yet whatever the truth of the
matter with regard to Tunisian draft camels, the most curious
aspect of the matter is the coincidence between the theory
that has just been propounded and one that has been adduced
to explain the invention of the horse collar in Central Asia.

It is not my intention nor is it within my powers to discuss
here the entire history of Central Asian harnessing. It is only
the involvement in that history of the two-humped camel that
is relevant. As has already been mentioned, camels have been
used to draw carts in Central Asia since the earliest domestication of the two-humped species. However, the point in question
now concerns the two-humped camel in its role as a pack
animal. André Haudricourt has shown by a convincing linguistic argument that the horse collar is of Central Asian origin

104 André Haudricourt's hypothesized evolution of modern harnessing.

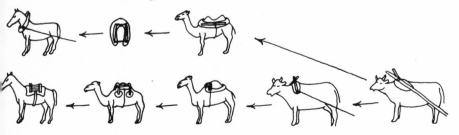

and reached eastern and northern Europe from the east.[63] His argument, in addition, links the invention of the horse collar in Central Asia to the type of pack saddle used there for two-humped camels. Observing that the relevant word relates solely to horse harnessing in a score of languages from English to Kirghiz but means both camel saddle and horse collar in Mongolian and Altai and only camel saddle in Manchu, Kazakh, and Tibetan, Haudricourt concludes that the original horse collar was a pack saddle turned vertically and put around a horse's neck.

This linguistic theory may possibly be confirmed or refuted by calling into evidence pictorial material regarding Central Asian saddle design. According to Haudricourt's theory, the camel saddle used in Central Asia from which the horse collar evolved consisted of a horseshoe shaped pad like that used for the South Arabian saddle and on top of it two long horizontal sticks, one on each side, attached to each other by thongs crossing the gap before and behind the humps. Nothing like the saddle-bows of the North and South Arabian saddles firmly binding together the framework is required since the animal's two humps necessitate a very long saddle and afford by their more precipitous slope comparatively abrupt protuberances for the saddle to rest against, both of which factors minimize the danger of a load slipping, which is the primary reason for the saddle-bow's existence. Haudricourt theorizes that set vertically and placed around a horse's neck, the horseshoe shaped pad became the cushion of the collar, and the two sticks the frame to which the shafts are attached.

Unfortunately, pictorial evidence for this type of pack saddle having been common in Central Asia during the period when modern harnessing developed does not abound. The many artistic funerary figurines of camels from the T'ang dynasty (618–907 A.D.) and the less numerous but similar figurines from the Northern Wei dynasty (386–534 A.D.) show, by and large, a quite different saddle.[64] A decorated covering, perhaps of felt, surrounds the animal's humps, but no pad can be discerned going around them either front or rear. As for the two sticks, they appear in actuality to be rather wide boards or bundles of reeds that curve in toward the camel's body at the midpoint and away from it at the ends of the humps.[65]

105 Northern Wei dynasty two-humped camel figurine from China. Note bound reed type saddle.

106 T'ang dynasty or Sui dynasty two-humped camel figurine from China. Note hemispherical load as in figures 75–77. *(facing page)*

107 T'ang dynasty two-humped camel figurine from China. Hemispherical load is transformed into fantastic face. *(facing page)*

108 Kirghiz camel equipped with bound reed saddle.

109 Mongol saddle using two horizontal poles.

The connection between these boards appears to go between the humps rather than around the ends where the boards diverge. Therefore it is difficult to see how this saddle could have been turned vertically and placed around a horse's neck.

The rigid poles called for by Haudricourt's theory do exist on camel saddles in use today in Central Asia, and can be found occasionally on T'ang figurines, but even when they are used, the pad that cushions them does not go around the humps but is in two parts, one on each side.[66] Furthermore, it may be recalled that the Chinese cave painting of a camel harnessed to a wagon circa 600 A.D. shows not a collar but a rigid horseshoe shaped device that suggests a yoke adapted for a single animal. And at the present time, the withers-strap is the invariable method of harnessing two-humped camels to wheeled vehicles. Thus, all in all, the weight of pictorial evidence is against Haudricourt's theory. However, it does present the alternative possibility, given the evident change in saddle design between T'ang times and the present, that the invention of the horse collar influenced the design of camel saddles and that this produced the anomalies in vocabulary noted in Haudricourt.

In conclusion, the camel as a draft animal has not presented a tidy topic for discussion. The phenomenon is geographically discontinuous and is clearly affected by local customs and conditions. Information on the subject is very difficult to find. It is particularly unfortunate that more data is not available relating to camels being used for turning mills and irrigation devices. It is observable that in some areas, such as the Egyptian delta and Arabia,[67] the harness used is essentially a South Arabian saddle while in others, such as Iran, the withers-strap can be found;[68] but there is nothing to suggest how these techniques evolved or where. Yet despite the limitations of the discussion, the phenomenon of the draft camel does appear to be compatible with the central argument of this book that the pack camel replaced the wheel in the Middle East and North Africa. India, Aden, Tunisia, and Morocco all afford examples of one-humped camels being used to pull carts, but only in Tunisia does the practice demonstrably date back to the period of rivalry between the camel and the wheel, and in that one area the wheel seems not to have disappeared. As for

110 Camel operating irrigation device in Egyptian delta.

the two-humped camel, its use as a draft animal is geographically remote from the arena of competition between the
camel and the wheel. Finally, the possible contribution of
Tunisian camel culture to the history of harnessing in Europe
remains to be confirmed or refuted, though that of Central
Asian camel culture appears to be unfounded. If confirmation
is forthcoming through future research, however, not only
will an additional footnote have been added to the role of the
camel in world history, but new evidence will have been
established pointing to a strong connection between Tunisia,
Sicily, and Italy from Roman through medieval times.

111 Camel harnessed by withers-strap operating linseed oil mill in
Isfahan, Iran.

8 A Society Without Wheels

This book began with the simple observation that a major civilized society at some point in time abandoned the use of the wheel for transportation. The explanation of when and why this event took place has involved many digressions and technical discussions that may not always have seemed germane to the subject, but hopefully the hypothesized evolution of camel breeding in the nexus of human activities has made the abandonment of the wheel seem reasonable within its historical context. Now the time has come to ask what difference it all made. If the wheel was as important an invention of primitive man as is generally supposed, it would seem to follow that abandonment of the wheel would have a marked and far-reaching effect upon the level of culture of the society that had taken such a great step backward. However, two special considerations diminish the force of this argument for the medieval Middle East and North Africa. First, the non-

vehicular use of wheels, and of rotating systems in general, **217**
suffered no regression. Quite the contrary; irrigation, milling,
potting, and other wheel-using occupations underwent
technological improvement if anything during the flourishing
period of the Islamic caliphate.[1] Secondly, the greater economy
of the pack camel marks its replacement of wheeled transport
as a technological advance rather than a step backward.
Therefore, it is perfectly within reason to ask whether widespread camel use really affected society very significantly or
whether its effect was a marginal one felt only in the transport
sector.

There are two ways in which this problem may be approached. One way is to look into material effects of the
change, significant concrete differences between wheeled and
wheelless environments. This approach will be followed up
in due course. The other way is to investigate intangible
changes in attitude. This is unquestionably a more difficult
undertaking and one which leads to less conclusive results, but
it may well be the more important one. Whereas the material
approach, as will be seen, is involved primarily with the
effects of the absence of wheels, the attitudinal approach centers primarily on the presence of camels. Camels are so much a
part of the Western stereotype of the Middle East and North
Africa that no illustration of the fact is needed. They are
regarded as humorous animals or, alternatively, as stupid and
nasty ones. Even the eleventh edition of the *Encyclopaedia
Britannica* sees fit to quote as authoritative Sir Francis Pal-
grave's opinion that the camel "is from first to last an
undomesticated and savage animal rendered serviceable by
stupidity alone, without much skill on his master's part, or any
cooperation on his own, save that of extreme passiveness.
Neither attachment nor even habit impresses him; never tame,
though not wide-awake enough to be exactly wild."[2]

Fortunately, camels are immune to the demoralizing effects
of slander. Less happy is the situation of Arab people who
have been plagued by the irrational identification in the Western mind of them with this allegedly ridiculous beast. Most
educated Arabs of today have little or no knowledge of camels
and even less association with them.[3] The insistence of
Westerners upon considering them to be only hours removed

from the camel herd is at best a bad joke and at worst an embarrassment.[4] Because the camel is derisively regarded by the West, it has come to be regarded by many Arabs as a symbol of backwardness, a symbol that has done much to produce a negative image of the Arab in motion pictures, literature, advertising, journalism, and so forth. Comparable phenomena would be the stereotype of American Indians as bloodthirsty savages and the now abated tendency to see the United States as a nation of cowboys, Indians, and gangsters.

The attitudinal effects of the rise of the camel in the Middle Eastern and North African transportation economy can only be appreciated if one purges one's mind of existing stereotypes of Arabs and camels. Throughout history some Arabs have bred camels while others have not. Those who have bred them have held them in high esteem. This applies to Somalis, Berbers, and other herders of one-humped camels as well.[5] Those who have not been involved in breeding them have tended to have no special regard for them. The difference in attitude toward camels of the Arab camel breeder and the Arab city-dweller is comparable to the difference in attitude toward cattle of the American cattle rancher and the urban American beef-eater.

The situation among two-humped camel breeders is somewhat different because of the rise of the horse in the first millenium B.C. as the most important and most highly esteemed herd animal. Camels do not seem to play as important a role in the intellectual and spiritual life of Central Asian Turkish and Mongolian nomads as they do in that of Arab nomads or, even more, in that of the Somalis and the Tuaregs. Jean-Paul Roux, who has made the most thorough investigation of the place of the camel in Turkish culture, provides some interesting examples of the stereotypical identification of camels and Arabs when he explains away a taste for camel meat among certain Turkish groups as being caused by contact with Arabs or with Islam, which as an initially Arab religion he regards as being inherently pro-camel.[6]

Looking at medieval Arab society with the distinction between camel breeder and indirect user of camel transport in mind, the same lack of special regard for the camel that exists today can be seen to have existed in urban, cosmopolitan

milieus. The camel was not a symbol of backwardness; it was **219**
simply a symbol of nomadism. By and large, people did not
think about camels. A few books about camels were written by
Arabs after the Islamic conquests; but although they have
not been preserved, it seems more than likely that they do not
reflect a great interest in the animal but rather belonged to
a genre of philological writing that aimed at elucidating Arabic
tribal poetry.[7] The latest recorded work on camels was by an
author who died in 966, and most such works were by authors
who lived over a century before that. As far as general works
on animals go, the camel does not receive an unusual amount of
attention; the most famous work of this sort, the *Kitāb al-
Ḥayawān* of al-Jāḥiẓ, mentions the camel only in the context of
speaking about other species.[8] Pigeons, for example, come
in for far greater attention. In pictorial art, too, the camel is
usually a bystander and rarely the central attraction.

Yet if the rise of the camel in the transportation economy
had little impact upon the attitude toward camels of either the
camel nomads themselves, who always admired them, or of
the sedentary people, who thought little of the benefits they
received from their strong backs, it certainly affected the
attitude of these two groups of people toward one another by
changing their economic relationship. From the side of the
nomads, as pointed out in chapter four, evidence of this change
in attitude is abundant and takes the form of wholesale
adoption of sedentary artistic standards, religious beliefs, and,
after the Islamic conquests had given them dominion, way
of life. Ultimately many tribes that participated in the conquests ceased to be camel breeders altogether and became
sedentarized. Bedouin life and mentality seem to have changed
little from pre-Islamic times until the coming of modernization,
but that is because the modifications made possible by changes
in camel technology and transport economy were basically
complete by the time of the conquests. To appreciate the effect
upon bedouin life of economic integration with settled society,
the relevant comparison is that between the desert society of
500 B.C. and 500 A.D. rather than between that of 500 A.D.
and 1900.

From the other side, that of sedentary, agricultural society,
the change in attitude is harder to document. Most dramatic,

naturally, was the forced acceptance in the seventh century of
nomadic Arabs as rulers with all that that eventually entailed
in terms of religious and linguistic change. Yet the directing
cadre of the Islamic conquests consisted of Meccan merchants
more than bedouin camel breeders. The Arab rulers became
sedentarized in a short space of time, and the effective prop-
agation of the Islamic religion and the Arabic tongue was
carried out by Arabs who were no longer camel breeders, if
they ever had been. Camel nomads continued to live in the
Arabian desert, of course, as they do today, and the recurrent
difficulties in dealing with them seem to have been little
different for Muslim rulers than they had been for pre-Islamic
rulers. With the passage of time even the linguistic and
genealogical link dissolved as Persians, Turks, Circassians, and
other non-Arab peoples rose to dominion in Islam. In North
Africa, of course, Arab rule encountered resistance from the
camel-breeding Berber tribes, and Arabic did not become the
dominant language until after the eleventh century when large
Arab tribal groups migrated to the area.

Superficially, then, looking at the ongoing relationship
between settled society and the camel nomad, as opposed to
the irrelevant relationship between Arab and non-Arab, little
change is noticeable in the attitude of settled society toward
the nomad. The former continued, more or less, to despise the
latter. As one noble Iranian put it early in the ninth century,
"I have become one of these people [the Arabs] in everything
which I detest, even unto the eating of oil, and the riding of
camels, and the wearing of sandals."[9] There was even a backlash against the strong cultural influence of tribal poetry.
Abū Nuwās, who died around 810, typified the backlash in this
parody of a tribal ode:

Let the south-wind moisten with rain the desolate scene
And Time efface what once was so fresh and green!
Make the camel-rider free of a desert space
Where high-bred camels trot with unwearied pace;
Where only mimosas and thistles flourish, and where,
For hunting, wolves and hyenas are nowise rare!
Amongst the Bedouins seek not enjoyment out:
What do they enjoy? They live in hunger and drought.

Let them drink their bowls of milk and leave them alone, **221**
To whom life's finer pleasures are all unknown.[10]

Taking a broader view, however, indirect evidence of an
underlying change in attitude can be seen. In particular, there
is a noticeable diminution during the Muslim period of the
pronounced effort made by previous governments to police
desert frontiers and drive the bedouin as far away as possible
from cultivated lands. Protection was afforded, whenever
politically possible, to commercial and pilgrim traffic passing
through or near bedouin territory, but this protection did not
consist of networks of fortified posts such as the Romans had
on their Syrian and Saharan frontiers and the Persians on
their Arabian frontier. Traffic had to be protected, but the right
of camel nomads to pasture their herds peacefully was also
taken for granted. There was a tacit recognition of the place of
camel breeders in the economy. Both nomad and camel were
considered natural, if not entirely desirable, parts of the environment. This amounted to an amelioration in the attitude of
settled society toward the bedouin.

A second and equally subtle change is perceivable in attitudes toward the desert itself. Although it was still desolate
and dangerous, the desert, whether the Arabian, Syrian, or
Saharan, never looms in the medieval Muslim mentality as the
formidable barrier it had been in pre-Islamic times. North
African Muslim states from the very beginning displayed an
easier and more comfortable relationship with the interior than
had their coast-bound predecessors. Camel-borne Saharan
trade grew rapidly. In the Middle East, the Syrian desert,
which had divided the Romans from the Persians, did not re-
emerge as a significant political barrier until the twentieth
century when the bedouin once again became economically
unimportant. The reason for this change is surely that the
widespread use of the camel in settled territories diminished
the age-old fear of the desert and of the nomads. The camel
breeder may not have become more attractive, but he became
more familiar. By becoming himself a part of the economic
nexus he forced sedentary society to the realization that the
desert, too, could be productive.

222   Finally, leaving camels aside, there appears to have developed throughout the area an unconscious prejudice against wheeled vehicles. Clear traces of this prejudice are hard to find, since the most obvious apparent effect, namely the slowness of Middle Eastern and North African society to readapt to the wheel in modern times, is intertwined with local resistance to Western customs of all sorts. Nevertheless, the fact that palanquins carried between two camels could still be seen in Cairo in the 1920's[11] or that wheelbarrows are almost unknown on construction sites in Tehran to this day, all burdens being carried instead on two-man litters, testify to a pervasive nonwheel mentality. Trucks may carry produce to market, but carts and wagons are still little used at the village level.

Whether or not this prejudice has ever been truly significant is difficult to say, but it was very likely a factor in the tardiness of Middle Eastern armies in developing mobile field artillery after their early development of siege artillery under the Ottomans. It is noteworthy that animal-borne artillery was, on the contrary, developed first in the Middle East and only later taken up by Europeans for mountain batteries. In 1722 an

112 Camel-borne palanquin in Cairo in 1923.

Afghan army defeated a much larger Persian force by means of one hundred small guns mounted upon camels and fired when the animals were in the couched position.[12] Units armed with these camel-mounted guns, called *zambūrak* (from *zambūr* meaning wasp), continued to exist in the Persian army well into the nineteenth century. The gun was small in size, of course, but together with its mount it weighed over eighty pounds, and one Frenchman observed that "it has replaced perfectly our light artillery."[13] Yet as late as 1838 the same Persian army for heavy artillery carried unformed metal on camel back to the scene of battle and there cast it into siege guns.[14]

The attitudes that have been described here as being legitimately traceable to the camel's supplanting the wheel may not form an exhaustive list. It is so difficult for someone reared in the United States in the second half of the twentieth century to grasp the full mental impact of a society devoid of wheeled vehicles that some obvious factor may have been overlooked. Nevertheless, the attitudinal factors that have been mentioned are sufficient to demonstrate that the impact of not having wheeled vehicles upon someone immersed in the wheelless society is entirely different from the impact upon an outside observer from a wheeled society. For a member of the wheelless society the situation presents no sensation of anomaly; whatever attitudes may be affected are unconscious ones. To the outside observer who becomes conscious of it, however, the wheelless society seems visibly peculiar; the camel caravan seems like a romantic wonder instead of a commonplace means of transportation. Yet what causes this outside observer's *feeling* of peculiarity is not the *feelings* of Middle Easterners and North Africans toward camels or wheels but rather certain physical differences in the environment. These differences are accepted as normative by members of the wheelless society, but they are remarkable in the eyes of outsiders.

The reason for spelling out in detail this self-evident distinction between the perceptions of insiders and outsiders is that very often in discussions of traditional Middle Eastern and North African society explanations for physical phenomena that are striking to the Western mind are sought for exclusively in the realm of ideas rather than in the material realm. This applies in particular to two physical phenomena that are in large part the products of the wheel's disappearance. These two phenomena which have engaged Western attention are a characteristic urban topography and the absence of roads.

Whoever has attempted to characterize medieval Middle Eastern and North African cities has sooner or later commented upon the narrow streets, the blind corners, the encroachment of buildings upon the public way, and in general upon the labyrinthine quality that strikes so forcibly the Western visitor. Many scholars have attributed this quality in some way to the Islamic religion and have implied that it is a universal feature of Islamic cities.[15] None has seen it as a characteristic of a society without wheels.

A rectilinear layout with streets of uniform width lined with buildings of similar height and design has until recently represented in Western thinking good order and intelligence of design. Even individuals not normally given to admiring this type of design are apt to feel the adjective "oriental" come to mind when confronted with a city composed of winding streets and narrow alleys.[16] Dirt, darkness, and crowding are thought of as inevitable and evil conditions of this "oriental" type of city, while parallel Western conditions such as motorized danger and the isolating quality of broad avenues are taken in stride. Islamic society is often described as turning its back on the street, hiding inside walled courtyards and behind windowless walls to shut out the cheerlessness and contagion of the public way. Private life is supposedly given precedence over communal life, which is seen by many to be deficient in the Islamic religion.[17] To an earlier generation such streets might be regarded as visible evidence of the supposed inadequacy of Islam.

This entire conception of the "oriental" city plan being generated by Islamic social principles runs counter both to logic and to fact. A great many factors, some deliberately planned and others unconscious and incremental, come into play in the development of a particular urban environment. Religious principles undoubtedly have their place among them. When it comes to the layout of streets, however, what cries out most for explanation is the rigid application of abstract geometrical forms. A particular shape or compass orientation might be dictated by religious belief, astrology, legal principle,

or the caprice of a ruler; but whatever the motive, it is
reasonable to expect it to be ascertainable.[18] The same cannot
be said of a city whose streets are not laid out in a formal
pattern but according to the lay of the land and the inclination
of the builder. Disorder requires explanation only if order is
taken to be normative.

Since from the Western viewpoint regular patterns in urban
topography are generally considered to be good and the absence of such patterns bad, it is not difficult to understand why
the feeling arose that the "oriental" city plan had to have an
explanation, particularly in view of the fact that Roman cities
throughout the Middle East and North Africa are known to
have exhibited a uniform rectilinearity.[19] But if narrow, winding streets are not inherently bad, the rationale for seeking an
explanation for this alleged falling away from perfection
evaporates. And in fact, narrow, winding streets have much to
recommend them. They easily follow the lay of the land; in
hot countries they provide shade; they diminish winds; they
permit a higher density of habitation which in turn makes a
sizable city accessible to pedestrians; they facilitate social relationships; and they are easily defensible. As for enclosed
courtyards with windowless exteriors, they provide secluded
open spaces where many household tasks are carried out, as is
desirable in a warm climate; and they allow for careful regu-
lation of water consumption, as is desirable in an arid climate.
There is privacy, too, of course, but that much familial privacy
is available in the large tenements built around courtyards
that are characteristic of North African cities is open to doubt.
A final observation on the sociability of streets of this character
may be gleaned from Roger Le Tourneau's monumental study
of the city of Fez in Morocco. He observes that the street is
the center of a quarter or neighborhood, while the demarcation
lines between neighborhoods follow the abutted backs of
houses.[20] By way of contrast, American residential neighborhoods often divide along street boundaries with residents
on the same side of a street knowing each other better than they
know their neighbors facing.

Since, then, the transition from Roman rectilinearity to
medieval disorder was not necessarily inherently bad, the need
to explain it in moral or ideological terms is greatly dimin-

ished and the way is open for a more prosaic physical explanation. Wheeled vehicles—and this can come as no surprise to today's city dwellers—are inflexible in the restraints they put on city life. Streets must be flat, without stairsteps or precipitous grades, and, if possible, paved. Moreover, they must be maintained in this state if circulation is not to be interrupted. They must always be as wide as a single axle—as wide as two if the citizens are to be spared immoderate language. Corners must not be too sharp or narrow to be maneuvered; dead ends must be eschewed. Encroachments on the public way either by buildings or by merchants displaying goods cannot be tolerated. And on top of all of these burdens is the fact that wheeled vehicles are noisy and dangerous.

Freed from this vehicular straitjacket by the disappearance of the wheel, it is scarcely a matter for wonder that Middle Eastern and North African cities gradually evolved types and arrangements of streets suited more closely to human needs. With only pedestrians and pack animals to accommodate, the street could become an open market or a narrow cul-de-sac giving access to residences. In the absence of any ideological sanction of constant widths and right angled turns, only enough legislation was needed to keep the streets passable. This is very different, needless to say, from having an ideological sanction for disorder. Indeed, on occasion Islamic rulers decreed explicit plans for cities, plans that on one occasion might call for broad thoroughfares and on another for great plazas;[21] but planning was not the rule because without wheeled vehicles the necessity for plans was negligible. As late as 1845 the width of a major new street in Cairo was determined by measuring the combined width of two loaded camels.[22]

The advent of Islam did not destroy previous city plans. Antioch and Herat are two examples of cities that to this day preserve long, straight thoroughfares traceable to pre-Islamic incarnations.[23] Alexandria was still described as being laid out like a chessboard in the thirteenth century.[24] But Islam came into being in a society that had recently abandoned the wheel, and hence it incorporated in its growth no ideological bias in favor of vehicular traffic. The evolution from a geometric to an organic urban design within the zone of the wheel's dis-

appearance followed as a natural consequence. Outside that
zone other, equally Islamic—or, rather, equally non-Islamic—
urban patterns arose. The dispersed cities of Indonesia made
up of discrete, villagelike *kampongs*; the precise rectilinear
design of Jaipur in India;[25] and the striking "skyscraper" cities
of southern Arabia illustrate the variety of urban design to be
found in Islamic lands and testify to the irrelevancy of Islamic
religious principles in this domain. It is the absence of the
wheel that goes furthest toward explaining this characteristic
feature of Middle Eastern and North African urban environments.

Roads are the second area in which the camel's impact on a
wheeled economy can be observed in concrete form. What
is important here is not which routes were traversed. In the
Middle East desert caravan tracks were in use for centuries
before the camel replaced the wheel. In North Africa the camel
would have become the common carrier on Saharan trade
routes regardless of its effect on wheeled transport. And in
Central Asia the camel dominated the caravan trade without
eradicating the wheel as it was used in agricultural districts or
for moving the belongings and portable homes of migrating
nomads. What is important is not the choice of routes; it is
their actual physical state.

Camels, donkeys, and pedestrians do not need paved roads.
Given that throughout the zone of the wheel's disappearance
the climate is dry during most of the year, it is more comfortable to walk on dirt. Furthermore, natural obstacles, such as
boulders, do not have to be removed to provide for a constant
minimum width, nor do ruts have to be filled in. Cost of
maintenance is as negligible as cost of construction. In a nonvehicular economy the most important physical features of a
road are its bridges. One bridge in place of a ford or ferry
can make an enormous difference in the ease and cost of transportation. After bridges, the most important features are
accommodations for travelers. A regular daily stage of travel
for a caravan does not exceed twenty miles, and a good road
will afford a stopping place at the end of every stage, whether
it be a town, a village, or a caravanserai. Beyond these two
things, bridges and caravanserais, the physical upkeep of roads
is insignificant; but bridges and caravanserais themselves can
be very costly.

The reflection of this state of affairs is everywhere apparent in the history of the Islamic Middle East. References to the upkeep of roads are almost nonexistent, but powerful dynasties frequently show their interest in promoting trade by building bridges and caravanserais.[26] Investment in these two things is functionally equivalent to roadbuilding in a wheelless society. There is no need to search for an ideological explanation for a nonexistent neglect of public ways. Middle Eastern governments acted with complete rationality in investing in bridges and caravanserais instead of in useless grading and paving.

In the case of roads, as in the case of medieval urban topography faced by modern automobile traffic, what was rational and desirable in a nonvehicular society has proved to be highly undesirable in the wheeled economy of modern times. In Europe, road improvement and advances in vehicular design went hand in hand. Heavy vehicles drawn by several animals meant that load size could be greatly increased over the quarter ton limit imposed by the pack camel, but their efficiency could only be fully realized on roads that were straight, level, and paved. Consequently, the infrastructure of carriageable roads that Europe took into the period of the industrial revolution far outstripped what the Middle East had going into the twentieth century.[27] Almost all non-Western countries, of course, have been faced with the need to build a network of motorable roads as a prerequisite for modernization, and many areas are endowed with much greater physical obstacles than is the Middle East, which is dry, devoid of forests, and relatively free of rivers. Strictly from the Middle Eastern perspective, however, it is evident that the area would have entered the period of modernization with a much better road system had it not been for the dominance of the pack camel and the absence of wheeled vehicles. Given the vital role of transportation in the industrialization process, both for centralizing manufacturing and distributing manufactured goods, it is possible that this deficiency was crucial.

Whether attitudinal or physical, the effects of the disappearance of the wheel as analyzed above imply the operation of a principle that should be more clearly stated. This is the principle that the state of technology and of the economy is the

prime determinant of people's attitudes and actions, at least
within the sphere of transportation. The counterargument to
this has already been noted in the discussion of urban topography. According to this counterargument Arabs, or Muslims
in general, can be viewed as constructing about them a certain
type of world wherever they go; the transport economy can
either be seen as a function of a positive ideological viewpoint,
a pro-camelline bias, or a physical consequence of negative
viewpoints such as absence of communal concern for roads and
urban orderliness. Obviously, I disagree with this alternative
approach, but the two arguments are actually subject to test,
so one need not rely upon an historian's predilections. The
test comes in looking at the transport economy of fringe areas
where camels and camel breeders encountered limits of one
sort or another. The three areas that will be briefly examined
are Spain, Anatolia, and India.

The number of camels in Muslim Spain seems never to have
been very substantial. The Arab troops that conquered North
Africa and pushed on eventually across the Strait of Gibraltar
were not the vanguard of important tribal migrations into the
area. Not until the eleventh century, three hundred years later,
did significant numbers of Arab camel breeders push into the
territory of modern Algeria and Morocco. Nor were the Berber troops that joined the Arabs in the conquest of Spain in
711 members of camel-breeding tribes. Camel breeding in
North Africa begins well south of the mountain ranges that
front the Mediterranean Sea, and the Arabs' early allies came
from coastal areas. Thus the few references to camels in the
first four centuries of Islamic rule in Spain do not signify the
establishment of substantial herds of camels in Europe but
pertain only to what camels were ferried across the Strait of
Gibraltar for special purposes or as part of military baggage
trains.[28] The first true camel breeders to reach Spain were the
Sanhaja Berber tribesmen from Mauretania who came in 1090
when the Almoravids invaded from Morocco. With their arrival camels become more noticeable in the sources,[29] but the
period of Almoravid ascendancy was brief. Scarcely fifty
years elapsed before their hold on Spain weakened, and by 1170
control had passed to the Almohads, a new Berber dynasty of
mountain rather than camel-breeding origin. Thus there never

was time for camel breeders to gain a foothold in the economy, and without a group of people specifically interested in breeding them, camels stood no chance of becoming established in the region on a large scale. Arab and Berber patterns of camel use depended upon the existence of camel-breeding tribesmen and did not leave room for other approaches to livestock management.

Despite the fact that there were insufficient camels either before or after the conquest to offer serious competition to wheeled transport, however, wheeled vehicles are never mentioned during the early centuries of Muslim rule.[30] One possible explanation for this would be that the Muslim invaders were prejudiced against the wheel, identifying it, perhaps, as a trait of the conquered population and therefore directly or indirectly suppressing its use. If this explanation were to be verified, the argument of this book that the disappearance of the wheel was largely a function of competition from camels would be brought seriously into question.

A second explanation is more substantiable, however. This is that wheeled vehicles did not exist in Spain in great numbers even before the conquest and hence did not have to suffer any decline in order not to be mentioned in Arabic sources. Roman Spain surely knew the wheel, since it was a normal part of the life not only of the Romans but of the native Celtiberians and pre-Roman Carthaginian colonizers as well.[31] However, successive invasions by Vandals, Alans, Suevi, and Visigoths brought about a severe decline in the economic life of the country as well as in the quality of its roads. By the time of the Muslim conquest little recovery had been made, and it is more than likely that vehicular traffic was at a low ebb.[32] Therefore, when the Muslims arrived, they had little incentive to adopt the use of wheeled vehicles, with which they were, in any case, unfamiliar; and they had equally little incentive to restore the road system since their pack animals, mostly native mules, did not require good roads.[33] As a consequence, the use of the wheel by the indigenous population probably declined still further.

It is unlikely that the wheel ever died out entirely in Muslim Spain. In the tenth century native Spaniards, both Christian and Muslim, can be found in historical sources making use of carts,[34] and the technological vocabulary of harnessing indicates a continuity in transportation developments across Spain, Sicily, and Tunisia.[35] Thus, the transport economy of Muslim Spain should properly be viewed as a case of unusually retarded recovery from the decline that accompanied the fall of the Roman Empire. Since the camel never became a factor, there was nothing to impede the gradual return of the wheel; and that return, when it came, did not depend upon technological influences from non-Muslim lands. Nevertheless, the virtual absence of wheeled transport during the first centuries of Muslim rule did leave traces in such things as nonvehicular city designs and the tendency of roads to follow short cuts by descending into valleys instead of following the longer, but vehicularly easier, crestline of ridges.[36]

While Spain presents the picture of a society with neither wheels nor camels, albeit one to which the wheel naturally returned in the course of time, Anatolia presents the opposite picture, a society with both camels and wheels peacefully coexisting. The explanation of this phenomenon, which seems to contradict the hypothesis that the camel is a competitively superior mode of transport, involves several factors, the most important of which is that Anatolia came under Islamic rule only after the battle of Manzikert in 1071 and consequently was occupied by Turkish rather than Arab tribesmen. The significance of this fact is that camel breeding in Anatolia has always been in the hands of a people who rarely exhibit a special concern for the animal and who customarily used it in conjunction with wheeled vehicles in their homeland of Central Asia. Particularly indicative of the Turkishness of Anatolian camel culture is the practice of camel wrestling—pitting two rutting males against each other—which always indicates a Turkish influence.[37]

Undoubtedly, climatic conditions were a factor as well. Al-Jāḥiẓ clearly notes in the eighth century that Arab camels could not live in Anatolia.[38] Yet in Assyrian and, judging from a coin of Trajan, Roman times two-humped camels were known there.[39] And by the fourth century a literary image involving a pack camel was perfectly understandable in western Anatolia.[40] Although concrete evidence of the kind available for Iran is lacking, it must be assumed that the practice of

113 Two-humped camel on coin of the emperor Trajan from central Anatolia.

hybridization reached Anatolia well prior to the Islamic conquests. Otherwise al-Jāḥiẓ would be making little
sense when he remarks that "camel owners desire to make use
of . . . Anatolia for camels . . . It is surprising that the people
of Anatolia get along well with camels in the desert since the
entry of camels into Anatolia means their [the camels'] destruction."[41] The camel owners clearly must have wanted to
expand into Anatolia because of the business of breeding hybrids since their own one-humped animals could not tolerate
the climate. As for the natives of Anatolia, their familiarity
with camels obviously was limited.

Historically, the optimism of the camel owners about business in Anatolia was fully justified. After the Turkish conquest,
economic contact with camel-breeding country in northern
Syria greatly increased. Moreover, the Turks brought with
them at least some two-humped animals which could be
used for breeding stock.[42] The result was the emergence of the
Turkoman camel, a hybrid, as the characteristic camel of
Anatolia.[43] The number of one-humped animals imported into
Anatolia from Syria and Arabia was 8,000 to 10,000 a year at
the beginning of the nineteenth century and still 7,000 or 8,000
at the time of World War I.[44] Contemporary with these latter
figures are others indicating a yearly sale of 32,000 camels from
Syria and Arabia to Egypt; this shows that the Anatolian

114 The emperor Bahram Gur riding a two-humped camel on thirteenth century Persian bowl. Compare figure 82.

camel trade, amounting, as it did, to a quarter of the Egyptian, was far from negligible in the eyes of the Arab camel breeders.[45] However, since all sources concur that only a few two-humped males existed in Anatolia for stud purposes, it is obvious that most breeding stock of both species had to be imported. From this it can only be concluded that Anatolian camels were comparatively expensive animals.

The distribution of oxcarts in Anatolia at the present day seems to confirm the importance of high breeding costs and the absence of a large body of dedicated camel nomads in the failure of the camel to replace the wheel. It is the areas that would have had the least access to camels coming from Syria that have the most oxcarts. The carts that existed on the Byzantine-Muslim border in northern Syria in the tenth century have been displaced by camels,[46] but camels are rare in northern and eastern Anatolia where oxcarts are commonplace. To the east camels are not found again in large numbers until

115 Solid-wheeled Anatolian oxcart.

one reaches the flat plateaus of Iranian Azerbaijan, a camel-   **235**
breeding area where oxcarts cease to be common.[47] The
superiority of the camel to the primitive Anatolian oxcart,[48]
therefore, was offset by high prices, with the result that the
camel's competition was felt predominantly in localities adjoining camel-breeding areas and along main caravan routes
where the high value of the merchandise justified using camels.
Elsewhere the oxcart remained supreme, and this applies in
particular to the European provinces of the Ottoman empire
which were too far from Syria to obtain breeding stock and consequently rarely saw camels except during military campaigns
when some from Anatolia and Syria were used, along with
many carts and wagons, in the army's baggage train.[49]

The effects of this coexistence of camels and wheeled vehicles may be found in the several different areas already investigated to show the effects of the wheel's disappearance.
Ottoman miniature paintings show accurately drawn vehicles.[50]
The Ottoman army used carts and wagons extensively.
Clearly there existed no antiwheel bias among the Ottomans.
After his conquest of Constantinople in 1453, Sultan Mehmet
gave orders for the repair of roads and bridges leading to the
city.[51] No comparable concern for repair of roads was ever
exhibited by the various Muslim rulers of Baghdad or Damascus. But the fullest appreciation of the difference between a
wheeled and a wheelless society can be gained by comparing
the ambience of Fez in Morocco and Kayseri, for example, in
Anatolia. Commonplaces about "oriental" cities with an im-
penetrable maze of streets make some kind of sense in Fez but
ring hollow in Kayseri and other Anatolian cities. To be sure,
most Anatolian cities inherited much from Byzantine and pre-
Byzantine times, but they also underwent much less "oriental-
ization" than equally ancient cities in Syria such as Aleppo.[52]

Finally, the situation of camels in India has been discussed
already in chapter seven. It is sufficient here merely to repeat
that the camel never replaced the wheel east of the Indus because the camel was instead harnessed for pulling carts and
wagons. This does not mean, of course, that pack camels were
not used in India; it simply means that instances of direct
competition between oxcart and pack camel could be resolved
by the use of a camel cart. As a result, Muslim India never

became a society without wheels, and Muslim Indian cities did not assimilate to the "oriental" city pattern.[53]

Taken altogether, what the examples of Muslim Spain, Anatolia, and India demonstrate is that economic and technological factors weigh heavier than ideological or religious factors in determining the transportation economy of a particular area and that the transportation economy affects other facets of society as well, even to the extent of affording plausible explanations for phenomena which are ordinarily attributed to ideological or religious causes. As a prime example, the pattern of urban design that is usually characterized as being "Muslim" or "oriental" can be explained more readily as a characteristic of a society without wheels than it can be by arguments from Islamic law or theology. Therefore, the abandonment of the wheel, even if it was at the time a step forward rather than backward, most assuredly caused significant and diverse changes in Middle Eastern and North African society and affected greatly both the image that society presented to other people and its capacity for adjusting to pressures for change in the nineteenth and twentieth centuries.

9 If Camels Are Such a Good Idea . . .

The final episode in the story of the camel and the wheel is
the reversal in the twentieth century of the process already
described. Instead of the camel replacing the wheel, the wheel
replaces the camel. But before embarking upon that final episode, a digression is called for both because it will illuminate
some of the questions that have already been touched upon
and because it may serve to bring the entire question of the
camel as an economic entity into closer focus for readers who
have never had much contact with the animal. This digression
concerns the many attempts made by Europeans and Americans to utilize camels for their own ends and to acclimatize
them to different parts of the globe. The question, essentially,
is if camels are such a good idea, why did their use not become
universal?

Few lasting results came of the experiments of Westerners
with camels; the establishment of feral camels as yet another

238   Western introduced animal pest in Australia is perhaps the
       only one. Many efforts were made, however, and the nature
       of these attempts and the thinking of the men who made them
       are worthy of attention. Basically, leaving aside importa-
       tion for zoos and menageries, Westerners have attempted to
       exploit camels in two different ways: for military transport
       and for general labor.[1] Camel products such as meat, milk, and
       fiber have been little exploited by the West, although camel's
       hair is used in some of the fabrics that go by that name, and
       before the development of superior rubber products, camel's
       hair imported from Central Asia through China provided the
       best known material for industrial belting.[2] This limitation
       in use is not surprising, however. Outside the domestic econ-
       omy of the camel-breeding tribes themselves, camel products
       have seldom been extensively utilized even in those countries
       that have had camels for centuries.

       That Europeans and Americans should think of the camel
       as a useful military and transport animal is, of course, entirely
       understandable. The animal's excellence was noted by almost
       every traveler who ventured into its domain, and not a few
       speculated upon its possible utilization in their home country.[3]
       There were even those who thought to improve upon indige-
       nous camel techniques in the Middle East. Englishmen in
       Bengal, for example, made plans to introduce camel-drawn
       carts, Indian style no doubt, on the route from Alexandria to
       Suez which was already frequented by camel caravans.[4]

116 Camels used for draft in nineteenth century Egypt.

Whether by their agency or someone else's, some draft camels did come to be used in Egypt in the late nineteenth century.[5] Yet experimenters and would-be experimenters were not blind to the fact that the camel could never compete economically with a railroad or with wheeled traffic in European countries endowed with good roads.[6] Nevertheless, they saw some possibilities in desolate parts of even the most developed countries, and the potential for camel use in colonial territories brought them to peaks of eloquence.

This interest in camels, which reached its height in the middle of the nineteenth century, must be seen in the context of a widespread movement, stimulated by the scientific spirit and by increased contact with non-Western countries, to promote the acclimatization of all sorts of animal and plant species both to Europe and to her colonies. A leader in this movement, the French zoologist Isidore Geoffroy Saint-Hilaire, foresaw the use of the yak and some of the larger African antelope as meat animals in France and fully expected to see the llama and the alpaca naturalized in the Pyrenees to provide not just meat but high grade wool as well.[7] His hopes for the camel were less sanguine as far as France was concerned, but for its use in colonial territories they were very high. Perhaps he was personally biased in favor of the camel as a result of his father's having accompanied Napoleon's expedition to Egypt as a zoologist, but he was probably completely sober when he wrote that the camel "even with the limited utility

which [he] attributes to it . . . [is] a beautiful gift made by Algeria to the motherland."[8]

It would be a mistake to interpret Geoffroy Saint-Hilaire's enthusiasm as that of a mere visionary. His energy was instrumental in the creation in 1854 of the very active Société Impériale Zoologique d'Acclimatation from whose publications much information on attempts to transplant camels and other animals may be derived. He also spearheaded the campaign to popularize horsemeat as a cheap food for peasants and laborers, a campaign which resulted in France becoming a country where horse is normally eaten, after being as late as 1861 a country without a single horse butcher where tons of horsemeat a year were used for feeding dogs and pigs or simply disposed of as garbage.[9] Such was the spirit of the times in the field of practical zoology.

The full catalogue of attempts to introduce the camel into new territories is long and certainly incomplete. It was known that camels were not native to North Africa, and its great utility there was frequently pointed to in the nineteenth century as proof that camels could be imported successfully to new areas and flourish;[10] but it was seldom realized that North Africa, like Somalia and India where camels were introduced at other periods, had the human resources necessary to make the transplantation succeed. By and large, efforts at acclimatization that did not make provision, at least unwittingly, for people who would devote themselves entirely to camel breeding have not been successful.

Europe has actually had two types of experience with camels. Many centuries before anyone thought to introduce the animal deliberately for economic reasons, it found its way there naturally as part of the herds of tribes migrating from the east. Mention has already been made of archaeological evidence of the two-humped camel's spread westward from Turkmenistan into the Russian steppes, and possibly even further if a swan-necked figurine of the first millenium B.C. found in Czechoslovakia is intended to represent a camel.[11] From this eastern fringe of Europe at least a few camels came into the possession of the Visigoths and other Germanic tribes who brought the species with them westward. The column of Arcadius (395–408) in Constantinople is often cited as evidence of camel herding among the Germans, but this is doubtful since the camels shown in surviving drawings of the column have Arab saddles and halters.[12] It is more likely that they were part of the baggage train of the Byzantine army. Nevertheless, Gothic does have a word for camel that is not obviously borrowed from any other language.[13] Camel bones found in Roman ruins at Vindonissa in Switzerland are probably also of Germanic provenance.[14]

At a somewhat later period camels were still known in Merovingian France. King Clotaire II (died 629) is reported to have paraded his queen Brunehaut before his army on the back of a camel before having her executed.[15] Traces of early familiarity with camels can be found as well in the folklore of eastern France.[16] Shortly thereafter the camel disappears from European sources. A single report of 1121 A.D. does place them in Poland in a context which may imply their use for drawing carts,[17] but there is little else to link the ancient and modern periods of European camel use.

Those few two-humped animals that accompanied the invading Germanic tribes did not establish the species, presumably because they were not very important to the tribes that owned them but possibly for climatic reasons as well. Hence all later attempts, outside of Muslim Spain, to introduce the camel to western Europe are of the nature of experiments in animal husbandry. The first of these was European in conception if not in locale. It was also the most permanently successful. In 1402 a French adventurer named Jean de Béthencourt pawned his estates in Normandy and with the money he received, and later with the support of King Henry III of Castile, he conquered the Canary Islands, off the coast of Africa. Before departing the islands forever in 1406 to enjoy his newly conferred title of king and any possible profits at home in Normandy, Béthencourt established a colony of Frenchmen there and imported camels from Morocco.[18] The importation was entirely successful, perhaps because the Canary Islanders took an interest in camel breeding; and several later attempts at acclimatization used Canary Island camels as their raw material.

The next experiment was made by Ferdinand II de Medici, one of the later and lesser members of the illustrious Florentine family, who ruled Tuscany from 1620 to 1670.[19] Although he is remembered primarily as the man who allowed the aged Galileo, his teacher, to be taken by the Pope's men and forced to recant his heretical theories, Ferdinand also established a camel ranch at San Rossore near Pisa which lasted until World War II when the remaining camels were transformed into meat.[20] Most accounts date the establishment of the herd vaguely to the middle of the seventeenth century, but an apparently reliable source specifies the year 1622 as the date the animals were introduced from Tunisia. Ferdinand II was only twelve years old at that time, and the state was under the control of his splendor-loving grandmother and mother, the Grand Duchess Christine and the Grand Duchess Maria Maddalena. Consequently, it is difficult to determine whether the importation of camels was a serious effort at introducing a new species or a mere extravagance prompted by the attention a camel drew when it was exhibited in Florence in that same year.

The interest of the Tuscan court in the camel herd at San Rossore flagged quickly. In the early eighteenth century the population was down to six. But more animals were then brought in from Africa, and in 1789 the number had risen to 196. In 1814 sixteen camels were sent from San Rossore to Naples to establish a herd there, and in 1820 two more were given to the Emperor of Austria for the same purpose. Interest in taking stock from San Rossore for establishing the animal in certain parts of France was expressed by the French government in 1830, but the project never came to fruition.

In Spain, as has already been mentioned, the camel never became well rooted during the Muslim period, but the substantial numbers in use in Huelva province in southern Spain near the mouth of the Guadalquivir may possibly trace back to the days of the Arabs.[21] Aside from these, thirty camels were brought to Barcelona in 1831 in an experiment by the captain general of Catalonia which ended when the animals died, and a breeding herd of Canary Island origin was maintained on the royal estates at Aranjuez from 1786 until the Spanish Civil War. In the middle of the nineteenth century it numbered twenty animals.

Further attempts to make use of the camel in Europe came in Poland and Russia toward the end of the nineteenth century.[22] The inspiration of these experiments, unlike those in western Europe, came from the Central Asian pattern of two-humped camel breeding with the result that the primary focus of utilization was the drawing of plows and wagons. Without more recent data the success or failure of the camel in eastern Europe is hard to judge, but the fact that the camels could be obtained without too much difficulty directly from traditional Central Asian breeding areas marks these experiments as being different in kind from those in which the intent was to acclimatize the animal to a new area on a self-perpetuating basis.

In the colonial arena most experiments met with as limited success as did those in western Europe. Several camels imported to Java died of liver disease.[23] In the middle of the sixteenth century an infantry captain named Juan de Reynaga transported a number of animals from the Canary Islands to Peru.[24] That experiment was brought to a halt by royal decree when complaints were raised that cheap camel transport would interfere with the profits to be made from hiring out the Indians at slave rates as human porters. Jamaica, too, was for fifty years the site of an unsuccessful camel experiment, as was Venezuela where the initial importation was made by Simon Bolivar's father-in-law.[25] The "jigger" was a hazard in the former area and snakebite in the latter. The camels were useful nevertheless in hauling sugar cane. In Cuba in 1841 seventy camels were in service in copper mines near Santiago, but they were made obsolete by a railroad and sent elsewhere in the island to be used in the sugar cane industry.[26]

Finally in the Caribbean area, the government of Brazil, after serious consideration, approached Geoffroy Saint-Hilaire's Société Impériale Zoologique d'Acclimatation in 1856 with a request that the society supervise the importation of camels into the dry northern province of Céara.[27] It is this request that prompted the study of the history of camel acclimatization from which much of the information in the preceding paragraphs has been taken, but the request brought practical results as well. On July 23, 1859, the three-masted *Splendide* unloaded on the beach at Céara fourteen camels and thirteen horses, all of Algerian origin. Nothing seems to have come of this effort,[28] but that is hardly surprising given the small number of camels imported.

In southern Africa the Germans, the Portuguese, and the British all tried using camels, and all met with some success.[29] The animals for German Southwest Africa came first from the

Canary Islands and later from North Africa. Some of the British animals were imported from Somalia. Despite their superior hardiness and strength, however, the effort began so late—not, it seems, until 1903—that successful establishment of the species could scarcely have been achieved before people's interest turned permanently to motorized transport. Whether anything survives of these experiments other than an old 150 reis stamp from Portuguese Nyassa I do not know.[30]

Two countries' camel experiences remain to be retold, Australia and the United States, and each is of particular interest, the first because of its uncommon success and the second because of its seemingly unnecessary failure. In both cases the very first efforts to introduce camels were indisputable failures. Two camels were brought to Virginia in 1701 by a slaver and never heard of again, and further north at around the same time a wealthy Salem sea captain named Crowninshield imported another pair which drew attention as curiosities but produced no lasting effect.[31] In Australia the first camel was the sole survivor of a group shipped from the Canary Islands.[32] It arrived in Port Adelaide, South Australia, in 1840 and was killed six years later after it had accidentally caused its owner's gun to fire, fatally wounding the owner. Also in the year 1840 a pair of camels reached Hobart, Tasmania, but nothing came of that importation either.

In North America no further attempts at importation were made until the mid-nineteenth century, which was about the same time that interest in such projects began to take hold in Australia. In both countries discussion of camel importation for useful purposes, as opposed to exhibition, long preceded implementation of the project. The colony of Western Australia is even reported to have offered a prize of £100 to anyone who would import a pregnant camel. The first substantial realization of these discussions did not come in Australia until 1860, however, when the *Chinsurah* reached Melbourne from Karachi with twenty-four camels aboard along with three so-called "Afghans"—a term that came to be used, with its abbreviation "Ghan," for all Asian camel men in Australia even though most of them were natives of Baluchistan or Rajasthan—and a British ex-soldier with camel experience. To this herd were added six other animals apparently already in the

TO THE CURIOUS!

To be seen at

TWO CAMELS,

MALE and FEMALE, imported from *ARABIA.*

THESE ſtupendous Animals are moſt deſerving the attention of the curious, being the greateſt natural curioſity ever exhibited to the public
on this continent.   They are nineteen hands high ; have necks near four
feet long ; have a large high bunch on their backs, and another under their
breaſts, in the form of a pedeſtal, on which they ſupport themſelves when
lying down ; they have four joints in their hind legs, and will travel twelve
or fourteen days without drinking, and carry a burthen of fifteen hundred
weight ; they are remarkably harmleſs and docile, and will lie down and riſe
at command.

117 Poster advertising camels imported by Captain Crowninshield
of Salem.

colony, with the result that later in the year an exploring expedition was able to set out from Melbourne with twenty-six camels in its baggage train.

The Burke and Wills expedition did not conclusively prove the superiority of camels to horses for desert exploration, but its experiences with the animals, added to those of the McKinlay relief expedition which was sent out to find Burke and Wills, convinced Thomas Elder, a large landholder in South Australia, of the wisdom of proceeding with a plan for importing camels that had entered his mind after traveling by camel from Cairo to Jerusalem in 1857. In January of 1866 Elder's camels, 124 of them including both riding and baggage types, reached Australia and inside a few months became the nucleus of Australia's first breeding herd on Elder's Beltana station.

The Beltana bred camels soon established a pattern that held true for later breeding stations as well, the superiority of the Australian bred camel over the imported animal. Selective breeding of riding animals had been known for centuries in Asia and Africa, but there had probably never been as much effort put into scientific breeding of work animals as was put in in Australia, where the camel's capacity for labor was admired far more than its riding qualities. Nevertheless, the camel having a long reproductive cycle, the demand for camels for exploring, packing, and carting was greater than domestic breeders could supply, and for many years new shipments were brought in from India.

Accurate figures are not available, but the data collected by Tom L. McKnight, upon whose work the preceding account has been based, indicates that from 65 in 1866 (after mange had wiped out half of Elder's herd) the number of camels in Australia rose to about 700 in the early 1880s and 1,600 in 1889. From there the population skyrocketed to an official peak approaching 13,000 by 1925 (real population closer to 20,000) and then in an even shorter period plummeted to 500 or fewer domestic animals in 1966.[33] What is hidden by the figures for domestic camels, however, is the tremendous growth in the feral camel population that came into being as camels supplanted by motorized transport were set free to fend for themselves. McKnight estimates the feral camel population of Australia at between 15,000 and 20,000. These animals are

classified as vermin, with a bounty offered in some states, because of their habit of going through rather than over wire
fences, and at present virtually no use is made of them.[34] These
camels, incidentally, would be the optimum source for any
renewed effort at acclimatization in the United States, since
they come from a land uncontaminated by hoof and mouth
disease.

Although only feral animals are left, during the period of
the camel's heyday in Australia the acclimatization effort was
spectacularly successful. Not only were camels used as pack
animals, but they were harnessed to wagons, buggies, and
farm equipment as well. The idea for this may have come from
seeing Indian camel carts, but the harnessing technique was
decidedly European in origin, being an adaptation of the idea of
the horse collar; and the "Afghan" camel men never engaged
in carting.[35] There is no reason to doubt the assertion that with
continued scientific breeding the camel would have surpassed
any other type of draft animal.[36]

Whether similar success would have been achieved in the
United States if the Civil War had not intervened is hard to
say. Although agitation for importing camels arose about the
same time, quite independently, in both countries, and the
nature of the first serious experiments was similar, there were
important differences between the two countries, not the least
of which was that the aboriginal population of one was pas-
sive and impotent while that of the other was energetic and
warlike.

The story of the importation of camels to the United States
has been retold many times. The potential value of the animal
for exploring the frontier was recognized as early as 1836
by Major George H. Crosman of the U.S. Army.[37] Major
Henry C. Wayne picked up the idea from him and in 1848
suggested to the War Department that camels be imported for
military use. It was Wayne who engaged the interest of Senator Jefferson Davis of Mississippi, and it was Davis, finally, as
Secretary of War in the cabinet of Franklin Pierce who for-
mally urged Congressional action in 1853. In 1855 a bill was
passed authorizing $30,000 for the importation of camels.

Chosen to implement the project were Major Wayne and
Lieutenant David Dixon Porter, later to achieve fame as an ad-

118 Australian camel harnessed to buggy by horse-collar.

119 Australian buggy with two-camel team.

miral in the Civil War. Porter had been urged to volunteer by his relative Edward Fitzgerald Beale, Superintendent of Indian Affairs in California and Nevada. Beale's interest in camels, in turn, had been stimulated by reading Abbé Évariste-Regis Huc's colorful and adventure-filled account of his travels as a missionary in Central Asia, China, and Tibet.[38] Wayne preceded Porter to Europe to learn what he could about camels in London and Paris. Porter, when he arrived in Italy, paid a visit to the camel ranch at San Rossore and there became convinced of the beast's utility as a work animal. Porter's *Supply* put in at many Mediterranean ports, and the two officers even went to the Crimea to observe the camels in use there in the British army. But they did not, oddly enough, visit the Canary Islands where so many other would-be camel importers acquired their stock and which would have reduced by almost 3,000 miles the distance they had to sail with the animals aboard.

120 Australian six-camel team. Note "spiders" around hump used to hold collar in place and carry the weight of the trace chains.

121 Australian riding camel with two-man Indian *pakra* saddle. Compare figure 92.

122 Loading camel bound for the United States aboard Porter's *Supply* in 1856. No two-humped camels survived the trip.

On May 14, 1856, the *Supply* unloaded thirty-four camels at a small Texas port twenty miles south of Galveston. Nine months later Porter completed a second trip by setting down in Texas an additional forty-four animals. Thus was established the U.S. Army's first and last camel herd at Camp Verde sixty miles northwest of San Antonio. Ten years later in 1866 the army quartermaster at New Orleans received orders to sell the sixty-six camels remaining in the Camp Verde herd at auction. At $31 a head, the U.S. government liquidated its decade-long camel experiment.

Half of the decade that the camels were given to prove their worth, needless to say, was taken up by the Civil War. In fact, only one true test of their usefulness was ever made, and that one was entirely positive. In the fall of 1856 the War Department ordered a survey made of a new wagon road from Fort Defiance in New Mexico to the Colorado River on the California border. Lieutenant Edward Fitzgerald Beale, the same man who had persuaded Porter to volunteer for the mission to buy the camels, was selected to conduct the survey expedition, and twenty-five Camp Verde camels were put at his disposal. The camels joined the survey party on June 21,

1857, and the Colorado River was crossed exactly four months later on October 21. During this time the camels repeatedly proved their superiority, even to the extent of swimming the Colorado without a loss, though ten mules and two horses drowned.

In California Beale did some further experimenting with the camels and found that they flourished on his estate even in two or three feet of snow. Then at the beginning of 1858 Beale began his return trip to test the practicability of his newly surveyed route during the winter. Once again the camels demonstrated their usefulness. Beale reported the results of his two long journeys to Secretary of War Floyd, who in December of the same year reported to Congress that "the entire adaptation of camels to military operations on the plains may now be taken as demonstrated." He urged the appropriation of funds for the purchase of 1,000 more animals. His appeal, repeated in 1859 and 1860, went unheeded.

Up to this point American and Australian experience roughly coincide. Official interest had led to the initial large-scale importation, and the animal's value had been proven by its use on exploring expeditions. Nor was there much difference in the efforts taken to follow up this start. As in Australia, a number of private American companies and individuals saw bright opportunities in camel importation. Unfortunately, a Thomas Elder was not among them. Such animals as were brought in, fifteen two-humped camels from Manchuria to San Francisco in 1860 and twenty-two more in 1862, were used immediately as pack animals instead of being used for breeding. The second group, in fact, was reshipped to British Columbia to serve in pack trains in the Cariboo region. However, even if a stud had been established, the small herds involved could scarcely have produced enough animals to popularize their use. Geoffroy Saint-Hilaire around 1860 heard in Paris of a plan to import 120 camels from Africa, but this scheme, which might have proved as significant as Elder's, never came to fruition.[39]

Thus at the point in time when the Civil War drove other thoughts out of the minds of most Americans, there was every reason to expect that an important, and perhaps decisive, advance in transplantation of camels to the U.S. was about to be made. Thoughtful people were not unaware that breeding was necessary to establish the animal. Major Wayne himself was reprimanded at the time of the first importation for conducting breeding experiments instead of feasibility studies by which the War Department might justify to Congress the expenditures made (far less than the $30,000 authorized). Yet the breakthrough never came, and the camel episode was short-lived. If the War Department had followed Wayne's initiative, the Camp Verde herd could easily have numbered over two hundred by 1866 instead of a meagre sixty-six.

May Humphreys Stacey, a young Philadelphian in Beale's surveying party, wrote in his journal on the day the camels first joined the expedition: "What are these camels the representation of? Not a high civilization exactly, but of the 'go-aheadness' of the American character, which subdues even nature by its energy and perseverance."[40] Unfortunately, the armies of the North and the South requisitioned all available energy and perseverance after 1860 and gave the lie to Stacey's hopeful words. After the war, the linkage of military camels with Jefferson Davis probably would have served to stifle any renewal of interest, but there seems to have been none to stifle. This does not mean, however, that camels would definitely have become a fact of American life had it not been for the war. In comparison with Australia, the United States was much farther away from any source of camels, a circumstance that could only have served to increase the cost and risk of importation. But a more crucial factor may well have proved to be a human one. For every three to eight camels brought to Australia there was an average of one "Afghan" camel handler.[41] The success of the acclimatization effort in that country must surely be attributed in large part to these men, since they provided the techniques of training and handling that were needed to demonstrate the animal's true potential. They must also have helped set up procedures in Australian camel studs, although, for the most part, they bred camels themselves on only a small scale in their new country.[42]

Camel handlers were brought to the United States, too, with those few batches of camels that were actually imported; but they were few and are described as being of several different nationalities.[43] They appear to have been recruited in the various Mediterranean ports visited by Porter and Wayne. While this does not necessarily impugn their competence as camel drivers, it does suggest that they did not have at their command the kind of expertise in breeding camels in the desert which Australia's Baluchi and Rajasthani "Afghans" had. Therefore, it is questionable whether an American camel stud would have been as successful in establishing the species as the Australian studs were.

Finally, there is the matter of Indians. In Australia the Aborigines took to using camels very slowly and played a relatively small role in their history.[44] What the American Indians would have done with the animal is another matter entirely. Perhaps nothing, but possibly there is more than hot air in the intriguing vision set forth in 1854 by one of America's first students of ecology and one of the camel's strongest and most thoughtful supporters, Senator George Perkins Marsh of Vermont:

> The habits of these Indians much resemble those of the nomade [sic] Arabs, and the introduction of the camel among them would modify their modes of life as much as the use of the horse has done. For a time, indeed, the possession of this animal would only increase their powers of mischief; but it might in the long run prove the means of raising them to that state of semi-civilized life of which alone their native wastes seem susceptible. The products of the camel, with wool, skin, and flesh, would prove of inestimable value to these tribes, which otherwise are likely soon to perish with the buffalo and other large game animals; and the profit of transportation across our inland desert might have the same effect in reclaiming these barbarians which it has had upon the Arabs of the Sinaitic peninsula.[45]

Marsh's two published works on camels are filled with the kind of optimism that pervades this quotation. It is the same sort of optimism that one finds throughout the work cited so frequently in this chapter on acclimatization of animals by Isidore Geoffroy Saint-Hilaire. Possible difficulties are minimized, and the camel's (or other animal's) virtues are praised out of proportion. The Los Angeles Star, for instance, reported on July 21, 1858, that the largest of the government's camels in California "pack a ton and can travel sixteen miles an hour."[46] This alleged rate of speed, under an absolute maximum possible weight, exceeds that claimed for the finest riding camels,[47] but preposterous reports such as this and the enthusiasm of even judicious observers like David Dixon Porter, who wrote that the 250 camels at San Rossore did "work equal to that of a thousand horses,"[48] served to inflate people's expectations and perhaps thereby to defeat attempts at importation in some countries. For a more cautious estimate of the value of the camel to the West one must look at the experiences and opinions of military men in colonial areas.

Apart from the American experiment, which Marsh visualized leading eventually to camel-borne mountain howitzers and light artillery,[49] no Western army ever made significant use of camels outside their native territory. Within camel territory, on the other hand, there is a long history of utilization by Westerners up to and including the German army's organization of camel trains in World War II to carry gasoline to their tanks stranded beyond their supply line in southern Russia.[50] However, no purpose would be served by simply recounting a large number of unconnected experiments. Instead three general observations will be made for the light they shed upon broader aspects of Western experimentation with camels.

The first observation is that European soldiers did not learn the art of handling camels very quickly. A. G. Leonard writes of a British officer put in charge of organizing a camel train in Egypt: "Neither he nor any of his assistants had the slightest idea how to do so, for they were entirely ignorant, even in the most rudimentary way, of the camel and its capacity, and of the necessary equipment required."[51] As a result, in some of the early campaigns in which camels were used, losses among the animals were extremely high. The camels were simply worked to death by men who did not know their limits. This was true in particular during the second Afghan war (1878–1880) when the British lost 70,000 animals, and matters were scarcely better on the campaign to relieve General Gordon at Khartum in 1885.[52] The Russians had similar experiences in their campaigns against the Turkmen tribes of the Kara Kum desert. In 1879 they lost 3,000 or 4,000

123 Italian camel corps machine gun borne by camel.

of their 10,000 baggage camels because of overwork.[53]
Eventually steps were taken to remedy this sorry situation, and
later campaigns, such as Allenby's invasion of Palestine in
World War I, made use of baggage camels in a rational way
and avoided unnecessary losses.[54] All of this serves to reinforce
the point made previously that camels were successfully
acclimatized on a large scale only in Australia where a deliber-
ate effort was made to import knowledgeable camel drivers
and breeders along with the animals.

The second observation is that European military men
recognized that their soldiers, by and large, could never equal
their nomadic enemies in military camel skills. French
experience in the Sahara made this fact very clear. Several
separate French camel corps were organized at different times.
The first was authorized by Napoleon in Egypt in 1798 and
brought into being by General Cavelier.[55] The second was
organized in 1843 in newly French Algeria by General
Carbuccia, but it lasted an even shorter time than its predeces-
sor.[56] Later in the century several French officers penned
strong pleas for new camel units, but not until the century's
close did these appeals bear fruit.[57] Regular camel units were
established in 1905 at Timbuctoo and other points on the
southern side of the Sahara, and in the following years more
units were created in the same area and in Algeria and Morocco
as well.[58]

The lessons of this long period of proposal and experimentation are contained in several works written around the turn
of the century. Some of the conclusions are that the animals
should be purchased or requisitioned locally; hired native
drivers should be used for pack animals in a ratio of one to
three;[59] Tuareg riding saddles, despite their superiority, should
not be used because they are too difficult to use well; and the
soldiers should always be infantrymen who fight dismounted
since they can never equal the enemy in riding.[60] In short,
in the combat field as in the baggage train, optimum use of
camels could only be attained by very experienced camel
people.

The final observation is that despite their recognition that it
was more difficult to make effective military use of camels
than originally thought, Western military men came to the

conclusion that they were worth the trouble because they were so superior, at least in dry climates, to any other animal. In fact, the British proved willing to ship camels from one country to another for use in different wars. In the Crimea, for example, the British army observed by Porter and Wayne on their camel buying expedition made extensive use of Syrian one-humped camels until they succumbed to the climate;[61] and between 1901 and 1904 Indian camels were shipped to Somaliland for use in fighting the so-called "Mad Mullah" Muḥammad b. ᶜAbd Allāh.[62]

On balance, taking both military and civilian experiments together, it would be difficult to conclude that the West made very effective use of the camel. Certainly the animal's impact upon the West, even in its most arid colonial possessions, never approached its impact upon the society of the lands to which it was native. In the colonial field the West, for the most part, stuck by the wheel rather than acquiescing to the camel's established position of dominance. Roads and carriages followed the flag of empire. In the Western countries themselves, attempts at acclimatization were more often than not overly optimistic, too small in scale, and naive in their failure to take into account the need for experienced handlers and breeders to go along with the animals.

Yet the tremendous amount of thought and effort that went into the experiments recounted above and the many others that have not been mentioned show how seriously the West took the camel. The West was dedicated to developing wheeled transport, but it was not blind to the fact that in many circumstances the camel might provide a superior alternative. Looking back from an era when motorized transport can penetrate with ease to any point on the globe, it is almost impossible to visualize a different history of transportation in modern times, a history in which the camel might eventually have become a significant factor in several countries where it had not before existed. But in the middle of the nineteenth century, it was not at all apparent that the wheel was about to bring to a quick and decisive end its two millennium long rivalry with the camel. The camel still looked like a good idea.

10 The Return of the Wheel
and the Future of the Camel

The era of the pack camel is very near its end. No longer can
animal energy compete successfully in the world transport
economy. In effect, what this means is that wheeled vehicles
have at last won their long contest with pack animals, won it
despite the grave disadvantages—smog, superhighways, con-
gestion, traffic deaths—that they entail. Yet the use of the
wheel in modern times must not be thought of as being in-
separable from motorized transport. Up until the twentieth
century most improvements in wheeled transport took for
granted the use of animal energy to provide the motive force.
Therefore, it is possible to look beyond the actual fact that
what has replaced the pack camel has been the motor vehicle
and question how the camel-wheel competition would have
developed had the internal combustion engine or its equivalent
not been invented. In other words, would the European car-

riage and wagon have replaced the pack camel if the motor car had not?

The answer to this question must be a qualified yes, yes because the wheel was an integral part of the culture being exported by Europe in the age of imperialism, and qualified because a few desert routes might never have been exploitable even by camel-drawn carts. That the triumphant return of the wheel would have been rapid and irresistible is not at all certain, however. The Turks who entered and settled in the Middle East in a dominating role from the eleventh century onward were perfectly familiar with efficient wheeled transport, including camel-drawn carts, from their homeland in Central Asia, yet they did not spark a revolution in the Middle Eastern transport economy. Vehicles of one sort or another did reappear somewhat in cities subject to Turkish rule or influence, but the countryside remained the realm of the beast of burden.[1] It is particularly indicative of the weakness of Turkish cultural influence in this field that the primitive, solid wheeled oxcart of the Anatolian peasant did not undergo any technological improvements despite the fact that the Turkish *araba* of Central Asia was a much more efficient vehicle.

Military technique shows the greatest evidence of a Turkish openness toward wheeled transport. The Ottoman army's use of carts and wagons is not particularly indicative since Ottoman campaigns were often conducted in Europe where wheeled transport had never been challenged, but the experimentation of the Safavid dynasty (a Turkish regime ruling in Iran in the sixteenth and seventeenth centuries) with wheel-borne guns is proof of an interest in using wagons for military purposes. The Safavids adopted from the Ottomans a technique that had been found effective during the Hussite wars in Central Europe in the fifteenth century. This technique consisted of mounting several small guns in a single wagon and then chaining the wagons together in a defensive circle or *laager* to ward off cavalry attacks. In 1528 the Safavids are reported to have used seven hundred of these *arabas* mounted with four guns (*zarbzan*) to turn a seeming defeat by the Uzbeks in eastern Iran into a tremendous victory.[2] After that date the experiment seems to have been abandoned.

124 Turkish *araba* in Central Asia.

125 Solid-wheeled oxcart of Circassian (Anatolian) settler in Jordan.

However, even taking these mostly fruitless military experiments into account, it cannot be said that there was a heavy Turkish influence in the transportation field. Wheels did not really begin to return to the Middle East and North Africa until the advent of European imperialism. The Turks were, by and large, assimilated into the existing cultural pattern of the Middle East. The Europeans did their utmost to assimilate the Middle East and North Africa into the existing cultural pattern of Europe. The ultimate success or failure of Western cultural impingement on the societies of the rest of the world is certainly far from being determined; but since efficient transportation is so much a part of Western ideas of manufacturing and marketing which have been among the most exportable of Western cultural traits, it is hard to imagine any society remaining wheelless for long once it had assimilated these Western notions.[3] Hence, the wheel's return may be seen as inevitable.

Nevertheless, if the carriage had remained the ultimate expression of Western thinking in land transportation instead of the automobile, the effect of the return of the wheel to the Middle East would have been entirely different. Heavy draft camels could have been adapted for pulling wagons just as they were in Australia,[4] and this would have preserved intact the traditional economic underpinning of some camel-breeding societies. Inevitable though it may have been given the impact of imperialism, the return of the wheel need not have radically altered the pattern of camel breeding in the Middle East and North Africa. It was the internal combustion engine that made the return of the wheel revolutionary by making traditional patterns of camel nomadism obsolete.

For centuries camel herding had proved a rational means of utilizing submarginal land. At no cost in agricultural resources the needs of the transportation economy had been adequately satisfied. All that was called for was the investment in human resources needed to carry on a productive level of camel breeding. Naturally, this was not the only or the original rationale for camel breeding, and even today a major camel-breeding culture in Somalia is not oriented toward supplying transportation. Still, the production of work animals played a significant enough role in the herding economy of many Arabian and

Saharan tribes for its obsolescence to bring those tribes' very existence into question. Even if a direct causal connection cannot always be traced, there is no doubt but that the sedentarization of camel nomads in the twentieth century is closely linked with a reduction in the demand for camels as beasts of burden.

By the 1920s it was already evident that camel populations were declining.[5] Raw data on world camel population is misleading since the accuracy of statistics from many camel-breeding countries has changed drastically over the years, but figures from three countries where the camel was once used primarily for labor are very suggestive.[6] Since the period 1947–1952, the camel population of Turkey has declined by 76,000 or 71 percent, that of Iran by 275,000 or 61 percent, and that of Syria by 68,000 or 90 percent. Yet worldwide the reported population of camels has increased during the same period from 10,273,000 to 14,595,000. This may be compared, incidentally, with Cauvet's estimate in 1925 of six million and an estimate in 1876 of one and a half million.[7] The increasing inadequacy of reported statistics as one goes back in time is clearly illustrated by these figures.

Figures to the contrary notwithstanding, therefore, there is reason to believe that the camel is on the road to decline and with it nomadic camel breeding as a way of life. All that separates the camel from an increasingly bleak future culminating, perhaps, in the reversion of abandoned herds to a feral state, as has happened in Australia, is its potential as a meat producer. On this potential there are conflicting opinions. Leaving aside questions of flavor and texture, the answers to which vary greatly according to the diet and condition of the animal and the prejudice of the consumer, the debate is whether the camel's ability to make desert land productive is valuable enough to offset certain disadvantages in using it as a meat animal.

Knut Schmidt-Nielsen has put the case for the meat camel most forcefully. "From the theoretical considerations," he writes, "it seems amazingly clear that the camel offers a most obvious solution to increased meat production in arid zones with a low natural vegetation density that cannot easily be increased."[8] He notes that besides being able to go for prolonged periods without water, which increases the area in which it can graze around a water source well beyond that of a sheep, the camel recycles urea recovered by its kidneys and converts it into protein, thus supplementing the low protein content of desert plants.[9] Yet while observing that the camel is ideally adapted to converting useless wasteland into usable rangeland, Schmidt-Nielsen gives passing recognition to the fact that with the camel declining as a transport animal and with the advantages of modern settled life being so broadly proclaimed, the camel nomads themselves may not long remain to produce the camels.

The negative side of camel breeding for meat production has been put by Thomas Stauffer in a mathematical comparison of the dynamics of sheep and goat herding and camel herding.[10] He points out that despite the camel's superior adaptation to submarginal land, the risk factor in camel breeding is extremely high. Camels rut once a year. The gestation period is one year so that the calves are dropped during the good pasture season which normally coincides with the rutting season. The nursing period lasts for another year thus making it impossible for a female camel to bear at a higher rate than one calf every two years. Finally, the young female camel is not normally expected to begin bearing until it is six years old.

By comparison both sheep and goats can begin bearing between one and two years of age; it is possible to breed them twice a year; and they frequently have twins. Consequently, if there is any kind of sudden drop in herd size due to adverse weather or disease, the sheep and goat herder is capable of replenishing his herds from natural increase much more rapidly than the camel herder. Historically, one outcome of this higher risk factor in camel breeding has been institutionalized raiding or rustling of stock from other tribes;[11] but this, obviously, could have no place in any program for exploiting camels for meat production at the present day.

Does a rosy future await the camel as a meat producer? Or is camel breeding for meat production too risky a proposition to be undertaken seriously? One possible answer might be gleaned from looking at the consumption of camel meat at the present day. In countries like Morocco and Libya camel meat is very common, and in Egypt some 36,000 camels are sold

each year on the Cairo camel market, mostly for meat.[12] Yet
this evidence of a substantial trade in camel meat may not be
truly indicative of the viability of the enterprise. Moroccan
camel meat comes from Saharan tribes in Mauretania and eastern Morocco, areas that have been touched very little by the
modern world. Libya until recently was a country with minimal
economic potential ruled in accordance with traditional concepts of society and economy. Egypt receives its camels from
the Sudan where nomadic tribal life has not yet felt the impact
of modernization. In short, it can be argued that the camel
merchants of today are simply reaping the last harvests of a
herding economy that is passing away. It is certainly significant
that fifty years ago the Cairo camel market was supplied from
Syria and Arabia as much as from the more distant Sudan. But
commercial camel breeding has virtually passed away in Syria
and in much of Arabia, and it seems destined to pass away
eventually in the Sudan for the same reasons. Once the camel
ceases being used for transportation, meat production alone
provides insufficient motivation to continue leading the life of
a camel nomad.

The Somalis, with their vast camel herds and a cultural pattern which stresses the intrinsic value of the camel more than
its carrying ability, may outlast the general decline of camel
nomadism, but otherwise there is every reason to believe that
with the passage of time camel nomadism will become increasingly unattractive as a way of life and the herding of camels by
this means a vanishing phenomenon. In the long run, if the
camel is to remain a significant domestic animal, new patterns
of exploitation must be developed. It is hard to believe that
eventually the world demand for animal protein will not make
the camel's ability to make good use of desert land economically profitable. Yet the low density of vegetation of desert
land makes necessary a broad dispersal of livestock if over-
grazing is to be avoided, and this engenders problems of control and delivery. Thus while tribal nomadism seems destined
to disappear as a mode of exploiting the domestic camel, the
modern techniques of livestock management developed for
cattle may not be easily adapted to providing an alternative
mode.

A few years ago it would have seemed whimsical to suggest

new experimentation with camel breeding in the United States. The fact that there might be a limit to the quantity of inexpensive beef this country could produce was not then generally recognized. Subsequent events, however, have brought the problems of feeding the world's population, and in particular of supplying it with animal protein, to the attention of everyone. Consequently, a suggestion that camels be reintroduced to this country with the ultimate intent of providing a new source of inexpensive meat may now be accorded a serious reception.

The camel converts low protein desert vegetation into meat. Plants that other meat animals will not or cannot eat afford a camel an adequate diet. One sight of a camel chewing up a prickly pear cactus, thorns and all, is sufficient to remove anyone's doubts about the animal's ability to flourish on desert vegetation. Since the United States has within its borders vast tracts of desert land, any possibility of using that land for food production seems worthy of consideration.

Immediate production of meat animals could scarcely be expected, of course. Experimentation of many different kinds would first have to be carried out. How are the animals best bred for meat production? How are they best fattened? What are the optimum techniques of range management? These and other questions would have to be answered before *chameau rôti au jus naturel* could be seen on a restaurant menu, or even camel sausage. But the experimentation should be undertaken. A valuable potential food resource should not be ignored simply because of an undeserved reputation for being stupid and nasty.

As stated at the beginning of this chapter, the era of the pack camel is very near its end, and an exciting and productive era it has been. A great many major historical events have been linked with the rise of the camel from a milk producer on the coast of the southern Arabia to a dominant figure in the world transport economy capable of driving the wheel out of existence over a vast area. Long distance caravan trading, which has barely been touched upon in this book, has been a factor of enormous significance in world economic history. The entire culture of large parts of the world has been visibly influenced by the use of the pack camel. Yet the fact that this era is ending does not mean that the camel is of no more use to man. If meat production does not kindle the same romantic flame in the breast that a caravan trekking across the Sahara does, it nevertheless fits into what remains of the once broad relationship between man and the animal world. The camel can remain in the service of man, and the disdainful expression on its face will ever call to mind the past era when the camel was superior to man's proud invention, the wheel.

Bibliographical Essay   Notes   Index

Bibliographical Essay

Geographically and chronologically this book has covered a very wide range and, as stated at the outset, no attempt has been made to be exhaustive or definitive in any given subject area. As a result of the breadth of coverage, the bibliography contained in the notes is extremely long. Yet most of the works in it contributed only tiny fragments of information to the discussion. Consequently, a simple compilation of these sources would be quite misleading to anyone who wished to explore further the history of the camel. What is proposed instead is to single out in the various subject areas dealt with a few specific works in which information on camels can be found in a more or less concentrated form or in which an introduction to the overall topic under discussion can be obtained.

The place to start is with the literature devoted exclusively to the subject of camels. Numerous books on camels have been written, but most of them are exceedingly difficult to locate. Once located, they seldom provide much enlightenment on historical questions. The authors' viewpoints are normally determined by career experience in veterinary medicine or military experience in colonial territories. What historical information on camels is contained in them is usually fragmentary, disjointed, and uncritical. One should not embark upon a study of camels in any specific context without a sound understanding of the animal's zoological characteristics, but aside from this there is often little to be gleaned of use to the historian from the general works on camels.

Within this group far and away the greatest breadth of perspective and knowledge is displayed by Commandant G. Cauvet of the French North African camel corps. His virtually unobtainable book, *Le Chameau* (Paris: J. B. Baillière, 1925–1926), 2 vols., is a mine of information, rather loosely organized and quite uncritically assembled from many sources, on almost every aspect of camel lore. Cauvet's strongly held but poorly substantiated views on various subjects diminish the work's authoritativeness, but it is an excellent source for references to other literature. Also in French is G. G. Curasson's *Le Chameau et ses maladies* (Paris: Vigot, 1947), perhaps the best available veterinary work but of quite limited interest for other matters.

In English the most valuable general work, although it bears no comparison to Cauvet, is A. S. Leese's *A Treatise on the One Humped Camel in Health and Disease* (Stamford, Eng.: Haynes and Son, [1927]). Leese was a camel veterinarian in the British army and writes from a great deal of experience. Only a small portion of the book is of general interest, the rest being devoted to veterinary matters. Leese was also founder of the Imperial Fascist League in Britain before World War II and has written a curious little memoir entitled *Out of Step; Events in the Two Lives of an Anti-Jewish Camel-Doctor* (Guildford: A. S. Leese, 1951).

Quite similar to Leese's book is H. E. Cross, *The Camel and Its Diseases* (London: Baillière, Tindall and Cox, 1917). Cross also gives a valuable account of camel stud farm management in India. A. G. Leonard, another British officer, wrote *The Camel: Its Uses and Management* (London: Longmans, Green, 1894). Unlike the first two, this book is written from the perspective of a transport officer rather than that of a veterinarian. Leonard's experience came in Egypt and the Sudan, but he does have a bit of information on South Africa as well.

Two other works get away from the military entirely and are both readable and informative. They do not, however, reflect firsthand experience. One is *The Camel: His Organization, Habits, and Uses* (Boston: Gould and Lincoln, 1856) by George Perkins Marsh, who was senator from Vermont and ambassador to Italy as well as being a noted gentleman scholar. Although Marsh was

interested in the camel importation experiment in this country, his **273**
book is primarily a general treatise on camels. The other work is an
article by C. Mirèio Legge, "The Arabian and the Bactrian
Camel," *Journal of the Manchester Geographical Society,* 46 (1935–
1936), 21–48. Though brief, this is one of the few general works
that says anything about the two-humped camel.

In Italian two outstanding works are Ivo Droandi, *Il Camello*
(Florence: Istituto Agricolo Coloniale Italiano, 1936) and M. A.
Vitale, *Il Cammello ed I Reparti Cammellati* (Rome: Sindicato
Italiano Arti Grafiche, [1928]). The former is written by a veterinarian, but the scope of its coverage is very broad, much more so
than any of the veterinary works referred to hitherto. The latter
is written by an officer in the Italian camel corps and contains
the fullest account of how a modern camel corps operated and
how the camel can be adapted for military service.

In the general area of the history of animal domestication, extensive introductory orientation is available in F. E. Zeuner, *A
History of Domesticated Animals* (New York: Harper and Row,
1963), and a broad variety of methodological viewpoints can
be examined in P. J. Ucko and G. W. Dimbleby, eds., *The Domestication and Exploitation of Plants and Animals* (London: Gerald
Duckworth, 1969).

On the specific question of the early domestication of camels,
two articles by Reinhard Walz are crucial, "Zum Problem des
Zeitpunkts der Domestikation der altweltlichen Cameliden," *Zeitschrift der deutschen morgenländischen Gesellschaft,* new series,
26 (1951), 29–51, and "Neue Untersuchungen zum Domestikationsproblem der altweltlichen Cameliden," in the same journal,
new series, 29 (1954), 45–87. These articles are written by an
orientalist and generally concur with and support the theories of
W. F. Albright. Also of interest are M. Mikesell, "Notes on the
Dispersal of the Dromedary," *Southwestern Journal of Anthropology,* 11 (1955), 231–245, and "The Coming of the Camel,"
chapter 4 of R. J. Forbes, *Studies in Ancient Technology* (Leiden:
Brill, 1965), vol. 2. The former reflects the interests of a geographer,
the latter those of a technological historian. Both are more compilations of information than expressions of ideas.

Geographically, the history of camel domestication has been
discussed much more extensively for some areas than for others.
The most noteworthy work pertaining to North Africa is É.
Demougeot, "Le Chameau et l'Afrique du Nord romaine," *Annales:
Économies, Sociétés, Civilisations,* 15 (1960), 209–247. Although
it concentrates upon the Roman period, it brings up to date a
variety of on-going arguments on the subject of camel domestica-

tion in that area. On the specific subject of Saharan rock art the best introduction is Henri Lhote, "Le Cheval et le chameau dans les peintures et gravures rupestres du Sahara," *Bulletin de l'Institut Fondamental d'Afrique Noire*, 15 (1953), 1138–1228. The literature on Saharan rock art is quite extensive, however, and Lhote's coverage of the subject should not be regarded as definitive.

From the numerous articles dealing with ancient Egyptian camels, or the lack thereof, one could select Joseph P. Free's "Abraham's Camels," *Journal of Near Eastern Studies*, 3 (1944), 187–193, as giving a broad selection of the pertinent evidence. Free's article is imbued with his conviction that camels did, in fact, exist in ancient Egypt.

The central areas of the Middle East are more or less covered by Walz's articles mentioned above. India is rather poorly surveyed in P. K. Gode, "Notes on the History of the Camel in India between B.C. 500 and A.D. 800," *Janus*, 47 (1958), 133–138, and China distinctly better treated, albeit from a largely literary standpoint, in Edward H. Schafer, "The Camel in China down to the Mongol Dynasty," *Sinologica*, 2 (1950), 165–194, 263–290.

The arcane subject of camel saddles has been best treated by T. Monod, "Notes sur le harnachement chamelier," *Bulletin de l'Institut Fondamental d'Afrique Noire*, series B, 29 (1967), 234–306; but for the impact of camel saddling on history it is important to read W. Dostal, "The Evolution of Bedouin Life," *L'Antica Società Beduina*, ed. F. Gabrieli, (Rome: Centro di studi semitici, Istituto di studi orientali, Università, 1959), pp. 11–34.

Harnessing, unlike camel saddling, has been a subject of academic interest for several decades. The still valuable pioneering work is Richard Lefebvre des Noëttes, *La Force motrice animale à travers les âges* (Paris: Berger-Levrault, 1924). A valuable updating and reconsideration of his work is contained in Joseph Needham and Wang Ling, *Science and Civilisation in China* (Cambridge, Eng.: Cambridge University Press, 1965), IV, part II, pp. 243–253, 303–328. Camel harnessing in particular seems never to have been made an object of study up until now.

Specific studies of camel-herding societies in modern times vary in availability from area to area, but they vary even more in the degree of attention paid to the livestock economy of the society in question. An exemplary work is Johannes Nicolaisen, *Ecology and Culture of the Pastoral Tuareg* (Copenhagen: The National Museum of Copenhagen, 1963). He discusses the breeding practices and overall livestock economy of the Tuareg of Niger and southern Algeria in sufficient detail to allow the reader to make sense of the bits and pieces of information scattered throughout the extensive

literature dealing with the Sahara. It is clearly the place to begin **275**
for this area.

Unfortunately, there is no equivalent work for the important
camel-breeding society of Somalia. Two books by I. M. Lewis,
Peoples of the Horn of Africa (London: International African Institute, 1955) and *A Pastoral Democracy* (London: Oxford University
Press, 1961) provide excellent orientation on all Somali topics, but
a detailed treatment of their camel-herding practices does not seem
to be available.

For the Arab bedouin there is, again, a vast literature and one
from which a detailed view of Arab camel culture can be extracted
with somewhat more ease than one can from the Saharan literature.
Yet no single work gives a thorough account, which leaves the problem of constructing a general picture from information drawn
from a broad geographical area in which there may be substantial
variation. Of particular value are the works of Alois Musil,
especially his *Manners and Customs of the Rwala Bedouins* (New
York: American Geographical Society, 1928), H. R. P. Dickson,
The Arab of the Desert (London: Allen and Unwin, 1949), and
Wilfred Thesiger, *Arabian Sands* (London: Longmans, Green,
1959). The first deals with a tribe from the area of Jordan and
northern Arabia, the second with Arabs from Kuwait, and the
third with tribes in the far south of the peninsula on the northern
and southern borders of the Rubᶜ al-Khali or Empty Quarter.
Among earlier works on the bedouin Arabs the most valuable is
J. L. Burckhardt, *Notes on Bedouins and Wahhabis* (London:
Henry Colburn and Richard Bentley, 1830). A large compilation of
useful information on specific tribes and their economy is *A
Handbook of Arabia*, 2 vols., put out by the Admiralty War Staff,
Intelligence Division, in 1916. A unique study of the caravan trade
on the fringes of the Syrian desert is C. P. Grant, *The Syrian
Desert* (London: A. & C. Black, 1937).

A great deal has been written about the Arabs in the time of
Muhammad, but the outstanding general description of bedouin
life at that time remains Henri Lammens, *Le Berceau de l'Islam*
(Rome: Pontificii Instituti Biblici, 1914). More a curiosity than a
useful reference tool is the exhaustive compilation of camel related
terms in classical Arabic by Josef Freiherr von Hammer-Purgstall,
Das Kamel, Denkschriften der kaiserlichen Akademie der Wissenschaften, Philosophisch-historische Classe, 6 (Vienna, 1855).

Classical Arabic literature seldom deals directly with camel breeding, although frequent mention of camels in early Arabic poetry
did give rise to some discussion of camel terminology in philological
works. The best medieval Arabic source on camels is al-Jāḥiẓ,

Kitāb al-Ḥayawān, ed. ᶜAbd as-Sallām Muhammad Hārūn (Cairo: Muṣṭafā al-Bābī al-Ḥalabī, 1938–45), 7 vols. The information on camels is widely scattered throughout the work, but the edition cited has a good index of animal species. A much less extensive and informative compilation of animal materials, but one which is available in English translation, is ad-Damīrī, *Ḥayāt al-Ḥayawān (A Zoological Lexicon),* tr. A. S. G. Jayakar (London: Luzac, 1906), 2 vols. Here the information is collected under the names of the separate animals, and the index identifies the species indicated by the Arabic terms.

There is surprisingly little written about camel culture in Central Asia, but the article of Jean-Paul Roux, "Le Chameau en Asie Centrale," *Central Asiatic Journal,* 5 (1959–1960), 35–76, is in general excellent. It concentrates upon the position of the camel in the history and world view of Central Asian Turkish society. A more recent, first-hand account, but one which is limited by the author's overriding interest in veterinary medicine and practical animal husbandry, is contained in articles by Viktor N. Kolpakov, "Ueber Kamelkreuzungen," and "Das turkmenische Kamel (Arwana)," *Berliner tieraerztliche Wochenschrift,* 51 (1935), 617–622, 507–573.

In Central Asia as in the Sahara and Arabia there is much to be gleaned from travel literature, but the information is widely scattered and hard to assemble into a general view. The outstanding works in the travel field dealing with camels are by Owen Lattimore, *The Desert Road to Turkestan* (London: Methuen, 1928) and *Mongol Journeys* (New York: Doubleday, Doran, 1941). The former gives a good picture of camel procedures used by Chinese caravan men and the latter an equally good picture of the somewhat different practices of Mongol camel herders. Several travel accounts from Central Asia discuss the question of the wild or feral camels in the Gobi and Lop Nor areas. There is also a body of literature dealing with the wild camels specifically. This includes A. G. Bannikov, "Distribution géographique et biologie du cheval souvage et du chameau de Mongolie *(Equus Przewalski* et *Camelus Bactrianus),*" *Mammalia,* 22 (1958), 152–160; G. Littledale, "Fieldnotes on the Wild Camels of Lob-Nor," *Proceedings of the Zoological Society,* 66 (London, 1894), 446–448; and Ivor Montagu, "Colour-Film Shots of the Wild Camel," *Proceedings of the Zoological Society,* 129 (London, 1957), 592–595.

Finally, the subject of acclimatization of animals to different parts of the globe in the nineteenth century is well introduced by Isidore Geoffroy Saint-Hilaire, *Acclimatation et domestication des*

animaux utiles (Paris: Librairie Agricole de la Maison Rustique, **277**
1861). For a bibliographical guide to the literature on camel use
in the United States see Albert H. Greenly, "Camels in America,"
The Papers of the Bibliographical Society of America, 46 (1952),
359–372. Anything important that one might wish to know about
camels in Australia is contained in Tom L. McKnight, *The Camel in
Australia* (Melbourne: Melbourne University Press, 1969).

Notes

Apologia

1. "Le chameau et la roue au Moyen-Orient," *Annales: économies, sociétés, civilisations,* 24 (1969), 1092–1103; "Why They Lost the Wheel," *ARAMCO World,* 24 (1973), 22–25.

1   The Camel and the Wheel

1. A recent general work is Lázló Tarr, *The History of the Carriage* (Budapest: Corvina Press, 1969).

2. C. F. Volney, *Voyage en Égypte et en Syrie* (Paris: Bossange Frères, 1822), II, 260.

3. Alexander Russell, *The Natural History of Aleppo* (London: G. G. and J. Robinson, 1794), p. 166.

4. Xavier Raymond, "Afghanistan," in Louis Dubeux and V. Valmont, *Tartarie, Beloutchistan, Boutan et Népal* (Paris: Firmin Didot Frères, 1848), p. 61.

5. Henry Baker Tristram, *The Great Sahara* (London: J. Murray, 1860), p. 295.

6. E. Lévi-Provençal, *Histoire de l'Espagne musulmane* (Paris: G. P. Maisonneuve, 1953), III, 93.

7. Jean Le Coz, *Le Rharb; fellahs et colons* (Rabat: Ministry of Education of Morocco and Ministry of Education of France, 1964), I, 354.

8. S. D. Goitein, *A Mediterranean Society*, vol. I, *Economic Foundations* (Berkeley: University of California Press, 1967), p. 275.

9. Prof. Hans Eberhard Mayer, personal communication.

10. One painting by the famous artist of the early sixteenth century Bihzad shows a completely realistic and credible horse-drawn cart. The design of the vehicle, however, shows it to be a Central Asian Turkish *araba*. This is a sign of the reintroduction of the wheel to the Middle East by the Turks, and the fact that the *araba* is so rarely depicted indicates how resistant the culture of the area was to this reintroduction. For further discussion see chapter 10. Thomas W. Arnold, *Bihzād and His Paintings in the Zafar-Nāmah Ms.* (London: Bernard Quaritch, 1930), pl. IX.

A second credible vehicle, one with four wheels, is shown in a Persian miniature of the sixteenth century (*Mostra d'Arte Iranica: Roma—Palazzo Brancaccio 1956*, [Milan: "Silvana" Editoriale d'Arte, 1956], pl. 103). Unfortunately, the horses drawing it have been so completely consumed by a dragon that the harnessing method cannot be determined.

11. Collection of the Fogg Art Museum #1955.12.

12. Ernst J. Grube, *The World of Islam* (London: Paul Hamlyn, 1966), p. 92.

13. René Patris, *La Guirlande de l'Iran* (n.p.: Flammarion, 1948), p. 30.

14. Arthur Upham Pope, ed., *A Survey of Persian Art* (Oxford: Oxford University Press, 1938), V, pl. 832D.

15. European depictions of vehicles and harnesses are not always highly accurate, either, but enough reasonably decipherable pictures exist to give a good impression of the main lines of technological development.

16. M. Rodinson, "ᶜAdjala," *Encyclopaedia of Islam*, new ed. (Leiden: E. J. Brill, 1960——), I, 205–206.

17. M. Rodinson, "Sur l'araba," *Journal Asiatique*, 245 (1957), 273–280; M. Rodinson and G. L. M. Clauson, "Araba," *Encyclopaedia of Islam*, new ed., I, 556–558.

18. Useful collections of photographs may be found in R. Lefebvre des Noëttes, *L'Attelage; le cheval de selle à travers les âges* (Paris: A. Picard, 1931), and Paul Vigneron, *Le Cheval dans l'antiquité gréco-romaine* (Nancy: Faculté des lettres et des Sciences humaines de l'Université de Nancy, 1968), II.

19. J. Sion, "Quelques problèmes de transports dans l'antiquité: **281**
le point de vue d'un géographe mediterranéen," *Annales d'Histoire
Économique et Sociale,* 7 (1935), 630–632.

20. R. Ghirshman, *Iran from the Earliest Times to the Islamic
Conquest* (Baltimore: Penguin Books, 1961), pp. 145–46, 187; R. J.
Forbes, *Studies in Ancient Technology* (Leiden: E. J. Brill, 1965),
II, 138.

21. Allan Chester Johnson, *Roman Egypt,* vol. II of *An Economic
Survey of Ancient Rome,* ed. Tenney Frank (Baltimore: Johns
Hopkins Press, 1936), p. 403.

22. Johnson, *Roman Egypt,* pp. 405, 407.

23. See chapter 5.

24. B. H. Warmington, *Carthage* (Harmondsworth: Penguin
Books, 1964), pp. 110, 130.

25. Forbes, *Ancient Technology,* II, 189.

26. Victor Chapot, *La Frontière de l'Euphrate de Pompée à la
conquête arabe* (Paris: Albert Fontemoing, 1907), pp. 172–173,
184, 222.

27. Chapot, *La Frontière,* pp. 181, 220; Johnson, *Roman Egypt,*
p. 631.

28. Roman Ghirshman, *Iran: Parthes et Sassanides* (Paris: Gallimard, 1962), pl. 367.

29. Rodinson, "°Adjala," p. 205; el-Bekri, *Description de
l'Afrique septentrionale,* tr. MacGuckin de Slane (Algiers: Adolphe
Jourdan, 1913), p. 36.

30. Forbes, *Ancient Technology,* II, 150.

31. J. G. Fevrier, *Essai sur l'histoire politique et économique de
Palmyre* (Paris: J. Vrin, 1931), pp. 31, 60–61.

32. A. H. M. Jones, *The Later Roman Empire, 284–602* (Oxford:
Blackwell, 1964), II, 841.

33. Forbes, *Ancient Technology,* II, 159.

34. In twelfth century Egypt the standard load was a scant 500
pounds. S. D. Goitein, *A Mediterranean Society* (Berkeley: University of California Press, 1967), I, 220, 335. For modern times
standard loads are given by A. S. Leese, *A Treatise on the One-
Humped Camel in Health and Disease* (Stamford, Eng.: Haynes
and Son, [1927]), pp. 114–115, for different types of camels in
different countries. A load of 430 pounds would be on the lower
side of the range of weights he gives, which extends up to 1,200
pounds for the very best animals.

35. Persuasive arguments in favor of a load limit higher than
500 pounds have been presented by J. Sion ("Quelques problèmes," pp. 628–629), and A. Burford ("Heavy Transport in Classical Antiquity," *Economic History Review,* ser. 2, 13 [1960], 1–18),

but even though the maximum load may well have exceeded 500 pounds, the standard load could still have been at the lower figure. In Australia, for example, the standard load for a draft camel was 1,000 pounds, although on occasion loads as heavy as 10,000 were pulled. H. M. Barker, *Camels and the Outback* (London: Angus and Robertson, 1964), pp. 91, 78. It has also been suggested (Tarr, *The Carriage*, p. 148) that loads were kept artificially low to save wear on the roads, but it is not at all clear that two carts carrying 1,000 pounds each would necessarily cause less wear than a single cart carrying 2,000 pounds.

36. In Egypt in the first century A.D. it cost 5 drachmae a day to have sheaves carried in a wagon and only 1.04 drachmae to hire a camel for the same purpose. Johnson, *Roman Egypt*, p. 405. Whether these figures are compatible in time and place is uncertain.

37. Owen Lattimore, *The Desert Road to Turkestan* (London: Methuen, 1928), p. 226.

38. Charles Issawi, ed., *The Economic History of Iran 1800–1914* (Chicago: University of Chicago Press, 1971), p. 204.

39. J.-L. Carbuccia, *Du dromadaire comme bête de somme et comme animal de guerre* (Paris: J. Dumaire, 1853), pp. 12–13.

40. Arthur Glyn Leonard, *The Camel: Its Uses and Management* (London: Longmans, Green, 1894), pp. 291, 295.

41. Leese, *The One-Humped Camel*, pp. 121–122.

42. Leonard, *The Camel*, pp. 329–330.

43. Johnson, *Roman Egypt*, pp. 230–232.

44. R. Lefebvre des Noëttes, *La Force motrice animale à travers les âges* (Paris: Berger-Levrault, 1924).

45. Forbes, *Ancient Technology*, II, 159; Leese, *The One-Humped Camel*, pp. 117–118.

46. There is a recorded instance of a mule wagon being sold in Roman Egypt for 80 drachmae, approximately one third the cost of an ox. Johnson, *Roman Egypt*, p. 407.

47. Plutarch, *The Lives of the Noble Grecians and Romans*, tr. J. Dryden (New York: Modern Library, n.d.), pp. 748–749.

48. Passenger vehicles were prohibited from Rome by the emperor Claudius and restricted in the rest of Italy. Tarr, *The Carriage*, p. 149. Cicero condemned Verres, governor of Sicily, for riding in a litter instead of on horseback as was appropriate for a military officer. 2 Verr., 4, 53; 5, 27, discussed in V. M. Scramuzza, "Roman Sicily," in *An Economic Survey of Ancient Rome*, ed. Tenney Frank (Baltimore: Johns Hopkins Press, 1937), III, 292–293.

49. In Syria some Roman roads underwent little deterioration; they simply fell out of use. Forbes, *Ancient Technology*, II, 150.

2 The Origin of Camel Domestication

1. Brief descriptions of the prehistoric development of the camel may be found in F. E. Zeuner, *A History of Domesticated Animals* (London: Hutchinson, 1963), p. 340, and Ivo Droandi, *Il Cammello* (Florence: Istituto Agricolo Coloniale Italiano, 1936), pp. 3–25.

2. Droandi, *Il Cammello*, pp. 29–30, 39–41; Georges Dennler de La Tour, "Zur Vererbung der Höcker beim Kamel, Dromedary und Tulu," *Säugetierkundliche Mitteilungen*, 19 (1971), 193–194; Viktor N. Kolpakow, "Ueber Kamelkreuzungen," *Berliner Tier-aertzliche Wochenschrift*, 51 (1935), 617–622.

3. The person primarily responsible for unraveling the age-old riddle of how the camel goes without water is Professor Knut Schmidt-Nielson, who has carried out his work primarily in Algeria and Australia where only the one-humped species is found.

4. The great Arabic writer al-Jāḥiẓ (d. 869) states quite clearly that camels, meaning one-humped Arab camels, die in Anatolia where the climate is colder and in many places moister than that of the camels' homeland. *Kitāb al-Ḥayawān*, ed. ᶜAbd as-Sallām Muḥammad Hārūn (Cairo: Muṣṭafā al-Bābī al-Ḥalabī, 1938–1945), III, 434; VII, 135. In modern times the same view is expressed by Henry J. Van Lennep, *Travels in Little-Known Parts of Asia Minor* (London: John Murray, 1870), II, 163. The inability of the two-humped camel, or more precisely the cross between the one-humped and two-humped camel, to bear heat is attested by a letter from H. Pognon, French consul at Aleppo, dated January 8, 1899, as quoted by F.-K. Lesbre, "Recherches anatomiques sur les camélidés," *Archives du muséum d'histoire naturelle de Lyon*, 8 (1900), 138.

5. Leese, *The One-Humped Camel*, p. 51, describes hill camels as having round, hard feet as opposed to the oval, soft feet of plains camels.

6. Camels in the Egyptian delta, for example, become accustomed to frequent waterings (Leese, *The One-Humped Camel*, p. 59), and the same is true of riverine camels generally (p. 52). The Bawāṭin breed of camel from Oman is said to desire water every day. G. Rentz, "Djazīrat al-ᶜArab," *Encyclopaedia of Islam*, new ed., I, 541. Among two-humped camels, those of Bukhara require frequent watering. Louis Dubeaux and V. Valmont, *Tartarie, Beloutchistan, Boutan et Népal* (Paris: Firmin Didot Frères, 1848), p. 18.

7. According to Herodotus (VII, 125) the lions of Thrace had a singular taste for the camels in the baggage train of Xerxes, preferring them, although they were previously unfamiliar with them, both to men and to other pack animals.

8. A good summary of scientific conclusions regarding the

284

camel's use of water is to be found in Knut Schmidt-Nielson's
"Animals and Arid Conditions: Physiological Aspects of Produc-
tivity and Management," *The Future of Arid Lands* (Washington,
D.C.: American Association for the Advancement of Science, 1956),
pp. 368–382.

9. Schmidt-Nielsen has observed that "it may also be of considerable significance that the camel, with progressing dehydration,
tends to expose as small an area as possible of the body surface to
the radiation from the sun by assuming a position sitting on the
ground with the legs under the body and the trunk oriented
lengthwise to the direction of the sun's rays." "Body Temperature
of the Camel and Its Relation to Water Economy," *American
Journal of Physiology*, 188 (1957), 108.

10. Somali camels are unique among one-humped camels in
developing flaccid humps. Droandi, *Il Cammello*, p. 381.

11. Reinhard Walz, "Zum Problem des Zeitpunkts der Domestikation der altweltlichen Cameliden," *Zeitschrift der Deutschen
Morgenländischen Gesellschaft*, n.s. 26 (1951), 43.

12. H. Gauthier-Pilters, "Quelques observations sur l'écologie
et l'ethologie du dromadaire dans le Sahara nord-occidental,"
Mammalia, 22 (1958), 145.

13. Genesis 12:14–16; 24:10–67; 31:17–35; 37:25.

14. See among other places W. F. Albright, *Archaeology and the
Religion of Israel* (Baltimore: Johns Hopkins Press, 1942), p. 96,
and by the same author, *The Archaeology of Palestine* (Baltimore:
Penguin Books, 1961), pp. 206–207.

15. Judges 6–8.

16. The important article of Reinhard Walz, "Zum Problem des
Zeitpunkts der Domestikation der altweltlichen Cameliden,"
generally supports Albright's view. It has been directly challenged,
on the other hand, by Joseph P. Free, "Abraham's Camels,"
Journal of Near Eastern Studies, 3 (1944), 187–193. Zeuner, *Domesticated Animals*, seems unaware of Albright's dictum.

17. A. Leeds and A. Vayda, eds., *Man, Culture, and Animals*
(Washington, D.C.: American Association for the Advancement of
Science, 1965), pp. 7–26, 87–128.

18. Camels molt every spring, and their wool can be collected
in tufts from bushes and the ground without the collector ever
coming into contact with the animal.

19. Systematic information on Somali camel culture is hard to
come by. I have used primarily I. M. Lewis, *Peoples of the Horn of
Africa: Somali, Afar, and Saho* (London: International African
Institute, 1955); L. G. A. Zöhrer, "Study of the Nomads of
Somalia," *Archiv für Völkerkunde*, 19 (1964–65), 129–165; and

I. L. Mason and J. P. Maule, *The Indigenous Livestock of Eastern* **285**
and Southern Africa (Farnham Royal: Commonwealth Agricultural
Bureaux, 1960), pp. 4–8.

20. Lewis, *Peoples,* pp. 70–71; Zöhrer, "Nomads," p. 151.

21. Massimo Adolfo Vitale, *Il Cammello d I Reparti Cammellati*
(Rome: Sindicato Italiano Arti Grafiche, [1928]), pp. 85, 237–238.
Zöhrer, "Nomads," p. 150, says "the nomads of the Somali Republic
consider the idea of mounting camels as simply ridiculous." Sir
Richard Turnbull, retired colonial administrator for northern
Kenya, remarked in an interview that the Somalis have no taboo
against riding but feel that it makes them good targets.

22. Vitale, *Il Cammello,* pp. 85–86, says "it is not uncommon to
see groups moving with all their camels unloaded while the
women carry small pieces of baggage."

23. Good mountain camels are found among other places in
Yemen and on Socotra.

24. Haroun Tazieff, "The Afar Triangle," *Scientific American,*
222 (1970), 32–40.

25. See chapter 5.

26. Lewis, *Peoples,* pp. 174–175; A. Paul, *A History of the Beja*
Tribes of the Sudan (Cambridge, Eng.: Cambridge University Press,
1954), pp. 147f.

27. In Senegal, for example, the density of camel population is
inversely related to the level of rainfall. R. Rousseau, "Le Chameau
au Senegal," *Bulletin de l'Institut Fondamental d'Afrique Noire,*
5 (1943), 69–79. Such precise correlations have not been made for
other countries, but the dependence of camels on dry weather for
breeding is generally assumed. On the other hand, the two-humped
camel's mating cycle may be keyed to temperature instead. According to letters I have received from the Moscow Zoo, the London
Zoo, and the Whipsnade Zoo, two-humped camels mate in Moscow
between March and May and in England between October or
December and March. The mean temperatures of London and
Moscow are comparable during these two periods. One-humped
camels mate in London from January to April and in Moscow from
March to May, but the animals come from different regions,
unlike the two-humped camels which all come from Central Asia.
A third possible triggering mechanism, photoperiodicity or number
of hours of daylight, has never been examined.

28. E. B. Edney, "Animals of the Desert," *Arid Lands: A Geo-*
graphical Appraisal, ed. E. S. Hills (London: Methuen, 1966),
p. 193.

29. Aden in Arabia and Berbera across the Gulf of Aden in
Africa have their greatest precipitation in February–March and

March–April, respectively. Jidda on the western coast of Arabia is affected by a different weather system and has its wettest month in November.

30. See chapter 5.

31. J. D. Clark, *The Prehistoric Cultures of the Horn of Africa* (Cambridge, Eng.: Cambridge University Press, 1954), pp. 311–315.

32. M. D. Gwynne, "The Possible Origin of the Dwarf Cattle of Socotra," *The Geographical Journal*, 133 (1967), 41. The information on Somali representations of short-horned cattle comes from a private communication to Gwynne and has apparently not been published in full. In Arabia a figure of a camel was found in low relief on a stone slab that also bore a depiction of a humpless bull. The site of this find in eastern Arabia is dated to the third millenium B.C., Geoffrey Bibby, *Looking for Dilmun* (New York: Knopf, 1969), p. 304.

33. Great antiquity is commonly attributed to the Indian Ocean coasting trade, but hard evidence for this is still wanting. Alan Villiers, *Monsoon Seas, the Story of the Indian Ocean* (New York: McGraw-Hill, 1952), chaps. 4–5. The use of this route for dissemination of domestication techniques in prehistoric times has been strongly suggested by Carl O. Sauer, *Seeds Spades, Hearths, and Herds* (Cambridge, Mass.: MIT Press, 1969), pp. 34–36. Since Clark assumes that all animals reached the horn of Africa from the north by land and dates his three periods of rock pictures according to this assumption, his suggested dates disagree with the ones proposed here and are out of keeping with his own data.

34. The case for Egyptian familiarity with the island of Socotra is put by Douglas Botting, *Island of the Dragon's Blood* (New York: Wilfred Funk, 1958), pp. 161–168. H. von Wissman, "Badw," *Encyclopaedia of Islam*, new ed., I, 881, summarizes the argument for including southern Arabia in the land of Punt.

35. Zebu cattle are found in Egyptian representations from the eighteenth dynasty (ca. 1570 B.C.) onwards. Zeuner, *Domesticated Animals*, p. 226.

36. D. Brian Doe, *Socotra: An Archaeological Reconnaissance in 1967* (Miami: Field Research Projects, 1970), pp. 5–6, 31–33, pl. 22. One figure is shown (fig. 10) that might possibly be a short-horned cow. The undeciphered writing of the graffitti found at the same site could hardly antedate the earliest inscriptions from southern Arabia, which date to approximately the tenth century B.C.

37. Several descriptions of Socotra mention a species of wild ass on the island. Unfortunately, none indicates whether it derives

from the Nubian or the Somali species, a fact which could be of   **287**
great importance to the matter at hand.

38. It is certain that later and more advanced techniques of camel
use reached Somalia. A camel operated mill in Mogadishu, Somalia,
for example (John Buchholzer, *The Horn of Africa* [London: Angus
and Robertson, 1959], plate opposite p. 193) can be seen to utilize
the same type of harness, derived from a South Arabian pack saddle, as that used by a similar mill in Arabia (François Balsan, *À
travers l'Arabie inconnue* [Paris: Amiot Dumont, 1954], photo
opposite p. 65). Presumably the inhabitants of the horn did not
adopt these later techniques because their outlook toward the camel
was not primarily utilitarian.

39. Von Wissman, "Badw," p. 882. Yemen in 1956 had only
70,000 camels as opposed to 8.5 million sheep and goats and
300,000 cattle. Omar Draz, "Improvement of Animal Production in
Yemen," *Bulletin de l'Institut du Desert d'Egypte*, 6 (1956),
79–110.

40. The *Periplus of the Erythraean Sea*, a Greek work written
sometime between the first and third centuries A.D., speaks of the
political connection between Socotra and Arabia (Doe, *Socotra*, pp.
xvii, 152–153), and the modern political situation is discussed in
Botting, *Island*.

41. M. Mikesell, "Notes on the Dispersal of the Dromedary,"
Southwestern Journal of Anthropology, 11 (1955), 244–245, argues
for the origin of camel domestication being in southern Arabia
but on slightly different grounds from those presented here.

42. H. Frankfort and others, *The Gimilsin Temple and the
Palace of the Rulers at Tell Asmar* (Chicago: University of Chicago
Press, [1940]), p. 212, #126f.

43. Bibby, *Dilmun*, p. 304; Charlotte Ziegler, *Die Terrakotten
von Warka* (Berlin: Gebrüder Mann, 1962), #194. The latter
example is also depicted in Burchard Brentjes, "Das Kamel in alten
Orient," *Klio*, 38 (1960), 35, #4, with a caption calling attention
to indications of a saddle. The indication is actually a black cross
painted on the back similar to painted designs on other animal
figurines of the period. There is no reason to suppose that a saddle
was intended.

44. Walz, "Zur Problem des Zeitpunkts," p. 47, is convinced
that central Arabia was the home of camel domestication, but he
does not offer any explanation of who did the domesticating and
why.

45. Ad-Damīrī, *Ḥayāt al-Ḥayawān (A Zoological Lexicon)*, tr.
A. S. G. Jayakar (London: Luzac, 1906), I, 27; Qur'ān XXIII:22.

288

46. Al-Jāḥiẓ, *Ḥayawān*, I, 152.

47. Al-Jāḥiẓ, *Ḥayawān*, VI, 246.

48. Ad-Damīrī, *Ḥayāt al-Ḥayawān*, I, 447.

49. Ad-Damīrī, *Ḥayāt al-Ḥayawān*, I, 32.

50. Ad-Damīrī, *Ḥayāt al-Ḥayawān*, I, 32.

51. Al-Jāḥiẓ, *Ḥayawān*, I, 154–155; VI, 23, 216; ad-Damīrī, *Ḥayāt al-Ḥayawān*, I, 28–29.

52. Yāqūt, *Muᶜjam al-Buldān* (Beirut: Dar Beirut and Dar Sader, 1955–1957), V, 356–359.

53. Ad-Damīrī, *Ḥayāt al-Ḥayawān*, I, 28.

54. W. F. Albright's chronology of southern Arabia as given by Wendell Phillips, *Qataban and Sheba* (New York: Harcourt, Brace, 1955), p. 247, has the first migration of Semitic people coming to southern Arabia from the north before 1500 B.C. and the second before 1200 B.C. Occasional finds of paleolithic and neolithic implements in southern Arabia show that there were previous inhabitants, however. See next note and Richard M. Gramly, "Neolithic Flint Implement Assemblages from Saudi Arabia," *Journal of Near Eastern Studies*, 30 (1971), 177–185. No comparable stone implements have been discovered on Socotra. Doe, *Socotra*, p. 151.

55. G. Lankester Harding, *Archaeology in the Aden Protectorates* (London: Her Majesty's Stationery Office, 1964), p. 5.

56. Botting, *Island*, pp. 218–219.

57. Bibby, *Dilmun*, pp. 303–304, 379. The site is dated very approximately between 2750 and 3000 B.C. A potsherd from the same site (p. 362) probably shows a camel.

58. Admiralty War Staff, Intelligence Division, *A Handbook of Arabia* (1916), I, 241; G. Rentz, "Djazīrat al-ᶜArab," *Encyclopaedia of Islam*, new ed., I, 541.

59. Butter and cheese are difficult to make from the milk of one-humped camels and are rarely eaten, but according to Èvariste-Regis Huc, *Travels in Tartary, Thibet, and China*, tr. W. Hazlitt (London: National Illustrated Library, n.d.), I, 209, the milk of two-humped camels supplies large quantities of butter and cheese. This may be another significant temperature related physiological difference between one- and two-humped camels. Mikesell, *Notes*, p. 245, argues that milk was not the purpose of domestication or else there would be evidence of selective breeding to increase milk yield. Since tribes living largely on camel's milk do have good milking breeds, such as the Edammah breed in Somalia (personal communication Sir Richard Turnbull), such evidence would appear to exist.

60. Wilfred Thesiger, *Arabian Sands* (London: Longmans, 1959), p. 42.

61. Alan Villiers, *Sons of Sinbad* (New York: C. Scribner's Sons, 1940).

62. *British Somaliland and Sokotra* (London: His Majesty's Stationery Office, 1920), pp. 38–39.

63. Leese, *The One-Humped Camel*, p. 112.

64. J. R. Wellsted, *Travels to the City of the Caliphs Along the Shores of the Persian Gulf and the Mediterranean* (London: Henry Colburn, 1840), II, 184.

65. James Theodore Bent and wife, *Southern Arabia* (London: Smith, Elder, 1900), p. 369.

66. Photograph in Freya Stark, *Seen in the Hadhramaut* (New York: E. P. Dutton, 1939), p. 98.

67. Leese, *The One-Humped Camel*, pp. 112–113.

68. Botting, *Island*, pp. 48–49, 51. Leese, *The One-Humped Camel*, pp. 114–115, gives average weights carried by pack camels in different countries. All are 300 pour.ds or more, up to 1,000 pounds, except the Somali, which is 240 pounds.

3 The Spread of Camel Domestication and the Incense Trade

1. See chapter 9.

2. Albright, *Archaeology and the Religion of Israel*, p. 96.

3. The best pictorial compilations are contained in Zeuner, *Domesticated Animals*, chap. 13, and Burchard Brentjes, "Das Kamel," pp. 23–52.

4. G. Caton-Thompson, "The Camel in Dynastic Egypt," *Man*, 34 (1934), 21.

5. P. Montet, *Byblos et l'Égypte* (Paris: P. Geuthner, 1928–29), p. 129, pl. LII, #179.

6. A single strap is most commonly depicted, but several clay figurines from the first half of the first millennium b.c. bear incisions indicative of a double strap. Ziegler, *Die Terrakotten*, pl. XXI, #308a, 313, 314.

7. A. J. B. Wace, *Chamber Tombs at Mycenae* (Oxford: The Society of Antiquaries, 1932), p. 112, pl. LIII, #1.

8. Arthur J. Evans, *Cretan Pictographs and Prae-Phoenician Script* (London: Bernard Quaritch, 1895), p. 72, #62b.

9. C. H. Gordon, "Western Asiatic Seals in the Walters Art Gallery," *Iraq*, 6 (1939), 21, pl. VII, #55. Whether the camel's feet are turned up, as suggested here, or it is standing upon snakes or birds may be debated. It seems, nevertheless, to be a plausible model for the Minoan seal even if that model was incorrectly understood.

10. Donald J. Wiseman, "Ration Lists from Alalakh VII," *Journal of Cuneiform Studies*, 8 (1959), 29, line 59; Albrecht

290

Goetze, "Remarks on the Ration Lists from Alalakh VII," *Journal of Cuneiform Studies*, 8 (1959), 37; I. J. Gelb, "The Early History of the West Semitic Peoples," *Journal of Cuneiform Studies*, 15 (1961), 27. I wish to thank Mr. A. Bernard Knapp for bringing this text to my attention and translating it for me.

11. Dog: Zeuner, fig. 13:15; donkey: Zeuner, fig. 13:16 and Brentjes, p. 36, fig. 1; horse: Zeuner, fig. 13:17 and Brentjes, p. 42, fig. 3; dragon (Mesopotamian variety): Brentjes, p. 30, fig. 3 and p. 50, fig. 2; pelican: Brentjes, p. 38, fig. 3.

12. Jean-Robert Kupper, *Les Nomades en Mesopotamie au temps des rois de Mari* (Paris: Les Belles Lettres, 1957).

13. The description here follows the main lines of that proposed by Carl Rathjens, "Sabaeica," *Mitteilungen aus dem Museum für Völkerkunde in Hamburg*, 24 (1953–1955), part II, pp. 11–19.

14. Villiers, *Monsoon Seas*, pp. 41–46.

15. Rathjens, "Sabaeica," part II, p. 16. A date this early seems hard to justify, but it is also hard to disprove.

16. Phillips, *Qataban and Sheba*, p. 247, summarizes the chronology worked out by W. F. Albright.

17. Genesis 25:1–4. Sheba and Dedan are both the names of Jokshan's sons and of principalities in southern Arabia and the Hijaz respectively; Midian is the name of Jokshan's brother and of the camel-breeding tribe mentioned in Judges.

18. Rathjens ("Sabaeica," part II, pp. 18, 115) suggests that the overland route was in use for over a thousand years, with asses doing the work, before the camel was introduced from somewhere in the north. Albright's chronology obviously has the Semitic migrations taking place without the use of camels (Phillips, *Qataban and Sheba*, p. 247).

19. Walter Dostal, "The Evolution of Bedouin Life," *L'Antica Società Beduina*, ed. F. Gabrieli (Rome: Centro di studi semitici, Istituto di studi orientali, Università, 1959), pp. 11–34; and by the same author, *Die Beduinen in Südarabien* (Vienna: Ferdinand Berger & Söhne, 1967). Théodore Monod, "Notes sur le harnachement chamelier," *Bulletin de l'Institut Fondamental d'Afrique Noire*, 29, ser. B (1967), 234–239, raises some questions about Dostal's theories. Wendell Phillips, *Unknown Oman* (London: Longmans, Green, 1966), p. 263, n. 2, ridicules them.

20. On the south side of the Sahara camels are ridden bareback in front of the hump and possibly they once were in Yemen as well. For further discussion of riding before the hump see chapter 5.

21. Rathjens, "Sabaeica," part II, pp. 114–117, 248–250.

22. Ziegler, *Die Terrakotten*, pp. 88–91, pl. 21. A damaged figurine found in Tigré province in eastern Ethiopia appears to

belong to this same category indicating that the South Arabian trade reached across the Red Sea as well. Unfortunately, the figurine was not found in a datable context. A. Caquot and A. J. Drewes, "Les Monuments recueillis à Maqallé (Tigré)," *Annales d'Éthiopie*, 1 (1955), 39–40.

23. It is very clear that a saddle is intended on most of the Yemeni examples. Ziegler does not mention a saddle in describing any of the Iraqi examples. She always considers the rise in the back to be a tail, although the similarity with the Yemeni figurines is certainly striking. Her #591 (photograph 309) shows the clearest evidence of a saddle except for #616 (photograph 320) which she believes to be part of a horse. Horse saddles, however, are not shown on the many Assyrian representations of horse riders, and the shape of the saddle is more like a behind-the-hump camel saddle than a horse saddle.

24. His argument is based partly on the fact that they were found in graves and cannot be considered conclusive.

25. The feminine identification is ascertainable in Ziegler's photograph 308b, but she mentions it also in describing nondepicted specimens #596 and 604.

26. Monod, "Notes," pp. 237–238. Monod also mentions on page 236, note 3, a variant which uses a light wooden frame instead of a cushion behind the hump, but I have not found further information on this.

27. L. W. King, *Bronze Reliefs from the Gates of Shalmaneser* (London: British Museum, 1915), pls. 23, 24.

28. G. Cauvet, *Le Chameau* (Paris: J. B. Baillière, 1925), pl. LXII; Johannes Nicolaisen, *Ecology and Culture of the Pastoral Tuareg* (Copenhagen: The National Museum of Copenhagen, 1963), p. 74, figs. 53–54.

29. Judges 6:5.

30. I Kings 10.

31. Daniel D. Luckenbill, *Ancient Records of Assyria and Babylonia* (Chicago: University of Chicago Press, 1926), I, 130.

32. Luckenbill, *Ancient Records*, I, 223.

33. Armas Salonen, *Hippologica Accadica* (Helsinki: Suomalainen Tiefeakatemia, 1956), pp. 87–90.

34. Luckenbill, *Ancient Records*, I, 293.

35. Luckenbill, *Ancient Records*, II, 208, 214, 218–219.

36. Luckenbill, *Ancient Records*, II, 75, 90. Also a relief reproduced in Brentjes, "Das Kamel," p. 42, fig. 1, shows camels in an Assyrian military camp.

37. Brentjes, "Das Kamel," p. 47, fig. 3. The mistakes in the drawing come from the strap under the tail being confused with

the tail itself, which is always shown rigid in Assyrian art, and the saddle bow being confused with the strap under the neck.

38. Leese, *The One-Humped Camel*, pl. 5.

39. British Museum #124908; illustrated in Jean Deshayes, *Les Civilisations de l'Orient Ancien* (Paris: Arthaud, 1969), fig. 76.

40. Max Freiherr von Oppenheim, *Tell Halaf* (Berlin: Walter de Gruyter, 1955), III, 48–49, pl. XXVII.

41. R. D. Barnett, *Assyrian Palace Reliefs* (London: Batchworth, n.d.), pls. 108–116; Salonen, *Hippologica*, pl. V, #2; C. J. Gadd, *The Stones of Assyria* (London: Chatto & Windus, 1936), pl. X. The last relief, from the reign of Tiglathpileser III (745–727 B.C.) seems also to show a cushion saddle. Two late Hittite reliefs of camel riders appear to fit with this group insofar as the riders are shooting bows and arrows and sitting on saddles that are only indicated by girths under the saddle blanket. D. G. Hogarth, Leonard Woolley, and R. D. Barnett, *Carchemish* (London: British Museum, 1952), part I, pl. B.16.b; part III, pl. B.50.a.

42. Salonen, *Hippologica*, pl. V, #2.

43. In the nineteenth century John Lewis Burckhardt observed of the Wahhabis in Arabia, "if camels are scarce, a man mounted upon one takes a companion . . . behind him." *Notes on the Bedouins and Wahābys* (London: Henry Colburn and Richard Bentley, 1830), p. 313.

44. British Museum #117716.

45. British Museum, Early Greek Room.

46. Dostal exaggerates the limitations of riding behind the hump ("Evolution," pp. 16, 22, 27) and is rightly criticized by Phillips, *Unknown Oman*, p. 263, n. 2. Some degree of inconvenience seems likely, however. Monod, "Notes," p. 236.

47. Luckenbill, *Ancient Records*, II, 317. The camel, of course, does not store water in its stomach as was long held to be the case. There is, however, some fluid that could be drunk in an emergency. For a discussion of the matter see Knut Schmidt-Nielsen, "The Question of Water Storage in the Stomach of the Camel," *Mammalia*, 20 (1956), 1–15.

4 The North Arabian Saddle and the Rise of the Arabs

1. There are several specimens in the collections of the American Numismatic Society and the British Museum. They are described by H. A. Grueber, *Coins of the Roman Republic in the British Museum* (London: British Museum, 1910), II, 589–590, and Gian Guido Belloni, *Le Monete Romane dell'Eta Repubblicana* (Milan: Comune di Milano, 1960), pp. 200–201, 210. An additional specimen is illustrated in Zeuner, *Domesticated Animals*, fig. 13:8. One

specimen with the name Bacchius makes the stomach girth into an
irrational vertical band at the withers which clearly indicates that
the die-cutter wasn't too familiar with his subject. Some coins
might be interpreted as having a double arch in front and a single
one in back, but none shows a saddle long enough to be a South
Arabian saddle. The same identification of the North Arabian
saddle has been made by Emilienne Demougeot, "Le Chameau et
l'Afrique du Nord romaine," *Annales: Économies, Sociétés,
Civilisations*, 15 (1960), 220.

2. M. Rostovtzeff, *Caravan Cities* (Oxford: Clarendon Press,
1932), chaps. I–II.

3. I Kings 10; II Chronicles 9. An Ishmaelite had charge of the
camels of King David (I Chronicles 27:30), but what these camels
were used for is not stated.

4. Strabo, *The Geography of Strabo*, tr. H. L. Jones (Cambridge,
Mass.: Harvard University Press, 1966), 16.4.19.

5. Strabo 16.3.3.

6. On Ptolemaic and Seleucid forays into Arabia see M. Cary,
A History of the Greek World from 323 to 146 B.C. (London:
Methuen, 1932), pp. 81–82. Strabo describes the campaign of the
Roman general Aelius Gallus (Strabo 16.4.22–24). For the debated
expedition against Mecca from Yemen see A. F. L. Beeston,
"Abraha," *Encyclopaedia of Islam*, new ed., I, 102–103.

7. Herodotus, *The Persian Wars*, tr. George Rawlinson (New
York: Modern Library, n.d.), 1.80.

8. Herodotus 7.69.

9. W. Pieper, "Ṣulaib," *Encyclopaedia of Islam*, IV, 514.

10. Strabo 16.1.26–27.

11. Strabo 16.4.24.

12. Strabo 16.4.23. Diodorus of Sicily says: "The remaining
part of Arabia, which lies towards Syria, contains a multitude of
farmers and merchants of every kind, who by a seasonable
exchange of merchandise make good the lack of certain wares in
both countries by supplying useful things which they possess in
abundance." Diodorus Siculus, *Diodorus of Sicily*, tr. C. H.
Oldfather (London: William Heinemann, 1933), 2.54.3.

13. *Livy*, ed. B. O. Foster and others (Cambridge, Mass.: Harvard
University Press, 1919–1967), 37.40.

14. *Herodian*, ed. C. R. Whittaker (Cambridge, Mass.: Harvard
University Press, 1969), 4.14.3–15.3. This reading is supplied by
an editor's correction, but long spears in the hands of camel riders
are mentioned in the alternative reading as well.

15. Diodorus 2.17.2. He also mentions the camels in her army
carrying disassembled river boats overland.

294

16. The basic word in Arabic for a riding saddle is *raḥl* from the verb *raḥala* meaning "to saddle a camel." *Shadād* refers specifically to the North Arabian type of riding saddle, although a more homely version is called *ghabīṭ*. Dostal ("Evolution," p. 20) seems to be reading too much into the word when he derives it from the verbal sense "to attack." For more on the terminology associated with this saddle see Julius Euting, "Der Kamels-sattel bei den Beduinen," *Orientalische Studien: Theodor Nöldeke zum siebzigsten Geburtstag (2.März 1906)*, ed. Carl Bezold (Gieszen: Alfred Töpelmann, 1906), I, 393–398.

17. Dostal, "Evolution," pp. 18–20.

18. British Museum #102601. This stone, dated approximately to the first century B.C., shows two men on a camel as in the Assyrian reliefs; but a projection upward behind the hump and before the tail appears to be the rising cushion of the South Arabian saddle.

19. Rostovtzeff, *Caravan Cities*, pl. III, #2.

20. There is a miniature by the painter Bihzad dated 1493 which shows a battle with long spears and swords taking place between riders mounted on South Arabian saddles. Since the scene illustrates a traditional romance and Bihzad passed his life in Afghanistan and Iran far from Arabia, the most likely reason for showing this saddle is that baggage saddles were commonly used for riding at that time in eastern Iran. Arthur U. Pope, *A Survey of Persian Art* (London: Oxford University Press, 1938), pl. 885c.

21. Vitale, *Il Cammello*, pp. 153–154. Vitale has the most precise and detailed description of camel movements and paces that I have found.

22. F. W. Schwarzlose, *Die Waffen der alten Araber aus ihren Dichtern dargestellt* (Leipzig: J. C. Hinrichs, 1886), pp. 46–47.

23. H. von Wissmann, "Badw," *Encyclopaedia of Islam*, new ed., I, 885. There is a south Arabian gravestone (Rostovtzeff, *Caravan Cities*, pl. III, #1) that shows a warrior with long lance riding a horse right alongside a camel.

24. There is a frequently cited saying of the Prophet to the effect that "camels are a glory to their people, goats and sheep are a blessing, and prosperity is tied to the forelocks of horses till the Day of Judgement." Ad-Damīrī, *Ḥayāt al-Ḥayawān*, I, 26.

25. Nicolaisen, *Ecology and Culture*, pp. 111–113.

26. Lewis, *Peoples*, p. 70; Zöhrer, "Nomads," p. 150.

27. Horses are included in booty from coalitions that include Arabs, but they are not specified as being from Arab tribes. Xenophon's observation (*Cyropaedia*, tr. Walter Miller [Cambridge, Mass.: Harvard University Press, 1968], 2.1.4) that in the army of

Cyrus an Arabian named Aragdus commanded 10,000 horses and **295** 100 chariots is difficult to interpret since the meaning of the word "Arabian" can vary.

28. Rostovtzeff, *Caravan Cities*, p. 28.

29. Strabo quotes this opinion (16.3.3) with an expression of doubt, since it seems to contradict what he knew about Gerrha from other and probably later sources.

30. Diodorus 3.42.5.

31. Werner Caskel, "The Bedouinization of Arabia," *Studies in Islamic Cultural History*, ed. G. E. von Grunebaum, *The American Anthropologist*, 56 (1954), memoir #76, p. 40. The inscription actually comes from the Lihyanic kingdom of Dēdan which adjoined the Nabataean kingdom on the south, but it would seem to represent a common phenomenon. The relevant portion reads, "Therefore, the assembly of the people has intrusted him for three years with the protection of the road."

32. Strabo 16.4.22–24. Augustus Caesar, who ordered the exploration, was specifically interested in finding the source of the caravan trade, "for he expected either to deal with wealthy friends or to master wealthy enemies."

33. Rostovtzeff, *Caravan Cities*, pp. 33–35.

34. Specimen in the collection of the American Numismatic Society.

35. Rostovtzeff, *Caravan Cities*, p. 151, pl. XXII; Kazimierz Michałowski, *Palmyre: Fouilles polonaises* 1960 (Warsaw: Państwowe Wydawnictwo Naukowe, 1962), pp. 143–147, figs. 158–159.

36. Edward Gibbon, *The History of the Decline and Fall of the Roman Empire*, chap. 11.

37. Caskel, "Bedouinization."

38. J. A. MacCulloch, "Incense," *Encyclopaedia of Religion and Ethics*, ed. James Hastings (New York: Charles Scribner's Sons, 1955), VII, 205.

39. The rise of Mecca for reasons of geographic determinism is suggested by, among others, Maxime Rodinson, *Mohammed* (London: Allen Lane The Penguin Press, 1971), p. 39; and W. Montgomery Watt, *Muhammad at Mecca* (Oxford: The Clarendon Press, 1953), pp. 2–3.

40. Most African products traded through Mecca came by way of Yemen, as did products from China, India, and Persia. Mecca did not have a port, and what little commerce came by sea was carried by foreigners. Hence it is unreasonable to consider Ethiopia as a separate compass point in the trade. Traffic in the direction of Iraq does not seem to have approached in volume that heading for

296   Syria, nor did Iraq receive Syrian goods, mostly grain, oil, cloth, and arms, by way of Mecca or vice versa. The actual trade routes were Syria-Yemen and Iraq-Yemen. Neither of these necessitated transshipment at a middle point. P. H. Lammens, *La Mecque à la veille de l'Hégire* (Beirut: Imprimerie Catholique, 1924), pp. 203–206, 284.

41. Watt, *Mecca*, pp. 2–3, 5.

42. For example: "Woe to every maligner, scoffer,
Who gathers wealth and counts it over,
Thinking that his wealth will perpetuate him!"
    —Qur'an 104.1–3

43. Beeston, "Abraha"; Watt, *Mecca*, pp. 13–16.

44. Caskel ("Bedouinization," pp. 40–41) seeks to minimize the Meccan trade, but Lammens (*La Mecque*, chaps. 8–13) provides convincing evidence that the trade was still appreciable and lucrative.

45. Demougeot, "Le Chameau et l'Afrique," p. 243.

46. John Bagot Glubb, *The Great Arab Conquests* (London: Hodder and Stoughton, 1963), pp. 61, 70.

47. C. Cahen, "ᶜAṭāʾ," *Encyclopaedia of Islam*, new ed., I, 729–730.

48. Nelson Glueck, *Deities and Dolphins* (New York: Farrar, Straus, and Giroux, 1965), pp. 379–380.

49. Fevrier, *Essai*, pp. 78–79. Cauvet (*Le Chameau*, I, 42) remarks of Elagabalus: "He invented a stew which consisted essentially of camels' feet; the success of this dish surely requires the hand of a consummate chef."

50. Strabo 16.4.26.

51. This caste of camel buyers is known as ᶜUqail, but there is no connection between them and the medieval tribe of that name. They all come from the Najd (northern Arabia) and either from minor tribes or from towns. Admiralty War Staff, Intelligence Division, *A Handbook of Arabia* (1916), I, 94–95; II, 17–18.

52. The ᶜAnazah tribe fulfilled this function in the early twentieth century. *Handbook*, I, 46.

5 The Camel in North Africa

1. *Annales: Économies, Sociétés, Civilisations*, 15 (1960), 209–247.

2. Cauvet, *Le Chameau*, I, 30–38; Vincent Monteil, *Essai sur le chameau au Sahara occidental* (St. Louis du Sénégal: Centre I.F.A.N., 1953), pp. 127–131. The word *méhari* is the French spelling of the Arabic *mahārī*, a plural of the word *mahrī* meaning

originally a camel from the district of Mahra in Arabia (see chapter 2). The French word for a camel-mounted soldier is *méhariste*. Cauvet tries to deny the Arabian origin of the word (I, 72), but it is attested with this meaning in Iraq as early as the seven century A.D. Dostal, *Die Beduinen*, p. 64.

3. The geographer E. F. Gautier writes: "It is Rome who has acclimated the camel to the Maghreb [North Africa]. This at least is not a hypothesis. There is no historical fact better established." *Les siècles obscurs du Maghreb* (Paris: Payot, 1927), p. 182.

4. *Caesar: Alexandrian, African and Spanish Wars*, tr. A. G. Way (Cambridge, Mass.: Harvard University Press, 1964), p. 251.

5. *Ammianus Marcellinus*, tr. John C. Rolfe (Cambridge, Mass.: Harvard University Press, 1965), 28.6.5. Demougeot ("Le Chameau et l'Afrique," p. 234) argues that the proper number may be 400. In the twentieth century, however, the camel population of Libya has numbered over 300,000; this makes 4,000 seem like a not unreasonable figure. *Production Yearbook 1971* (Rome: Food and Agriculture Organization of the United Nations, 1972), p. 338.

6. Demougeot, "Le Chameau et l'Afrique," pp. 241–247.

7. Cauvet, *Le Chameau*, I, 14, 37, 608; Yolande Charnot, *Répercussion de la déshydratation sur la biochimie et l'endocrinologie du dromadaire* (Rabat: Institut Scientifique Chérifien, 1960), p. 8.

8. Josef Freiherr von Hammer-Purgstall in his exhaustive compilation of Arabic terms relating to camels cites one meaning "weiss- und schwarzgesprenkelten," but he does not say where the term is used. *Das Kamel*, Denkschriften der kaiserlichen Akademie der Wissenschaften. Philosophisch-historische Classe, 6 (Vienna, 1855), 22.

9. Henri Lhote, "Le Cheval et le chameau dans les peintures et gravures rupestres du Sahara," *Bulletin de l'Institut Fondamental d'Afrique Noire*, 5 (1953), 1138–1228.

10. Cauvet, *Le Chameau*, I, 30–31. Cauvet extends to the Sahara the argument originally made for Egypt by E. Lefébure, "Le Chameau en Égypte," *Actes du XIVe Congrès International des Orientalistes: Alger 1905* (Paris: Ernest Leroux, 1907), part II, sec. VII, pp. 55–62. Lefébure's thesis is that the Coptic Christian practice derives from pre-Christian Egyptian religious practice, but there is virtually no evidence to support this contention since the ancient Egyptian language did not have a word for camel and hence could not express a prohibition against eating or drawing the animal.

11. Cauvet, *Le Chameau*, II, 165.

12. Nicolaisen, *Ecology and Culture*, pp. 63–65, 100, 103.

13. At the mouths of the Indus River in Pakistan and, formerly,

298

of the Guadalquivir in Spain camels feed on water plants while standing in deep swamp water. Leese, *The One-Humped Camel*, p. 55; Abel Chapman, *Wild Spain* (London: Gurney and Jackson, 1893), pp. 94–101.

14. The classic geography of the Sahara desert is that of Robert Capot-Rey, *L'Afrique blanche française*, vol. II, *Le Sahara français* (Paris: Presses universitaires de France, 1949–1953). A good shorter account (except for the chapter on camels) is E. F. Gautier, *Sahara: The Great Desert* (New York: Columbia University Press, 1935).

15. Cauvet, *Le Chameau*, I, 29; Leese, *The One-Humped Camel*, p. 59.

16. Lefébure, "Le Chameau en Égypte," pp. 36–38. Demougeot ("Le Chameau et l'Afrique," pp. 218–219) casts strong doubt upon the tale that Alexander the Great used camels to visit the oasis of Siwa in the western desert of Egypt.

17. Lefébure, "Le Chameau en Égypte," pp. 47–49; Strabo, 16.4.24; 17.4.45, 65; Pliny, *Natural History*, tr. H. Rackham (Cambridge, Mass.: Harvard University Press, 1969), 6.102, 168.

18. M. Cary, *A History of the Greek World*, p. 296.

19. M. P. Charlesworth, *Trade-Routes and Commerce of the Roman Empire* (Cambridge, Eng.: Cambridge University Press, 1924), p. 22.

20. Zeuner, *Domesticated Animals*, figs. 13:20–21.

21. H. A. R. Gibb, "ʿAydhāb," *Encyclopaedia of Islam*, new ed., I, 782; A. J. Arkell, *A History of the Sudan from the Earliest Times to 1821* (London: University of London, the Athlone Press, 1961), pp. 170–171, 178–179.

22. Strabo, 16.4.24.

23. The Beja language is related only very distantly to Arabic. Their word for camel, *kām*, may or may not be related to Arabic *jamal*. On tribes of this region see A. Paul, *A History of the Beja Tribes of the Sudan* (Cambridge, Eng.: Cambridge University Press, 1954), and P. M. Holt, "Bedja," *Encyclopaedia of Islam*, new ed., I, 1157–1158. On the word *kām* see I. M. Diakonoff, *Semito-Hamitic Languages: An Essay in Classification* (Moscow: Nauka, 1965), pp. 55–56. I wish to thank Dr. Marina Tolmacheva for this last reference.

24. Dows Dunham, *Royal Tombs at Meroë and Barkal* (Boston: Museum of Fine Arts, 1957), p. 127, fig. 82, pl. XLIXf. The saddle design on this figurine suggests a possible influence from Somalia.

25. Demougeot, "Le Chameau et l'Afrique," p. 243.

26. Among those who have made this comparison is Zeuner, *Domesticated Animals*, pp. 342, 352. Some people must have come with the camels, of course, as bearers of skills and techniques, and it

should be pointed out that Thamudean (early Arabic) inscriptions have been found along the trade routes in the Egyptian eastern desert. H. von Wissmann, "Badw," *Encyclopaedia of Islam*, new ed., I, 887–888.

27. G. E. M. Hogg, in "Camel-Breeding," chap. II of H. E. Cross, *The Camel and Its Diseases* (London: Baillière, Tindall, and Cox, 1917), pp. 36–37, writes: "All those *dachis* [female camels] which I pointed out to you just now as being pregnant leave the group [around the stallion], walking away with their tails up in the air . . . A *dachi* is said always to do this if pregnant."

28. Theodore Monod, "Notes sur le harnachement chamelier," *Bulletin de l'Institut Fondamental d'Afrique Noire*, 29, ser. B, (1967), 234–306.

29. From rock art it is known that horse- and ox-drawn chariots were in use in the Sahara prior to the introduction of the camel, and there are also depictions of horses being ridden; but cavalry in the sense of an organized military force could not have existed since the animal was ridden bareback and guided by a stick. Lhote, "Le Cheval et le chameau."

30. The camel-related vocabulary in the area where the *rahla* saddle is used is 90 percent Arabic. Monteil, "Essai." The Tuaregs who use the *terik* and *tahyast* saddles have no Arabic terms in their camel vocabulary. Nicolaisen, *Ecology and Culture*, pp. 92–102.

31. Vitale, *Il Cammello*, pp. 253–254; Lt.-Col. Venel and Capt. Bouchez, *Guide de l'officier méhariste au territoire militaire du Niger* (Paris: E. Larose, 1910), pp. 100–105.

32. British Museum #125682. A saddle design utilizing the position before the hump seems to be in use at the present day in Yemen, but I have been unable to locate either a description or an adequate photograph of it. A partial photograph appears on the back cover of Richard Gerlach's *Pictures from Yemen* (Leipzig: Edition Leipzig, n.d.). Whether this indicates a south Arabian role in the invention of this type of saddle or is an isolated local design cannot be determined without further information.

33. Monod, "Notes," figs. 16–20; M. Benhazera, *Six mois chez les Touareg du Ahaggar* (Algiers, 1908), p. 40; Nicolaisen, *Ecology and Culture*, fig. 75.

34. Dostal, *Die Beduinen*, p. 154.

35. Monod, "Notes," figs. 21–23. Monod (p. 265) also classifies the Tuareg shoulder saddles as deriving from the North Arabian saddle rather than the South Arabian.

36. Hans Winkler draws careful distinctions between the style of camel drawing of the Blemmyes in Upper Egypt and that of the later Arabs, but he does not make note of the fact that the former

300

group shows the rider sitting before the hump and the latter group above the hump. Hans A. Winkler, *Rock-Drawings of Southern Upper Egypt* (London: Egypt Exploration Society, 1938), I, 15, pls. I, III–IV.

37. Demougeot, "Le Chameau et l'Afrique," pp. 212–213.

38. Winkler, *Rock-Drawings*, II, 20, pls. XXX, XXXIII.

39. Theodore Monod, ed., *Contributions à l'étude du Sahara occidentale* (Paris: Librairie Larose, 1938).

40. Henri Lhote, "Nouvelle contribution à l'étude des gravures et peintures rupestres du Sahara Central; la station de Tit (Ahaggar)," *Journal de la Société des Africanistes*, 29 (1959), 147–192.

41. Peter Fuchs, "Felsmalereien und Felsgravuren in Tibesti, Borku und Ennedi," *Archiv für Völkerkunde*, 12 (1957), 110–135.

42. Winkler, *Rock-Drawings*, I, pls. III–IV; O. F. Parker and M. C. Burkitt, "Rock Engravings from Onib, Wadi Allaki, Nubia," *Man*, 32 (1932), 249–250.

43. Monod, *Notes*, fig. 57.

44. Cauvet, *Le Chameau*, I, 37; Monteil, *Essai*, pp. 127–131.

45. This route of dissemination has been suggested by others, as well, including H. von Wissmann, "Badw," p. 889, and Paul Huard and Jean-Claude Féval, "Figurations rupestres des confins Algéro-Nigéro- Tchadiens, " *Travaux de l'Institut de Recherches Sahariennes*, 23 (1964), 86.

46. The main east-west motor route passes through Darfur and then south of the desert through Fort Lamy and Kano to the Niger River. The route connecting the highland areas is, for the most part, a recognized and marked track, rather than a formal road.

47. The absence of any abrupt change in rock art accompanying the introduction of the camel has been affirmed by Lhote ("Le Cheval et le chameau," pp. 1216–1217) and by Monod who shows graphically the overlap in subject matter ("Peintures rupestres du Zemmour français [Sahara occidental]," *Bulletin de l'Institut Fondamental d'Afrique Noire,* 13 [1951], 200).

48. Al-Balādhurī, *Futūḥ al-Buldān,* ed. Ṣalāḥ ad-Dīn al-Munajjid (Cairo: an-Nahḍa al-Miṣriya, [1956]), p. 280.

49. Winkler, *Rock-Drawings*, I, pl. III.

50. Demougeot, "Le Chameau et l'Afrique," pls. II A-C. These figurines bear a striking resemblance to one found at Nippur in Iraq. Leon Legrain, *Terra-cottas from Nippur* (Philadelphia: University of Pennsylvania Press, 1930), pl. LXI, #325. There is also a later Christian lamp from Gabès in southern Tunisia which bears a stamped figure of a camel with a saddle on top of the hump. *Catalogue du Musée Alaoui (Supplement)* (Paris: Ernest Leroux,

1910), p. 246, pl. XCVII #6. A chapel in the necropolis at al-Bagawāt in the Kharga oasis in Egypt has several pictures of loaded and ridden camels in Old Testament scenes. These pictures all show North Arabian saddles and are dated to the first half of the fourth century A.D. Ahmed Fakhry, *The Necropolis of el-Bagawāt in Kharga Oasis* (Cairo: Government Press, 1951), pp. 50, 60, 65.

51. Zeuner, *Domesticated Animals*, fig. 13:21.

52. For a detailed discussion see chapter 7.

53. Procopius, *History of the Wars*, tr. H. B. Dewing (Cambridge, Mass.: Harvard University Press, 1961), 3.8.23–27; 4.11.17–56. In one case a ring of camels twelve deep was formed.

54. The difference between the two areas in particularly noticeable in the draught harness, where the Egyptians use basically a South Arabian saddle and the Tunisians simply a woven band across the shoulders.

55. Demougeot, "Le Chameau et l'Afrique," p. 218. Most of her evidence pertains to the route from the Nile to the Red Sea (p. 244), and it is difficult to see why the desert route she portrays (opposite p. 232) from Thebes to Grande Oasis (?) to Siwa to Augila should ever have been preferred to the cheap and comfortable water route down the Nile to Alexandria and along the coast by sea.

56. S. D. Goitein, *A Mediterranean Society*, vol. I, *Economic Foundations* (Berkeley: University of California Press, 1967), pp. 275–276.

57. Demougeot, "Le Chameau et l'Afrique," pp. 241–242; Ch.-André Julien, *Histoire de l'Afrique du Nord* (Paris: Payot, 1961), I, 200–201.

58. Sijilmasa becomes important only in the eighth century. Julien, *L'Afrique du Nord*, II, 39. It eventually became the main northern terminus of trans-Saharan trade in the western Maghreb. Ghadamès served the same function for trade in the eastern Sahara, but it never became as important politically as Sijilmasa. Trade through Ghadamès dates back to the Roman period, but it enjoyed much greater prosperity under Muslim rule. J. Despois, "Ghadamès," *Encyclopaedia of Islam*, new ed., II, 991–992.

59. See chapter 2.

60. On the Garamantes see Charles Daniels, *The Garamantes of Southern Libya* (New York: Oleander Press, 1970).

61. Nicolaisen, *Ecology and Culture*, pp. 54–105.

6 Iran: One Hump or Two?

1. The best extensive treatment of camels in the east is Jean-Paul Roux, "Le Chameau en Asie Centrale," *Central Asiatic Journal*, 5 (1959–60), 35–76, but he deals primarily with the place of the

302   camel in Turkish and Mongolian culture and hence does not discuss
the earlier problems involving Iran.

2. An important article on this by Viktor N. Kolpakov, a camel
specialist at the veterinary medicine institute in Saratov on the
Volga, is available in German translation; "Ueber Kamelkreuzungen," *Berliner tieraerztliche Wochenscrift*, 51 (1935), 617–622.
Other references may be found in Annie P. Gray, *Mammalian Hybrids: A Check-List with Bibliography* (Slough, Eng.: Commonwealth Agricultural Bureaux, 1971), pp. 161–162.

3. For a discussion of the camel in Anatolia see chapter 8.

4. Most of the information listed under Persian comes actually
from India in the time of the Mogul Empire around 1590. The
source is Abū al-Faḍl ᶜAllāmī, *Āʾīn-i Akbarī* ed. H. Blochmann
(Calcutta: Asiatic Society of Bengal in the Bibliotheca Indica, 1872),
I, 146–147. Blochmann's translation (2d ed., Calcutta: Asiatic
Society of Bengal, 1939, pp. 151–152) is not entirely accurate.

5. Kolpakov, "Ueber Kamelkreuzungen," p. 620, figs. 6–10.

6. The word *bukhtī* for the hybrid camel is usually said to come
from the word Bactria (Arabic and Persian: Balkh), but this is not
certain. It could come instead from the Indo-European root *bheug*
meaning "to swell or bend." *Bukhtī* is often mistakenly taken to
mean two-humped camel.

7. For some of the extensive bibliography on this subject see
the Bibliographical Essay.

8. A. G. Bannikov, "Distribution géographique et biologie du
cheval sauvage et du chameau de Mongolie (*Equus Przewalski* et
Camelus Bactrianus)," *Mammalia*, 22 (1958), 152–160.

9. The camel's calluses have been described as a trait acquired
through domestication and caused by the heavy weights the animal
is made to carry. That they are actually a genetic trait is pointed
out by Ernst Mayr, *Populations, Species, and Evolution* (Cambridge,
Mass.: Harvard University Press, 1970), pp. 109–110, who
compares them with the calluses of the ostrich and warthog.

10. The Soviet archaeologist V. I. Sarianidi has written me that
he intends to publish an article on camel domestication based on
archaelogical work in this region and has summarized the evidence
he will use.

11. R. Ghirshman, *Fouilles de Sialk* (Paris: Paul Geuthner,
1938–39), I, pl. LXXIX, A2, also possibly pl. LXXVI, A12. Zeuner,
Domesticated Animals, p. 359, has made the suggestion that the
animal shown is a camel, but judging from a remarkably similar
pottery motif from northern Baluchistan, the animal could just as
well be bovine. See Walter A. Fairservis, Jr., *The Roots of Ancient
India* (New York: Macmillan, 1971), p. 153, fig. 38 (A-4). A cylinder

seal from Siyalk illustrated by Brentjes ("Das Kamel," p. 46, #1; Ghirshman, *Fouilles*, II, pl. XXX, 6) looks more like a bird or winged beast than a camel (see Ghirshman, *Fouilles*, I, pls. XIII, 3; XVII, 5).

12. The sites in question, including Altyn-tepe, Ulug-tepe, and Namazga, are located on the plain just north of the Kopet Dagh mountains which form the border between Iran and the Soviet Union. On the wagons see V. M. Masson and V. I. Sarianidi, *Central Asia: Turkmenia before the Achaemenids* (London: Thames and Hudson, 1972), pp. 109, 120, pl. 36.

13. For information and photographs on finds at Shahr-i Sukhta I wish to thank Dr. Maurizio Tosi of the Missione Archaeologica Italiana, Zabul, Iran.

14. Masson and Sarianidi, *Central Asia*, pp. 94–96.

15. Bibby, *Looking for Dilmun*, pp. 303–304; P. V. Glob, *al-Bahrain* (Copenhagen: Gyldendal, 1968), p. 167.

16. In modern times, the nose peg has become standard on one-humped camels in India, Afghanistan, and Baluchistan (Leese, *The One-Humped Camel*, pp. 104–105), but these were originally two-humped camel territories. Elsewhere in one-humped camel territory the nose peg or ring is used on an occasional basis, but the halter is predominant. Cauvet, *Le Chameau*, I. 369–371; Nicolaisen, *Ecology and Culture*, p. 73.

17. This is a revision by C. C. Lamberg-Karlovsky of the date he suggested in "Further Notes on the Shaft-hole Pick-axe from Khurāb, Makrān," *Iran: Journal of the British Institute of Persian Studies*, 7 (1969), 163–168. A date of 2000–1800 B.C. is advanced by K. R. Maxwell-Hyslop, "Note on a Shaft-hole Axe-pick from Khurab, Makran," *Iraq*, 17 (1955), 161.

18. Zeuner, *Domesticated Animals*, p. 360, and "The identity of the Camel on the Khurab Pick," *Iraq*, 17 (1955), 162–63.

19. Lamberg-Karlovsky, "Further Notes," p. 168.

20. I have been informed by Dr. Tosi of the discovery of a clay figurine of a one-humped camel at Shahr-i Sukhta in Sistan, but I have seen no dating or photograph of the figurine.

21. Masson and Sarianidi, *Central Asia*, pl. 36.

22. Letter from Dr. Tosi.

23. J. Ulrich Duerst, "Animal Remains from the Excavations in Anau," in Raphael Pumpelly, ed., *Explorations in Turkestan, Expedition of 1904: Prehistoric Civilizations of Anau* (Washington: Carnegie Institution, 1908), II, 342. The entire bone sample numbered 1,300.

24. B. Prashad, *Animal Remains from Harappa*, Memoirs of the Archaeological Survey of India #51 (Delhi: Manager of Publications, 1936), pp. 58–59. Prashad believes the bones come from

304

one-humped camels descended from the prehistoric species of the Siwalik hills in India, but there is no evidence that that species was one-humped and little more that these bones are closely related to it. See also F. R. Allchin, "Early Domestic Animals in India and Pakistan," *The Domestication and Exploitation of Plants and Animals*, eds. P. J. Ucko and G. W. Dimbleby (London: Gerald Duckworth, 1969), p. 320.

25. The fact that camels played no significant role in the hunting economy is confirmed by the absence of camel bones in deposits of wild animal bones and by the absence of camels among the wild animals depicted on painted pottery.

26. I wish to thank Dr. Prem Singh for indispensable help in analyzing the meaning of the word *ushtra*.

27. Otto Schrader, *Reallexikon der indogermanischen Altertumskunde* (Strassburg: K. J. Trübner, 1901), p. 405; G. Redard, "Notes de dialectologie iranienne, II: Camelina," *Indo-Iranica* (Wiesbaden: Harrassowitz, 1964), pp. 155–162.

28. Tadeusz Sulimirski, *Prehistoric Russia* (New York: Humanities Press, 1970), pp. 261–266.

29. It is regarded as a loanword by Friedrich von Spiegel, *Die arische Periode und ihre Zustände* (Leipzig: Wilhelm Friedrich, 1887), p. 49.

30. The most authoritative statements of this view are Hermann Grassmann, *Wörterbuch zum Rig-Veda* (Wiesbaden: Harrassowitz, 1964), p. 269, and Manfred Mayrhofer, *Kurzgefasstes etymologisches Wörterbuch des Altindischen* (Heidelberg: Winter 1956), I, 113–114. Among those who have been led astray is Reinhard Walz, "Neue Untersuchungen zum Domestikationsproblem der altweltlichen Cameliden: Beiträge zur ältesten Geschichte des zweihöckrigen Kamels," *Zeitschrift der Deutschen Morgenländischen Gesellschaft*, 104 (1954), n.s. 29, 45–87.

31. Only Spiegel (*Die arische Periode*, pp. 49, 51) cites texts to prove the *ushtra* was a buffalo, and his citations are either unconvincing or based upon misreadings.

32. Roland G. Kent, *Old Persian* (New Haven: American Oriental Society, 1953), pp. 118 (DB 86–87), 178. Salonen, *Hippologica*, pp. 85–86. Phonetically, it is difficult to derive *uduru* from *ushtra*, but the linguistic evidence available is too scanty to rule it out.

33. T. Burrow, *The Sanskrit Language* (London: Faber and Faber, 1955), p. 150.

34. The use of the word *azhrī* is given by Xavier Raymond, "Afghanistan," p. 9. It is not mentioned by Viktor N. Kolpakov, "Das turkmenische Kamel (Arwana)," *Berliner tieraertzliche Wochenschrift*, 51 (1935), 570–573.

35. Kent, *Old Persian*, p. 118.
36. Herodotus, 1.80.
37. V. S. Agrawala, *India as Known to Pānini* (Lucknow: University of Lucknow, 1953), pp. 148–149; *The Laws of Manu*, tr. G. Bühler, *Sacred Books of the East*, ed. Max Müller, vol. XXV (Oxford: Oxford University Press, 1886), pp. 67, 472.
38. Strabo, 15.1.43. The correct reading of the Greek is uncertain, but this is the most reasonable translation.
39. Walz, "Neue Untersuchungen," pp. 61–62. In Aleksandr Belenitsky, *The Ancient Civilization of Central Asia* (London: Barrie & Rockliff, 1969), pl. 27, there is pictured a brazier with two two-humped camels in the center and a procession of lions around the rim. This brazier is noted as coming from Kazakhstan in the first millennium B.C., but no detailed information is provided. For a largely philological account of camels in ancient China see Edward H. Schafer, "The camel in China down to the Mongol Dynasty," *Sinologica*, 2 (1950), 165–194, 263–290.
40. Sulimirski, *Prehistoric Russia*, p. 337.
41. Salonen, *Hippologica*, p. 86, and personal communication from Prof. A. Leo Oppenheim.
42. Salonen, *Hippologica*, p. 85.
43. Salonen, *Hippologica*, p. 86; Luckenbill, *Ancient Records*, I, 122 (Adad-Nirāri II, 911–891 B.C.), 130 (Tukulti-Ninurta II, 890–884 B.C.), 145 (Assur-Nāṣir-Pal II, 883–859 B.C.), 211, 214 (Shalmaneser III, 858–824 B.C.), 256 (Shamsi-Adad V, 823–811 B.C.), 271, 286 (Tiglath-Pileser III, 745–727 B.C.); II, 76 (Sargon II, 721–702 B.C.), 130, 133 (Sennacherib, 704–681 B.C.), 209, 215 (Esarhaddon, 680–669 B.C.).
44. Brentjes, "Das Kamel," pp. 29, #2; 30, #1.
45. Franz Hančar, "Aus der Problematik Urartus," *Archiv Orientální*, 17 (1949), 302. Walz ("Neue Untersuchungen," p. 73) corrects Hančar's figure of 150 camels to 115, but the correction makes little difference.
46. Jean Deshayes, *Les Civilisations de l'Orient Ancien* (Paris: Arthaud, 1969), fig. 208; Roman Ghirshman, *Perse* ([Paris]: Gallimard, 1963), fig. 99.
47. L. Vanden Berghe, *Archéologie de l'Iran ancien* (Leiden: E. J. Brill, 1959), p. 109, pl. 135e.
48. Strabo, 15.3.1.
49. The firmest identification of the tribute delegations is that of Erich F. Schmidt, *Persepolis*, vol. III, *The Royal Tombs and Other Monuments* (Chicago: University of Chicago Press, 1970), pp. 148–149.
50. Burckhardt, *Bedouins and Wahābys*, p. 110; Henry J. Van

Lennep, *Travels in Little-Known Parts of Asia Minor* (London: John Murray, 1870), II, 162–164. Burckhardt mistakenly refers to the two-humped camel as a dromedary. Van Lennep does not mention the Crimea as the source of two-humped breeding stock.

51. The only published evidence I have found of two-humped camels in Iran in recent years is a photograph of several of them in the town of Birjand in the eastern part of the country. Lotte and Gustav Stratil-Sauer, *Kampf um die Wüste: Ein Bericht über unsere Fahrten in die ostpersische Lut* (Berlin: Reimar Hobbing, 1934), p. 43. Dr. Michael Bonine of the University of California at Davis has seen and photographed male two-humped camels in a hybrid breeding herd in Azerbaijan province in northwestern Iran.

52. Yasna 44 translated by Jacques Duchesne-Guillemin, *The Hymns of Zarathustra* (Boston: Beacon Press, 1963), p. 73, and Vendīdād 9.37 translated by Louis H. Gray, "Camel," *Encyclopaedia of Religion and Ethics*, ed. James Hastings (New York: Charles Scribner's Sons, 1955), III, 175.

53. The standard history of Central Asia during this period is William M. McGovern, *The Early Empires of Central Asia* (Chapel Hill: University of North Carolina Press, 1939).

54. N. Pigulevskaja, *Les Villes de l'état iranien aux époques Parthe et Sassanide* (Paris: Mouton, 1963), pp. 82, 161.

55. Ziegler, *Die Terrakotten*, pp. 137–138, 187, pl. 43, #545; Wilhelmina Van Ingen, *Figurines from Seleucia on the Tigris* (Ann Arbor: University of Michigan Press, 1939), pp. 6, 320, pl. 76, #556–557.

56. Many Chinese figurines are extant from the period of the Northern Wei (386–534) and T'ang (618–907) dynasties; for representative illustrations see Brentjes, "Das Kamel," pp. 26, #5; 46, #2; Rostovtseff, *Caravan Cities*, pl. IV, #1; Osvald Sirén, *Histoire des arts anciens de la Chine* (Paris: G. van Oest, 1930), III, pls. 32–33, 100. The Northern Wei specimens are much less stylized than the T'ang ones; one of them (Sirén, pl. 32) indicates that the round load may have originated as basketry.

57. P. V. L. Baur, M. I. Rostovtzeff, and A. R. Bellinger, eds., *The Excavations at Dura-Europus; Preliminary Report of the Fourth Season of Work, October 1930-March 1931* (New Haven: Yale University Press, 1933), pl. XXIII, 2. Two-humped camels still reached northern Syria on rare occasion in caravans from Baghdad in the eighteenth century. Russell, *Natural History of Aleppo*, p. 170. One-humped camels, naturally, were also used at Dura-Europus; see lamp shown in *Excavations . . . October 1931-March 1932*, pl. XXI, 1.

58. Diodorus, 2.54.6. If Diodorus had to explain how the two

humps were distributed on the animal, his audience must have   **307**
been quite unfamiliar with it.

59. Rathjens ("Sabaeica," part I, fig. 121, photo 62) shows a
graffito from Yemen that looks to be a two-humped camel, but he
correctly identifies it (p. 117) as a one-humped camel with a South
Arabian saddle.

60. Van Ingen, *Figurines from Seleucia*, p. 320, pl. 76, #556.

61. Diodorus, 2.54.6. It seems unlikely that grain would have
been a major item in the caravan trade because its value would
have been so low in comparison to transportation costs.

62. A. Wylie, tr., "Notes on the Western Regions; Translated
from the 'Tsëen Han Shoo,' [Annals of the Former Han Dynasty],
Book 96, Part 1," *Journal of the Anthropological Institute*, 10
(1881), 33, 40.

63. Specimen illustrated in Zeuner, *Domesticated Animals*,
fig. 13:36.

64. Islay Lyons and Harald Ingholt, *Gandhāran Art in Pakistan*
(New York: Pantheon, 1957), p. 30, figs. 145, 150; Bruno Dagens
and others, *Monuments Préislamiques d'Afghanistan* (Paris: G.
Klincksieck, 1964), pl. VI, #21–22.

65. H. E. Cross, *The Camel and Its Diseases*, p. 1.

66. Al-Iṣṭakhrī, *Kitāb Masālik al-Mamālik*, ed. M. J. de Goeje
(Leiden: E. J. Brill, 1927), p. 176.

67. Yāqūt, *Muᶜjam al-Buldān* (Beirut: Dar Sader and Dar Beirut,
1957), V, 279. He calls the people the Nudha instead of the Budha.
For an English translation of another version of the same report by
the geographer al-Idrīsī see S. Maqbūl Ahmad, *India and the
Neighboring Territories in the "Kitāb Nuzhat al-Mushtāq
fi'Khtirāq al-'Afāq" of al-Sharīf al-Idrīsī* (Leiden: E. J. Brill, 1960),
p. 52.

68. Al-Jāḥiẓ, *Ḥayawān*, VII, 242.

69. In addition to the sources cited in notes 67–68, see Guy Le
Strange, *The Lands of the Eastern Caliphate* (London: Frank Cass,
1966), pp. 349–350; Ṭabarī, *Ta'rīkh*, ed. Muḥammad Abū al-Faḍl
Ibrāhīm (Cairo: Dār al-Maᶜārif, 1960–1969), IV, 180.

70. Burckhardt, *Bedouins and Wahābys*, p. 110; Van Lennep,
Travels, II, 162–164; Kolpakov, "Ueber Kamelkreuzungen."

71. Al-Jawālīqī, *al-Muᶜarrab min al-Kalām al-Aᶜjamī*, ed. A. M.
Shākir (Tehran, 1966), pp. 154–155.

72. Rafā'īl Nakhla al-Yasūᶜī, *Gharā'ib al-Lugha al-ᶜArabiya*
(Beirut: Imprimerie Catholique, [1960]), p. 229.

73. For a detailed account of this relationship from the Arabic
chronicler Ṭabarī see Theodor Nöldeke, tr., *Geschichte der Perser
und Araber zur Zeit der Sāssāniden* (Leiden, 1879).

74. Brentjes, "Das Kamel," p. 47, #1; *Tāq-i Bustān* (Tokyo, 1969), I, pls. 81, 102.

75. Richard N. Frye, *Sasanian Remains from Qasr-i Abu Nasr* (Cambridge, Mass.: Harvard University Press, 1973), I.221, I.286, D.118, D.155, D.306, D.354. Professor Frye has also given me access to photographs of several unpublished sealings of this type. Two seals have been found dating back to the Parthian period; evidently the motif was one that grew in popularity along with the caravan trade. Robert H. McDowell, *Stamped and Inscribed Objects from Seleucia on the Tigris* (Ann Arbor: University of Michigan Press, 1935), p. 124, pl. V, #89.

7 The Camel as a Draft Animal

1. Herbert M. Barker, *Camels and the Outback* (London: Angus and Robertson, 1964); Tom L. McKnight, *The Camel in Australia* (Carlton, Victoria: Melbourne University Press, 1969), pp. 45–47, pls. 4–5, 8.

2. The pioneer in the history of harnessing is Richard Lefebvre des Noëttes, *La Force motrice animale à travers les âges* (Paris: Berger-Levrault, 1924) and *L'Attelage: le cheval de selle à travers les âges* (Paris: A. Picard, 1931). The most important reconsideration and expansion of his work is by Joseph Needham and Wang Ling, *Science and Civilisation in China* (Cambridge, Eng.: Cambridge University Press, 1965), IV, part II, pp. 243–253, 303–328.

3. Needham and Wang, *Science and Civilisation*, p. 306

4. Modern harnessing spread during the early Han dynasty; Needham and Wang, *Science and Civilisation*, pp. 308–312.

5. Lefebvre des Noëttes reproduces a photograph of a throat-and-girth harness in use apparently in Afghanistan (*La Force motrice*, fig. 195); and I possess a photograph of a donkey pulling water from a well in Arabia by means of this harness at the present time.

6. A pair of camels pulling a plow by means of a yoke in upper Egypt are depicted in Clement Robichon and Alexandre Varille, *Eternal Egypt* (London: Gerald Duckworth, 1955), fig. 79. The yoke seems to rest on a great pad filling in the dip in the neck. It seems unlikely that this expedient would prove very satisfactory for a vehicle harness where the weight of the load pressing down on the neck would be much greater.

7. For pictures of oxen harnessed singly by yokes see Lefebvre des Noëttes, *La Force motrice*, figs. 211–214, and Needham and Wang, *Science and Civilisation*, fig. 537.

8. André G. Haudricourt and Mariel Jean-Brunhes Delamarre,

L'Homme et la charrue à travers le monde (Paris: Gallimard, 1955), **309**
pp. 155–164.

9. Needham and Wang, *Science and Civilisation*, pp. 308–312.

10. Needham and Wang, *Science and Civilisation*, p. 327.

11. Barker, *Camels and the Outback*, pp. 20–21, describes these
straps and explains their purpose. McKnight, *Camel in Australia*,
has good photographs of them (pls. 5 and 8) as well as a photograph showing how a single camel could be harnessed to a buggy
by means of a horse collar (pl. 4).

12. Masson and Sarianidi, *Central Asia*, pl. 36.

13. Anatol Démidoff, *La Crimée* (Paris: Ernest Bourdin, 1855),
p. 157.

14. For example, a team of twenty-two oxen is shown drawing
a vehicle. D. T. Rice, *Islamic Art* (New York: Praeger, 1965), p. 63.

15. For a discussion of the possibility that the practice did spread
from India to Aden see below.

16. Tarr, *The Carriage*, p. 103.

17. Karl Jettmar, *Art of the Steppes* (New York: Crown, 1967),
pp. 65–81.

18. Needham and Wang, *Science and Civilisation*, pp. 308–312.

19. Needham and Wang, *Science and Civilisation*, fig. 569.

20. Needham and Wang, *Science and Civilisation*, p. 327.

21. Lefebvre des Noëttes, *L'Attelage*, fig. 371.

22. P. K. Gode, "Notes on the History of the Camel in India
between B.C. 500 and A.D. 800," *Janus*, 47 (1958), 137. The value
of this article is largely nullified by the author's failure to
recognize that *ushtra* originally meant two-humped camel and not
one-humped camel.

23. R. N. Frye, "Balūčistān," *Encyclopaedia of Islam*, new ed., I,
1005.

24. Otto Spies, *An Arab Account of India in the 14th Century*,
Bonner orientalistische Studien #14 (Stuttgart: W. Kohlhammer,
1936), p. 48. The source is Egyptian, al-Qalqashandī's *Ṣubḥ
al-Aᶜshā*, and therefore perhaps too remote to be very reliable.

25. Leese, *The One-Humped Camel*, pp. 126–127, pl. 6.

26. ᶜAllāmī, *Āʾīn-i Akbarī*, translation pp. 225–226, 285. The first
reference is to the parading of camels in which they appear in order
of value. Hybrids come first and then one-humped camels; two-
humped camels are not listed at all.

27. Pack camels are cheaper than modern camel carts on Central
Asian routes; Lattimore, *Desert Road to Turkestan*, p. 226.

28. Demougeot, "Le Chameau et l'Afrique," p. 230, pl. II-D.

29. Ibn Taghrībirdī, *An-Nujūm as-Zāhira fī Mulūk Miṣr wa
al-Qāhira* (Cairo: Dar Kutub Misriya, 1930), II, 307.

310

30. The Revised Standard Version and The Jerusalem Bible have the corrected reading.

31. F. M. Hunter, *An Account of the British Settlement of Aden in Arabia* (London: Trübner & Co., 1877), p. 79. For a good photograph see Ameen Rihani, *Around the Coasts of Arabia* (London: Constable, 1930), pl. 24.

32. There is a photograph of two near Mārib in Ahmed Fakhry, *An Archaeological Journey to Yemen* (Cairo: Government Press, 1951), part III, pl. XXXIX-B. An equally unexpected aspect of traditional life in Yemen is the use of a single camel to pull a plow. The harness involved looks surprisingly like those in use in Tunisia. Whether this is a recent innovation or an ancient practice cannot be determined from the evidence available. Richard Gerlach, *Pictures from Yemen* (Leipzig: Edition Leipzig, n.d.), illus. [43].

33. Gilbert Boris, *Documents linguistiques et ethnographiques sur une région du sud tunisien (Nefzaoua)* (Paris: Adrien Maisonneuve, 1951), pp. 16, 19, illustrates the use of the camel plow among bedouin. See also F. Couston, "Le Chameau de trait dans le Sahara algérien," *Journal d'Agriculture Pratique,* n.s. 31 (1918), 408–411.

34. Boris, *Documents,* p. 19.

35. Haudricourt and Delamarre, *L'Homme et la charrue,* pp. 260–261.

36. This can be seen in the Egyptian delta where camels sometimes plow in tandem with other animals.

37. Max Ricard, *Le Bossu au pied mou: conférence prononcée le 23 decembre 1951* (Fez: Editions Amis de Fès, 1953), p. 15. Ricard also mentions (p. 13) the occasional use of a single camel harnessed to a plow, but he does not describe the harness.

38. É. Laoust points out the Latin words underlying the harnessing terminology of Moroccan Berber in *Mots et choses berbères* (Paris: Augustin Challamel, 1920), pp. 291, 293.

39. Demougeot, "Le Chameau et l'Afrique," pp. 230–233, 236–240, pls. III-A, IV-B-C; O. Brogan, "The Camel in Roman Tripolitania," *Papers of the British School at Rome,* 22 (1954), 126–131; P. Romanelli, "La Vita Agricola Tripolitana Attraverso le Rappresentazioni Figurate," *Africa Italiana,* 3 (1930), 53–75.

40. The earliest generally accepted breast-strap harness is from the eighth century. Lynn White, *Medieval Technology and Social Change* (Oxford: Oxford University Press, 1962), pl. 3.

41. William MacGuckin de Slane, ed., *Histoire des Berbères* (Algiers: Imprimerie du Gouvernement, 1847), I, 105; in his translation (Algiers, 1852), I, 164.

42. See chapter 5.

43. Needham and Wang, *Science and Civilisation*, pp. 315–319, 326–328.

44. Haudricourt and Delamarre, *L'Homme et la charrue*, p. 185.

45. The lamp is not mentioned in the museum's published catalogue. I wish to express my gratitude to Monsieur Ben Ahmed Abdel Hadi, the museum's director, for providing me with a photograph.

46. Needham and Wang, *Science and Civilisation*, figs. 552–554.

47. Lefebvre des Noëttes, *La Force motrice*, pp. 54–56; Needham and Wang, *Science and Civilisation*, pp. 315–318.

48. For example, Lefebvre des Noëttes, *L'Attelage*, figs. 140–144, 148.

49. Romanelli, "La Vita Agricola," figs. 4–5.

50. Demougeot, "Le Chameau et l'Afrique," pp. 240–241. Cauvet is apparently referring to the same inscription (*Le Chameau*, I, 35) when he cites a toll from Roman Tunisia for a loaded camel and driver. His translation of the word *carricatus* is incorrect according to Demougeot's more scholarly reading.

51. Mohamed Talbi, *"L'Émirat aghlabide* (Paris: Adrien Maisonneuve, 1966), pp. 287–288.

52. Talbi, *L'Émirat aghlabide*, p. 295.

53. Michele Amari, *Storia dei Musulmani di Sicilia* (Florence: Felice le Monnier, 1858), II, 446. The source is the life of St. Filareto which refers to mules *ad vehicula trahenda aptissimi.*

54. Jean Despois in *La Tunisie Orientale; Sahel et Basse Steppe* (Paris: Les Belles Lettres, 1940), pp. 168–169, speaks of horse-driven mills in eleventh century Qairawan. His source is not exactly clear, but if accurate, the observation would again imply the existence of modern horse harnessing of some type.

55. Needham and Wang, *Science and Civilisation*, pp. 316–317. For pictures of Sicilian and Maltese carts see, respectively, Cecilia Waern, *Mediaeval Sicily* (London: Duckworth, 1910), p. 313, and Augustus Hoppin, *On the Nile* (Boston: J. R. Osgood, 1874), pl. V.

56. Clauson and Rodinson, "Araba."

57. Petrus Hispanus, *De Lingua Arabic Libri Duo*, ed. Paul Lagarde (Göttingen: Dieterich Arnold Hoyer, 1883), p. 142.

58. É. Littré, *Dictionnaire de la langue française* (Paris: Hachette, 1881), I, 417.

59. The Latin root word *lanx* denotes the flat dish of a balance (*bi-lances* = two dishes) while the Arabic root has more a connotation of ease and smoothness, but it is easy to imagine that local semantic usage made them virtually synonymous.

60. Haudricourt and Delamarre, *L'Homme et la charrue*, pp. 177, 262. Maltese plows are also equipped with whippletrees (p. 262).

61. Needham and Wang, *Science and Civilisation*, p. 322, fig. 560.

62. A. Dareste, "Rapport sur l'introduction projetée du droma-daire au Brésil," *Bulletin de la Société Impériale Zoologique d'Acclimatation*, 4 (1857), 190. John D. Latham has suggested in "Towards a study of Andalusian Immigration and Its place in Tunisian History," *Les Cahiers de Tunisie*, 5 (1957), 232, that the *kirrīta* was introduced to Tunisia in the thirteenth century by refugees from Spain. While he presents sufficient evidence to prove that these refugees knew and used carts, he does not firmly establish that the vehicles were not known in Tunisia prior to the immigra-tion. His suggestion is by no means implausible, but it must be weighed against the data already presented relating to vehicular use prior to the thirteenth century. I am indebted to Professor James Monroe for bringing this article to my attention.

63. André G. Haudricourt, "Contribution à la géographie et à l'ethnologie de la voiture," *La Revue de Géographie et d'Ethnolo-gie*, 1 (1948), 61.

64. Published specimens include Brentjes, "Das Kamel," pp. 26, #5; 46, #2; Rostovtseff, *Caravan Cities*, pl. IV, #1; Sirén, *Arts anciens de la Chine*, III, pls. 32, 33-B, 100-A. Other specimens have been studied in the British Museum and the Victoria and Albert Museum.

65. This type of saddle made of reeds exists among the Kirghiz to the present day but appears to be rare. *Aziatskaia Rossiia* (St. Petersburg: Tovarishchestvo A. F. Marks, 1914), I, 158.

66. An interesting T'ang figurine with this type of saddle shows a camel carrying a troupe of musicians. *Historical Relics Unearthed in New China* (Peking: Foreign Language Press, 1972), pl. 143.

67. For an Arabian example see François Balsan, *A travers l'arabie inconnu* (Paris: Amiot Dumont, 1954), photo opposite p. 65.

68. Dominique and Janine Sourdel, *La Civilisation de l'Islam classique* (Paris: Arthaud, 1968), illus. 97.

8 A Society Without Wheels

1. The various types of rotating systems in use in traditional Middle Eastern society are well described by Hans E. Wulff, *The Traditional Crafts of Persia* (Cambridge, Mass.: MIT Press, 1966).

2. *Encyclopaedia Britannica*, 11th ed., V, 103.

3. The only recent general work on camels in Arabic is an article by Jibrā'īl Jabbūr, "Al-Jamal: Rukn min Arkān al Badāwa," *Kitāb al-ᶜId* (Beirut: American University of Beirut, 1967), pp. 1–28.

4. An apt example of this sensitivity is a small article that

appeared in *Le Revue du Liban*, August 4, 1973, p. 21. A Westerner **313**
living in Beirut is called to task for sending to friends in Canada a
photograph of a camel with a caption saying that this was how he
went to and from work in Beirut. The photograph and caption
found their way into a magazine and back to Beirut where they
were interpreted as an example of tasteless and insulting propa-
ganda. I wish to thank Ms. Leila Fawaz for bringing this article to
my attention.

5. For examples of poetry extolling camels see Nicolaisen,
Ecology and Culture, p. 106; J. von Hammer-Purgstall, "Das
Kamel," *Denkschriften der kaiserlichen Akademie der Wissenschaften, Philosophisch-historische Classe*, 6 (Vienna, 1855),
73–83; I. M. Lewis and B. W. Andrzejewski, *Somali Poetry: An
Introduction* (Oxford: Clarendon Press, 1964), especially poem
number 19. On the role of the camel in the religions of the Arabs
see Hammer-Purgstall, pp. 46–48, and M. Gaudefroy-Demombynes,
"Camel—in Arabia," *Encyclopaedia of Religion and Ethics*, pp.
173–174.

6. Jean-Paul Roux, "Le Chameau en Asie Centrale," *Central
Asiatic Journal*, 5 (1959–60), 71–72.

7. Hammer-Purgstall, "Das Kamel," pp. 1–2, lists the known
Arabic works on the camel.

8. Hammer-Purgstall, "Das Kamel," p. 2, comments with
surprise upon the absence of a section devoted to camels in
al-Jāḥiẓ' work.

9. E. G. Browne, *A Literary History of Persia* (Cambridge, Eng.:
Cambridge University Press, 1956), I, 332.

10. Reynold A. Nicholson, *A Literary History of the Arabs*
(Cambridge, Eng.: Cambridge University Press, 1956), p. 286.

11. See photographs in *Asia*, XXIII, 830; XXV, 569.

12. F. Colombari, *Les Zemboureks. Artillerie de campagne à
dromadaire dans l'armée persane* (Paris, 1853), summarized in L.
Voinot, *L'Artillerie à dos de chameau* (Paris: Berger-Leorault,
1910), pp. 62–70. Voinot discusses the history of camel artillery in
the course of presenting a brief for transforming mule-borne
artillery into camel-borne artillery for use in the Sahara. The
Italians also made use of camel-borne artillery in their African
colonies. Vitale, *Il cammello ed i reparti cammellati*, photographs in
chap. IX.

13. A Dareste, "Rapport sur l'introduction projetée du dromadaire au Brésil," *Bulletin de la Société Impériale Zoologique
d'Acclimatation*, 4 (1857), 70. Burckhardt, *Bedouins and Wahābys*,
p. 267, comments favorably upon these weapons which were also
used somewhat in Iraq and Syria.

14. Dareste, "Rapport," pp. 68–69.

15. For example, Xavier de Planhol, *The World of Islam* (Ithaca: Cornell University Press, 1959), pp. 14–22. He is forced to observe (p. 22) that Mecca itself does not look like an Islamic city since it has straight streets.

16. Lewis Mumford so describes fifth century B.C. Athens in *The City in History* (Harmondsworth: Penguin Books, 1966), p. 192. One nineteenth century British lady traveler wrote of Cairo: "Only a few narrow streets and old houses are left . . . where you can yet dream that the 'Arabian Nights' are true." Norman Daniel, *Islam, Europe and Empire* (Edinburgh: Edinburgh University Press, 1966), p. 50.

17. Planhol, *The World of Islam*, pp. 7–8.

18. For an extensively illustrated analysis of the rationale for specific urban designs see Sibyl Moholy-Nagy, *Matrix of Man* (New York: Praeger, 1968).

19. See, for example, the plans of Roman Timgad and Cuicul in Julien, *Histoire de l'Afrique du Nord*, I, 168–169.

20. Roger Le Tourneau, *Fès avant le Protectorat* (Casablanca, 1949), p. 229.

21. For Baghdad, a round city, see K. A. C. Creswell, *A Short Account of Early Muslim Architecture* (Harmondsworth: Penguin Books, 1958), pp. 164–170; for Samarra, a city centered on a long, wide axial street, see J. M. Rogers, "Sāmarrā: A Study in Medieval Town-planning" in *The Islamic City*, eds. A. H. Hourani and S.M. Stern (Oxford: Bruno Cassirer, 1970), pp. 119–155.

22. Marcel Clerget, *Le Caire: étude de géographie urbaine et d'histoire économique* (Paris: Paul Geuthner, [1934], I, 289.

23. For comparative maps of Roman and Islamic Antioch see Glanville Downey, *Ancient Antioch* (Princeton: Princeton University Press, 1963), pls. 4–5; for a map of Herat showing its crossed north-south, east-west main streets see Alexandre Lézine, "Hérat: Notes de Voyage," *Bulletin d'Études Orientales*, 18 (1963–64), fig. 1.

24. Yāqūt, *Muꜥjam al-Buldān*, I, 186.

25. Moholy-Nagy, *Matrix of Man*, fig. 170.

26. One of the few individuals who ever displayed an interest in the upkeep of roads was the Persian heretic Bihāfrīd who was executed in northeastern Iran in 749. The fact that upkeep of roads and bridges was remembered as one of his prescriptions would seem to testify to its being an unusual concern at that time. E. G. Browne, *Literary History*, I, 308–310.

27. The mileage of carriageable roads in Iran in 1914 was still

extremely limited. Issawi, ed., *The Economic History of Iran, 1800–1914*, pp. 203–204.

28. E. Lévi-Provençal, *Histoire de l'Espagne musulmane* (Paris: G. P. Maisonneuve, 1950–1953), I, 284; III, 97, 286.

29. Lévi-Provençal, *L'Espagne musulmane*, III, 286.

30. Lévi-Provençal, *L'Espagne musulmane*, III, 98.

31. The Celtic cart was called an *essedum* in Latin. How extensively it was used in Spain is unknown.

32. Gaul, too, suffered a decline in wheeled traffic until the Carolingian period. Tarr, *The Carriage*, pp. 156–160.

33. Lévi-Provençal, *L'Espagne musulmane*, III, 285–286.

34. Lévi-Provençal, *L'Espagne musulmane*, III, 98.

35. See chapter 7.

36. Lévi-Provençal, *L'Espagne musulmane*, III, 319–320.

37. Camel wrestling is a regular, yearly spectator sport in Turkey. The technique is to cross necks and force the opponent to the ground. Fighting camels appear as an artistic motif in Muslim art (for example, Ernst J. Grube, *Muslim Miniature Painting* [Venice: Neri Pozza, 1962], pl. 59), but there as elsewhere they are a sign of Turkish influence. The practice is unknown among Arab, Berber, and Somali tribes.

38. Al-Jāḥiẓ, *al-Ḥayawān*, III, 434; VII, 135.

39. There is one specimen of this coin in the collection of the American Numismatic Society and another illustrated in Otto Keller and Friedrich Imhoof-Blumer, *Tier-und-Pflanzenbilder auf Münzen und Gemmen* (Leipzig: Teubner, 1889), pl. II, #32.

40. Eunapius, *Lives of the Philosophers*, in *Philostratus and Eunapius*, tr. W. C. Wright (London: William Heinemann, 1922), p. 419. Eunapius (346–414) lived in Sardis and is not known to have visited the Middle East. I wish to thank Dr. Clive Foss for this reference.

41. Al-Jāḥiẓ, *al-Ḥayawān*, III, 434. Fernand Braudel is badly misguided in attributing the failure of the Arabs to conquer Anatolia to his notion of the inferiority of the one-humped camel. *The Mediterranean and the Mediterranean World in the Age of Philip II* (London: Collins, 1972), I, 96.

42. The prevalence of two-humped camels in the herds of the Turks cannot be documented in numbers, but there is a marked increase after the twelfth century in representations of the animal in Persian art. In particular, the motif of the Sasanian emperor Bahram Gur riding on a camel with his slave girl behind him undergoes a change of mounts. Pope, *Survey of Persian Art*, V, pls. 664, 679. The most noteworthy prior appearance of the two-

316

humped camel in Islamic art is in a frieze from Samarra which seems to be inspired by the Persepolis friezes of tribute delegations. Ernst Herzfeld, *Die Malereien von Samarra*, vol. III of *Die Ausgrabungen von Samarra* (Berlin: Dietrich Reimer, Ernst Vohsen, 1927), pp. 100–105, pls. LXXV-LXXXVIII.

43. Alexander Russell, *Natural History of Aleppo* (London: 1794), pp. 167, 169; L. A. O. de Corancez, *Itinéraire d'une partie peu connue de l'Asie Mineure* (Paris: J. M. Ebehrard, 1816), pp. 79–80; Burckhardt, *Bedouins and Wahābys*, p. 110.

44. Burckhardt, *Bedouins and Wahābys*, p. 257; Admiralty War Staff, Intelligence Division, *A Handbook of Arabia* (1916), II, 19–20.

45. *A Handbook of Arabia*, II, 19–20.

46. Masᶜūdī, *Murūj adh-Dhahab* (Beirut: Publications of Lebanese University, 1966), II, 124.

47. In crossing the border from Turkey to Iran the change from oxcart country to camel country is particularly noticeable, but oxcarts do exist in farming villages in Iranian Azerbaijan. Wulff, *Traditional Crafts*, figs. 131, 378, 388. The population on both sides of the border is ethnically Turkish.

48. Although the Turks used wheeled vehicles in Central Asia, the Anatolian oxcart is a more primitive vehicle than the Turkish *araba*. It is called a *kağni*, and the technological vocabulary associated with it is of Byzantine rather than of Turkish origin. Speros Vryonis, *The Decline of Medieval Hellenism in Asia Minor* (Berkeley: University of California Press, 1971), p. 476.

49. V. J. Parry, "Ḥarb—Ottoman Empire," *Encyclopaedia of Islam*, new ed., III, 191–192. Ordinarily camels were not found in the Ottoman European provinces outside of Thrace. Corancez, *Itinéraire*, pp. 80–81.

50. See, for example, Emel Esin, *Turkish Miniature Painting* (Rutland, Vt.: Charles E. Tuttle, 1960), pls. 10–11.

51. Halil Inalcik, "The Rise of the Ottoman Empire," *The Cambridge History of Islam* (Cambridge, Eng.: Cambridge University Press, 1970), I, 307.

52. The best study of the progressive stages in the evolution from Roman city to "oriental" city is Jean Sauvaget, *Alep* (Paris: Geuthner, 1941).

53. Urbanism in Muslim India has still not been well studied, but traditional Hindu concepts relating to city planning can be found in Binode Behari Dutt, *Town Planning in Ancient India* (Calcutta: Thacker, Spink, 1925).

9 If Camels Are Such a Good Idea . . .

1. Igino Cochhi remarks, "thus the use that is made of it is uniquely to serve as beast of burden." "Sur le naturalisation du dromadaire en Toscane," *Bulletin de la Société Impériale Zoologique d'Acclimatation,* 5 (1858), 479.

2. C. Mirèio Legge, "The Arabian and the Bactrian Camel," *Journal of the Manchester Geographical Society,* 46 (1935–36), 44–45; M. F. Davin, "Notice industrielle sur le poil de Chameau," *Bulletin de la Société Impériale Zoologique d'Acclimatation,* 4 (1857), 253–257; J. Merritt Matthews, *Textile Fibers,* 5th ed. (New York: John Wiley and Sons, 1947), pp. 632–636. My thanks to Ms. Lillian Eliot for the last reference.

3. An Englishman named Robert Swinhoe, for example, saw camels in use in Peking in 1860 and wrote: "I should say that they would form an acceptable addition to the beasts of burden at home, where in flat portions of the country they might be usefully and economically employed." *Narrative of the North China Campaign of 1860* (London: Smith, Elder & Co., 1861), p. 369.

4. A. Dareste, "Rapport sur l'introduction projetée du dromadaire au Brésil," *Bulletin de la Société Impériale Zoologique d'Acclimatation,* 4 (1857), 191.

5. See photographs in Giulio Cervani, *Il "Voyage en Egypte" (1860–1862) di Pasquale Revoltella* (Trieste: ALUT, 1962), figs. 48, 55. In some cases harnessing was achieved through the use of a South Arabian saddle as in Aden. The practice seems to have remained strictly within the European sector of the economy.

6. Dareste, "Rapport," pp. 191–192; Isidore Geoffroy Saint-Hilaire, *Acclimatation et Domestication des Animaux Utiles* (Paris: Librairie Agricole de la Maison Rustique, 1861), pp. 24, 26.

7. Geoffroy Saint-Hilaire, *Acclimatation,* pp. 277–296 (Yak), 317–347 (Llama and Alpaca).

8. Geoffroy Saint-Hilaire, *Acclimatation,* p. 26.

9. Geoffroy Saint-Hilaire, *Acclimatation,* pp. 126–138.

10. Geoffroy Saint-Hilaire, *Acclimatation,* pp. 22–23, 302; Dareste, "Rapport," pp. 130–132.

11. J. Poulík and W. and B. Forman, *Prehistoric Art* (London: Spring, [n.d.]), pl. VII.

12. Dareste, "Rapport," p. 135; Giulio Q. Giglioli, *La Colonna di Arcadio a Constantinopoli* (Naples: Gaetano Macchiaroli, 1952), pls. 25–26, 35–36.

13. Gothic *ulbandus* may be related somehow to the word elephant, but the significance of this etymological connection is a

318   mystery. Sigmund Feist, *Vergleichendes Wörterbuch der Gotischen Sprache*, 3d. ed. (Leiden: Brill, 1939), p. 515.

14. Karl Heschler and Emil Kuhn, "Die Tierwelt," in *Urgeschichte der Schweiz*, ed. Otto Tschum, vol. I (Frauenfeld: Huber, 1949), p. 342.

15. See paragraph 42 of Fredegarius's continuation of Gregory of Tours's chronicle, *Grégoire de Tours et Frédégaire*, tr. M. Guizot (Paris: Didier, 1862), II, 204.

16. Roux, "Le Chameau en Asie Centrale," p. 55.

17. P. Jaffé, *Bibliotheca rerum germanicarum*, V, 748. I am indebted to Professor Giles Constable for this reference.

18. Dareste, "Rapport," p. 196.

19. For a general account of the life of Ferdinand II, see G. F. Young, *The Medici* (New York: E. P. Dutton, 1913), II, 390–458. Young says the camels came from India (p. 449), but more reliable authors cite Tunis as the source. A good account of the Tuscan camels in particular is that of Igino Cochhi (see n. 1 above).

20. Zeuner, *Domesticated Animals*, p. 358.

21. Dareste, "Rapport," pp. 189–190; M. P. Graells, "Sur l'acclimatation des animaux en Espagne," *Bulletin de la Société Impériale Zoologique d'Acclimatation*, 2 (1854), 109–116; Legge, "The Arabian and Bactrian Camel," pp. 31–32.

22. Jean Vilbouchevitch, "Emploi du chameau en Russie," *Bulletin de la Société Impériale Zoologique d'Acclimatation*, 40 (1893), 477, and by the same author, "Emploi du chameau en Russie comme animal agricole," *ibid.*, 41 (1894), 337–342; Cauvet, *Le Chameau*, I, 45.

23. Geoffroy Saint-Hilaire, *Acclimatation*, pp. 301–302.

24. Dareste, "Rapport," p. 196.

25. Dareste, "Rapport," p. 197; Leese, *The One-Humped Camel*, pp. 43–44.

26. Dareste, "Rapport," p. 198.

27. Geoffroy Saint-Hilaire, *Acclimatation*, pp. 309–316.

28. Leese, *The One-Humped Camel*, p. 43.

29. Leese, *The One-Humped Camel*, p. 44; Leonard, *The Camel*, pp. 325–333; Droandi, *Il Cammello*, p. 349; Cauvet, *Le Chameau*, I, 48–50.

30. Cauvet, *Le Chameau*, II, 164.

31. Dareste, "Rapport," p. 197. The handbill advertising Crowninshield's camels has been preserved in the Peabody Maritime Museum in Salem, Massachusetts.

32. The following brief history is summarized from Tom L. McKnight, *The Camel in Australia* (Melbourne: Melbourne University Press, 1969), pp. 17–24.

33. McKnight, *The Camel in Australia*, pp. 71–76, 98–105.   **319**
34. McKnight, *The Camel in Australia*, pp. 105–122.
35. McKnight, *The Camel in Australia*, pp. 45–47, 52–56.
The memoirs of a camel teamster, H. M. Barker *(Camels and the Outback)*, are of interest throughout for the picture given of camel utilization in Australia. In particular, he comments upon the disinterest of "Afghans" in carting (p. 207) and gives a detailed description of the harness (pp. 20–21). The riding saddle described by McKnight (p. 42) is obviously derived, unlike the draft harness, from the Indian *pakra* saddle, for which see Leese, *The One-Humped Camel*, pp. 126–127, pl. 6.
36. Barker, *Camels and the Outback*, p. 208.
37. The following account is taken from Lewis Burt Lesley, *Uncle Sam's Camels* (Cambridge, Mass.: Harvard University Press, 1929), pp. 3–17, 119–136. An exhaustive bibliography on the subject has been compiled by Albert H. Greenly, "Camels in America," *The Papers of the Bibliographical Society of America*, 46 (1952), 359–372.
38. Évariste-Regis Huc, *Travels in Tartary, Thibet and China*, tr. W. Hazlitt (London: National Illustrated Library, 1852).
39. Geoffroy Saint-Hilaire, *Acclimatation*, pp. 308–309.
40. Lesley, *Uncle Sam's Camels*, p. 43.
41. McKnight, *The Camel in Australia*, p. 57.
42. McKnight, *The Camel in Australia*, pp. 65–71.
43. Lesley, *Uncle Sam's Camels*, pp. 10–11, 129–130.
44. McKnight, *The Camel in Australia*, pp. 90–91, 98–102.
45. George P. Marsh, *The Camel: His Organization, Habits and Uses* (Boston: Gould and Lincoln, 1856), p. 189. This small book is an expanded version of Marsh's lecture "The Camel" published in *Ninth Annual Report of the Board of Regents of the Smithsonian Institution* (Washington: Beverley Tucker, 1855), pp. 98–122. The same passage appears on page 120 of the lecture.
46. Lesley, *Uncle Sam's Camels*, p. 122.
47. The largest load ever recorded in Australia, where camels were bred for strength, was just short of a ton, 1,904 pounds. (McKnight, p. 44). All sources mark the pack camel's walk at 2.5 miles per hour or less. The speed records collected by Marsh (pp. 123–128), a camel enthusiast, for fine riding camels never exceed 10 miles an hour; and the highest rates claimed elsewhere are very suspicious.
48. Lesley, *Uncle Sam's Camels*, p. 8.
49. Marsh, *The Camel*, p. 188. Marsh also notes (p. 192) the military advantage accruing to the camel rider, on a North Arabian saddle, from sitting higher than a horseman.

320

50. B. H. Liddell Hart, *The Other Side of the Hill* (London: Cassell, 1951), p. 305.

51. Leonard, *The Camel*, p. 259.

52. Leese, *The One-Humped Camel*, pp. 45–46; Leonard, *The Camel*, pp. 277–279; Count A. E. Gleichen, *With the Camel Corps up the Nile* (London: Chapman & Hall, 1888), pp. 40–41, 177–178, 185–201.

53. Robert Edwin Berls, Jr., "The Russian Conquest of Turkmenistan," Ph.D. thesis, Georgetown University, 1972, pp. 136, 147. I wish to thank Professor John Emerson for bringing this work to my attention.

54. Leese, *The One-Humped Camel*, p. 46. A personal acquaintance, Mr. George Kendle, was a veterinary sergeant-major in charge of camels during the Allenby campaign and remembers with pride the excellent health record that was maintained.

55. M. Jomard, "Le Régiment des Dromadaires à l'armée d'orient (1798–1801)," pp. 219–244 of General Jean-Luc Carbuccia *Du Dromadaire comme bête de somme et comme animal de guerre* (Paris: J. Dumaire, 1853).

56. Geoffroy Saint-Hilaire, *Acclimatation*, pp. 296–299.

57. Examples of this literature are H. Wolff and A. Blachère, *Les Régiments de Dromadaires* (Paris: Challamel Ainé, 1884), and P. Wachi, *Rôle militaire du chameau en Algérie et en Tunisie* (Paris: H. Charles-Lavauzelle, 1900).

58. Lt.-Col. Venel and Capt. Bouchez, *Guide de l'officier méhariste au territoire militaire du Niger* (Paris: E. Larose, 1910), pp. 11–13; General Duboc, *Méharistes coloniaux* (Paris: L. Fournier, 1946), p. 8.

59. Wachi, *Rôle militaire*.

60. Venel and Bouchez, *Guide*, pp. 100–105, 221; Capt. Moll, *Infanterie montée à chameau: notes sur l'organisation d'une compagnie montée à chameau dans les 1er et 3e territoires militaires de l'Afrique occidentale* (Paris: H. Charles-Lavauzelle, 1903), pp. 6–7.

61. Lesley, *Uncle Sam's Camels*, p. 9; Leese, *The One-Humped Camel*, p. 45.

62. Leese, *The One-Humped Camel*, pp. 46, 124.

10 The Return of the Wheel and the Future of the Camel

1. Mr. Norman N. Lewis has been kind enough to furnish me information from a book he is writing on *The Frontier of Settlement in Syria in the Nineteenth Century* showing that carts were reintroduced into Syria at that time by Circassian settlers from eastern Anatolia. Their typical vehicle was the solid wheeled oxcart.

Turks had been known in Syria since the eleventh century but had never popularized the use of their vehicles.

2. Martin B. Dickson, *Shah Tahmasb and the Uzbeks*, Ph.D. thesis, Princeton University, 1958, pp. 127, 129 (University Microfilms, Ann Arbor, Mich.). "Cavalry," *Encyclopaedia Britannica*, 11th ed., V, 564–565.

3. In Iran the capital and initiative for building carriage roads early in the twentieth century came primarily from Europeans. Issawi, *The Economic History of Iran*, pp. 200–202.

4. In the nineteenth century outside of Australia numerous experiments were made on a small scale with harnessing camels to vehicles. The Persians even tried camel-drawn artillery. Dareste, "Rapport," p. 72; Cauvet, *Le Chameau*, I, 665.

5. Cauvet, *Le Chameau*, II, 192–193.

6. *Production Yearbook, 1971* (Rome: Food and Agriculture Organization of the United Nations, 1972), p. 338.

7. Cauvet, *Le Chameau*, I, 780–782.

8. Schmidt-Nielsen, "Animals and Arid Conditions," p. 380.

9. Schmidt-Nielsen, "Animals and Arid Conditions," p. 377; "Urea Excretion in the Camel," *The American Journal of Physiology*, 188 (1957), 477–484.

10. Thomas Stauffer, "The Dynamics of Middle Eastern Nomadism: Traditional Pastoralism and Schultzian Rationality" (unpublished).

11. Stauffer, "Dynamics of Middle Eastern Nomadism," pp. 1, 22–23; Louise E. Sweet, "Camel Raiding of North Arabian Bedouin: A Mechanism of Ecological Adaptation," *American Anthropologist*, 67 (1965), 1132–1150.

12. Helen Gibson, "40-Day Walk to the Camel Market," *International Herald Tribune*, November 25, 1971.

Index

323

Index